D1739209

REFLECTIONS OF A CIVIL WAR HISTORIAN

Shades of Blue and Gray Series
Edited by Herman Hattaway and Jon L. Wakelyn

The Shades of Blue and Gray Series offers Civil War studies for the modern reader—Civil War buff and scholar alike. Military history today addresses the relationship between society and warfare. Thus biographies and thematic studies that deal with civilians, soldiers, and political leaders are increasingly important to a larger public. This series includes books that will appeal to Civil War Roundtable groups, individuals, libraries, and academics with a special interest in this era of American history.

REFLECTIONS OF A CIVIL WAR HISTORIAN

Essays on
Leadership,
Society,
and the
Art of War

Herman Hattaway
Foreword by Frank E. Vandiver

University of Missouri Press
Columbia and London

Copyright © 2004 by
The Curators of the University of Missouri
University of Missouri Press, Columbia, Missouri 65201
Printed and bound in the United States of America
All rights reserved
5 4 3 2 1 08 07 06 05 04

Library of Congress Cataloging-in-Publication Data

Hattaway, Herman.
 Reflections of a Civil War historian : essays on leadership, society, and the art of
war / Herman Hattaway.
   p.   cm. — (Shades of blue and gray series)
Includes bibliographical references and index.
ISBN 0-8262-1487-8 (alk. paper)
  1. United States—History—Civil War, 1861–1865—Miscellanea. 2. Generals—
United States—Biography. 3. Generals—Confederate States of America—
Biography. 4. United States—History—Civil War, 1861–1865—Campaigns.
5. Command of troops—History—19th century. 6. United States—History—Civil
War, 1861–1865—Social aspects. 7. Military art and science—United States—
History—19th century. I. Title. II. Series.
E468 .H34 2003
973.7—dc22

                                                                    2003016712

♾ This paper meets the requirements of the
American National Standard for Permanence of Paper
for Printed Library Materials, Z39.48, 1984.

Designer: Jennifer Cropp
Typesetter: Crane Composition, Inc.
Printer and binder: The Maple-Vail Book Manufacturing Group
Typefaces: Palatino and Diotima

To

all of my LSU professors

my doctoral students
Mark A. Snell
Ethan S. Rafuse
Michael J. C. Taylor
Ron G. Machion
Steven A. Gregson
Nola M. Sleevi

my master's degree students
with whom I collaborated
Michael Gillespie
Lloyd A. Hunter

CONTENTS

FOREWORD

For more than forty years Herman Hattaway has thought about the Civil War, about such special facets of it as command, leadership, tactics, and innovations. This splendid volume offers an apparently eclectic collection of his essays that touch on varied parts of the war. A close reading, though—and these essays deserve a close reading—shows a personal concern running through the book. Hattaway is interested in people in war, at war, and affected by war. That is not surprising since his mentor, T. Harry Williams of Louisiana State University, had mostly similar predilections.

Biography is his forte; his scholarly career began with a life of Confederate General Stephen D. Lee and progressed to a recent study of Jefferson Davis. Beyond biography he has been concerned with the Civil War armies, with the way the war changed tactics, and with such war innovations as balloons. Especially useful are his careful studies of numbers and casualties. He blazes an important new trail in this book with his essay on "State Rights and Local Defense"; he takes sharp issue with Frank L. Owsley's famous book *State Rights in the Confederacy*, especially in its condemnation of local defense forces. Hattaway's careful research offers a fresh interpretation of the entire matter of state rights and the Southern war effort.

Equally cogent is his critique, in "We Shall Cease to Be Friends," of U.S.-British relations after the *Trent* affair. The threatened war would have forced British efforts in Canada, where operations would have been difficult on the Great Lakes and along the upper Union coastline. Clearly the United States had the power to fight a two-front war and Hattaway adroitly suggests that a stalemate seemed likely and would have been too costly for Victoria's exchequer.

Deftly written, boldly insightful, certainly controversial, this is a must read for anyone willing to think seriously about the war that changed the United States and perhaps the world.

FRANK E. VANDIVER

PREFACE

This is my "late-in-career vanity piece." That is, it is a compilation of writings which I have composed over the years, most of them previously published, but some in rather obscure outlets and thus not easily available for present-day readers. A few of the pieces herein have never until now appeared in print.

It is usual in works of this sort to open with a chapter-length autobiographical essay. However, since I look forward to collecting essays of a more personal nature in another volume, I will open with only the briefest description of who I am.

I was born in New Orleans, Louisiana, on December 26, 1938. As a young adult I found my way into Professor T. Harry Williams's classes at Louisiana State University. He changed my life, for until then I had no idea what I wished to do in a career. His lectures and writings were so inspiring that I became his disciple, receiving a B.A. in 1961, an M.A. in 1963, and a Ph.D. in 1969, all under his valuable and much-admired direction.

I have found collaboration to be enormously useful and helpful in researching and writing. Only two of my books—the biography *General Stephen D. Lee,* which was my revised dissertation, and *Shades of Blue and Gray: An Introductory Military History of the Civil War* (1997)—were written alone. I also had collaborators for many of my articles, encyclopedia entries, and other short pieces. Richard Beringer and I worked together for many years and finally finished in 2002 our *Jefferson Davis, Confederate President.*

I believe that in some cases, and definitely in my case, collaborations have become greater than the sum of their parts: that is, neither collaborator could possibly have done the same job alone, because each had special talents, insights, and so on that the other lacked. In some cases it was just a matter of time-saving convenience. But working in a foursome, as I did on *Why the South Lost the Civil War,* was a tricky business, a nerve-racking experience which I would never attempt again and would not recommend to anyone.

During my time in higher academia, jobs have been scarce and hard to come by. This was especially true in my fields: Civil War, military history, Southern history, and religion studies. So I was very lucky to have landed a job at the University of Missouri–Kansas City in 1969. Some of my former classmates were not able to find employment at all as university professors. Concurrently, over the past decades there also has been little or no mobility possible. So, despite my wanderlust, I was obliged to stay for the entirety of my teaching career at my first post.

At least it has proved to be pleasant living in Kansas City. There are 2,500 four-year institutions of higher education in the United States, more or less (a few new ones are created and a few die out every year). At least 2,000 of them are in remote places which I would regard as unfit to live in. I have always mused that being trapped at the University of Nameastate–Podunkville would be a special taste of hell. A tour of one such while returning from vacation during the summer of 2002 confirmed my suspicions. I am hopelessly an urbanite.

I was fortunate to be awarded an appointment as Visiting Professor of Military Art, 1990–1991, at the U.S. Military Academy, West Point. That was the finest of all my years in teaching. The cadets were wonderful students and we much enjoyed each other. I am proud and gratified to still be in touch with some of them as well as a few of my colleagues on the faculty. I am also proud to have on the front of my automobile the infantry license plate which one of the latter gave me. (The guards at the West Point gate began saluting me! When I told that to my wife, she said they saluted her too. I asked if she returned the salutes, as indeed I did, and she said no— she just waved.)

As will be perceived by looking over my selections herein, my primary interest has been biography. I have been equally interested in studying the lives of people with well-known names and reputations and individuals of lesser rank. Burl Noggle, one of my LSU professors, agreed with me during my comprehensive oral examinations that any human being is worthy of a biography if sufficient and worthwhile sources exist. It is amazing how many people there were who lived at the time of the Civil War for whom that is the case.

My second interest, running a close second to my primary one— and it may be that my contributions here are more important to the field of history in general—has been macrocosmic synthesis. That is, I have written some books which, while based somewhat on research in primary sources, are rather more summations, evaluations, and extrapolations of the best extant works on large topics.

Finally, I have been much inclined to study new and innovative areas, such as the military use of balloons, high-level reform in military organization, the relevance of religion in warfare, the concept and significance of civil religion, the nature of good (and bad) military leadership, and why people find it interesting and important to remember, and sometimes to try to "relive," history.

I have been very involved in trying to evaluate the work of my fellow historians through the formal review process. My published reviews total in the hundreds. I have written several forewords to books which I think are exceptionally good and interesting. I have served as the "hired gun," or initially anonymous reader-evaluator of books, for various presses. I am a member of the boards of editorial advisors both for the distinguished magazine *Civil War Times Illustrated* and the George Tyler Moore Center for the Study of the Civil War, located at Shepherd College in Shepherdstown, West Virginia. Lastly, I served a five-year term as editorial advisor for *The Historian*, the journal of the professional fraternity Phi Alpha Theta.

I fondly recall all of my LSU professors and include them in my dedication. But it is my graduate students to whom I now convey the warmest regards. I have, in what proved to be a 32½-year teaching career, been blessed with some wonderful master's degree seekers, quite many of whom produced exemplary theses. It was much for the best, too, that my university did not have a doctoral program in history for my first three decades in harness. Any recipients of Ph.D.'s from my place of employment, before my rise to a fair measure of national prominence, would surely have had a hard time securing desirable employment. But, as it has turned out, all of those who received doctorates under my direction have been blessed with good fortune in their job searches. I am very, very proud of them.

REFLECTIONS OF A
CIVIL WAR HISTORIAN

PART 1
LEADERSHIP AND COMMAND

❧ CIVIL WAR LEADERSHIP

This piece has not been previously published. I do not now re-member what I wrote it for; my best guess is that it was a Civil War Roundtable talk or a piece for one of the many panel discus-sions I have served on. It comprises much of the germ for my initial input for *How the North Won: A Military History of the Civil War* (1983). It emphasizes the South much more than the North, reflecting my greater interest. I thought perhaps I might acknowledge this tendency with a new and more specifically descriptive title, but decided not to do so.

Good leadership ranked equally with adequate manpower as a factor in determining the Civil War's outcome. This was especially true at senior-level, general-grade appointments. The Confederacy ultimately named eight full generals, seventeen lieutenant generals, and seventy-two major generals. It is my opinion that blame for the eventual Confederate defeat cannot be placed upon this group. That is so either collectively or with any individuals or groups of in-dividuals.

I believe that Confederate generalship compared rather closely and favorably with Federal generalship. It is true, however, that some of the generals on both sides were less than exemplary. Sound and discernible military reasons typically prompted a general's ele-vation in rank, but both opposing presidents occasionally granted promotions for broader considerations, usually political in nature.[1]

The age of a general can have much bearing upon his ability to

1. It has been typical of Civil War scholars to denigrate nearly all of the polit-ical generals, but Thomas J. Goss offers a good argument that there were sound and compelling reasons for the naming and retention of the political generals in *The War within the Union High Command: Politics and Generalship during the Civil War* (Lawrence: University Press of Kansas, 2003).

perform well; it is important that he be neither too old, and hence lacking in vigor and flexibility, nor too young, and hence unseasoned and possibly incapable of eliciting the necessary level of confidence, not only in his own estimation but also particularly in his subordinates. This is an especial truth in a war such as the U.S. Civil War, because nearly all of the general officers typically and frequently were in the field, often in direct contact with the troops they commanded, led, and managed. The average age of the higher-ranking, active-duty Civil War general trended downward as the war progressed. This resulted because of retirement by many elderly men, resignation, casualties, and the addition of new slots for general officers.

By the end of the war's first full year, forty-eight Southern generals had been given a rank above brigadier. The average age for Southern generals was 44.8 years; Northerners were slightly younger. At the war's end, seventy-six Confederate officers with major generalcies or higher remained in service. The average age, after four years of war, had decreased to 42.5 years in both armies.

Five states within the Confederacy (Virginia, North and South Carolina, Georgia, and Tennessee) contributed two-thirds of the Southern generals elevated above brigadier. The remaining six states, comprising the Gulf Coast area, could boast of only five higher generals. But this uneven distribution by states in truth rather accurately reflected the population distribution; only a few slight variations appear. Also, like the population as a whole, most Civil War generals (78 percent) were born in rural areas or small towns with under 3,000 residents.

There is no apparent correlation between a man's receiving a Civil War generalship and the occupation his father had pursued; but interestingly, about one-quarter of the generals who gained promotion above brigadier came from families with professional ties. Modern wars—and the Civil War sometimes has been called "the first modern war"—require at least as much managerial skill from the generals who conduct them as they require in leadership (or charismatic) capability. The charisma factor (crucial in olden times) becomes less significant in modern war, but educational attainment—or pure intellectual power, however attained—increases in significance.

Regardless of social class, which varied considerably on both sides, few Civil War generals who lacked formal education gained promotion. Eighty percent of the total had graduated from college. More than one-half of those above brigadier had graduated from West Point. Of the twenty-five highest-ranking Southern generals, only Nathan Bedford Forrest was not a college graduate. Experience— that is, prior military experience—was an important factor: promotion to the higher grades of general proved almost impossible for men without any military experience predating the Civil War. Of the top twenty Confederates, only two were new to the military, Forrest and Wade Hampton, both of whom had attained considerable economic success and status before the war. All of the top twenty Union generals had become well-qualified military men before hostilities began.

There is at least one statistical indication that Northern generals as a group were more scholarly than Southern generals: of the generals who had attended West Point, the Union officers boasted a much higher academic standing; almost 40 percent of the North's West Point generals finished in the top quarter of their class, whereas only 25 percent of the South's generals ranked that high. And conversely, 23 percent of the South's generals ranked in the bottom quarter of their class; while only 6 percent of the North's West Pointers ranked that low. The top assignments, however, did not go to the low achievers: only three of the Confederacy's poor former students (John B. Hood, James Longstreet, and Theophilus Holmes) attained rank beyond major general.

Though some historians have called the United States's war with Mexico a "rehearsal for conflict," statistical investigation reveals that Mexican War service by itself offered little of value in propelling a man upward in general-grade rank. Mexican War service *and* a West Point education were most effective aids to promotion, but only in combination. Individuals who lacked either variable did discernibly less well in attaining high Civil War rank. Seventeen of the top twenty-five Confederate generals possessed both qualifications.

Experience outside the military might provide an added dimension of potential capability in any given general officer. In 1860 only one-half of the men who later became Civil War generals were in active military service. The others, the civilians who became general officers, can be divided into three categories: those with no military experience other than militia duty, those who had resigned from the U.S. Army at some previous time, and those with some other type of military service. None of the three categories stands out as having produced more generals than did the others; they are almost equally divided. The move upward from major general in the Confederacy, however, quite typically was limited only to former regular-army officers. (This was owing to a particular bias of President Jefferson Davis.) At least half of the civilians who became generals had taken an active part in politics before the Civil War, and men with political experience tended to begin the war with higher ranks. But significantly, the very highest ranks attained by civilians went to politicians who also had Mexican War experience.

Promotion to the various upper grades of general did not always result from logical progression through regular advancement. To be sure, all of the Confederate lieutenant generals had previously held the rank of major general, but several of the major generals never had held the rank of brigadier. The year 1862 saw the most rapid expansion of the list of senior generals (for both sides): during that time new appointments to major generalcies and above numbered thirty-eight for the Confederacy. That same year the Confederacy promoted its first lieutenant generals and named Braxton Bragg a full general, the last man to attain that rank in the South's regular army. (In 1864 Hood was named a full general, but the Confederate Congress later asserted that rank to be a temporary one—*not* in the Confederacy's regular army.) Fewer, though some crucial, adjustments came in 1863 and in 1864; for the most part, later elevations were necessitated by attrition.

Civil War generals had little job security. In addition to dangerous working conditions which resulted in numerous fatalities and severe or disabling wounds (one thinks especially of the dilemma faced by Robert E. Lee and the Army of Northern Virginia as a result of the heavy toll taken by the Chancellorsville campaign), political misfortune or combat ineffectiveness might result in loss of command. Nevertheless, few generals were actually dismissed unwillingly from service; even John C. Pemberton continued on active duty after the Vicksburg debacle, though not as a lieutenant general—he selflessly accepted a lieutenant colonelcy. Like Pemberton (and, in the North, John Pope, relegated to Indian-fighting duty following Second Bull Run), most of those who demonstrated themselves to be truly inept in high command subsequently were allowed either to languish in staff assignments or at remote locations or they resigned.

The attrition rate for all Confederate general officers amounted to nearly 30 percent. The South suffered 18 percent of its generals either killed in action or dying from wounds. The position of Confederate brigadier general carried more danger than the other generalcies: 20 percent of them died in combat. Relatively few of the Confederate generals, 4.5 percent, resigned. Despite resignation, retirement, and deaths, the number of generals in grade grew as the war wore on. These increases came gradually, with the exception of the high incidence of appointments during 1862. The Confederate president named 425 individuals to one of the South's four grades of general; 299 remained in grade at the return of peace.

With only a minute nucleus of regular officers, actually both the North and the South managed very well. Warfare often seems a contest to see who can outblunder whom; but, in spite of such tragedies as Union Maj. Gen. Ambrose Burnside's egregious attack at Fredericksburg and Confederate Lt. Gen. Pemberton's disastrous retreat into Vicksburg, both sides conducted the war rather competently and realistically. If we are going to absolve Ulysses S. Grant for Cold Harbor, as well I think we must, it seems correct to forgive R. E. Lee his decisions on the third day at Gettysburg.

As might have been expected in view of the common parentage of both armies, their respective leadership did not differ significantly in outlook and doctrine. Indeed, there was really not a great deal of difference as a group between the Northern generals and the Southern generals. A vast percentage of them educated at West Point, the professional leaders were conditioned by their engineering-oriented schooling, their Mexican War experiences, and their reading of history. Their familiarity with Napoleonic campaigns caused their belief in the attainability of decisive battle, but their realization of the tactical power of the defense also convinced them that they probably could not gain such a result in a frontal fight. If they took too long to learn the value of entrenchments and field fortifications, they surely did learn and thereafter almost universally employed them. The efficacy of these strategies only reinforced what West Point and Professor Dennis Hart Mahan had already taught them, and confirmed their conviction of the tactical supremacy of the defensive.

They had learned the turning movement, seen as the key to victory in battle, as much from Winfield Scott and Zachary Taylor in Mexico as they had from Napoleon. For a battle to be decisive, the attacker must reach the enemy's rear with his entire force, inducing the enemy to make a frontal attack in order to extricate himself and recover his communications. This was a feat so difficult that even Napoleon achieved it only rarely, and so it was that the Civil War generals did not do so very many times either.

The war's greatest general—this was U. S. Grant, I long ago concluded, despite my Southern upbringing, parentage, and family ties—achieved it three times: at Fort Donelson, Vicksburg, and Appomattox, though in every case either with the aid of inept or weakened opposition. Count Alfred von Schlieffen's later tongue-in-cheek observation could well apply to Grant's Fort Donelson and Vicksburg successes: in order to attain a Cannae, "a Hannibal is needed on the one side and a Terentius Varro on the other, both cooperating." But the Confederacy did not often pit a general possessed of Varro's inferior qualifications against a Hannibal, nor a Grant or a Sherman!

The Southern generals enjoyed a certain axiomatic advantage: they frequently could choose to fight on the tactical defensive as they attempted to protect their territory. Tactical realities caused most leaders on both sides to make territory their objective. Confederate generals anxiously desired to conserve *all* their territory (a mistake) and its essential logistical resources (probably crucial). The Southern people and politicians favorably reacted to this strategy, one which seemed well adapted to the weaker side, which clearly, as everyone could see, the South was. But territory was a defensive asset for the South: the vast size of the Confederacy, its poor roads, and its somewhat limited production of food and fodder that an invader could appropriate would have made a Union strategy of inflicting defeat primarily by conquering territory very difficult in any case; but in addition, the limited rail and water routes of invasion made obvious the potential Union lines of operation, enabling the Confederates easily to concentrate against them.

Rebel guerrilla activity and early Confederate strength in cavalry were both significant advantages enjoyed by the Southern commanders at the outset. Most important in the Tennessee theater, raids by guerrillas and by substantial forces of regular cavalry could destroy the fragile railroads upon which the supply of invading armies depended. Though obsolete on the battlefield, cavalry, as brilliantly led by Forrest and John Hunt Morgan, well displayed its potential for its other traditional role—attacking the enemy's logistics. Even an inferior mounted force was formidable in this role, and the near parity enjoyed by Confederate cavalry early in the war permitted them temporarily, but completely, to stop Union advances in the West.

The necessity for keeping communications open along the secure water route of the Mississippi River in late 1862 made Grant's line of operations so obvious that the Confederates could force him to approach them head on. A Union frontal attack failed at Chickasaw Bayou.[2] That battle later lent some credence to the myth—popular in some quarters, particularly many parts of the postwar South—that Southern generals in the main were superior to Northern generals, and that the latter triumphed only because of "overwhelming numbers and resources." Many years after the war's end, die-hard rebel sympathizers still remembered and spoke of campaigns like this one where Brigadier General Stephen D. Lee, as they put it, "gave old Sherman a good drubbing." Indeed, one Southern newspaper proclaimed that the Chickasaw Bayou battles "deserve as historic a place in history as that of Thermopylae." The campaign is indeed an interesting illustration of how a great general like William Tecumseh Sherman, even with a vastly superior force—as was the case here—could be defeated by an adversary of lesser ability, the difference being that the victor momentarily performed almost perfectly, while the defeated functioned in a flawed manner.

2. Not Chickasaw *Bluffs* as it is so frequently misidentified; Chickasaw Bluffs are in Tennessee, Chickasaw Bayou is just north of Vicksburg.

In the East, a similar situation prevailed. The lines of operation by rail in Virginia were easily discernible, though the Confederates could turn the Union army on the west, and the Union forces could turn the Confederates on the east. R. E. Lee used this advantage in 1862 and 1863, and George B. McClellan and Grant, each in his own way, exploited the Union ability to turn the Confederates. Because of the short lines of communication in Virginia, guerrillas and cavalry raiders mattered less in that congested theater.

In discussing generalship, one needs, to be sure, also to include in the discussion the civilians who, according to both the American and the Confederate scheme, occupy places in the military chain of command. In the Confederacy, just as was the case in the Union, the president—the commander in chief—made the ultimate determinations concerning grand strategy. Unlike Abraham Lincoln, Jefferson Davis had no powerful and vocal radicals advocating their strategic ideas and pushing to greater prominence certain favored generals. Though Davis was pressured to provide for the defense of *every* locality, this caused no distortion in Confederate policy, because almost every Confederate geographic area had some crucial importance as a source of recruits and supplies.

Under Davis's leadership the Confederacy skillfully reconciled the defense of exposed territory against raids with powerful resistance on the main lines of operation. The fortunate location of Southern railroads made possible a uniting of the major and minor theaters. Thus the Confederacy could integrate the defense of the Atlantic seaboard with the defense of northern Virginia by converting the railway lines from Richmond to Savannah into a "pipeline" full of troops which they could concentrate at any threatened point.

The Confederacy applied a similar concept less systematically to the defense of the line from Richmond to Chattanooga, a mountainous and less vulnerable frontier. State militia forces, largely composed of men otherwise exempt from Confederate military service, well supplemented the South's ability to reinforce rapidly. Thus the Confederates united powerful resistance on the main lines by using the railways to combine dispersion with concentration.

They succeeded well in joining to the national effort the concern for local defense, which had compelled the states to create and maintain their own emergency forces. Composed of men from vital occupations, or otherwise exempt, and of those unfit or beyond the age suitable for field service, these formations received a significant augmentation in 1864. The reserves provided at all times some form of protection, even when all regular troops were deployed elsewhere. Though they might do no more than man fortifications, they possessed psychological importance in that they maintained local morale and demonstrated to the enemy the presence of organized defensive forces.

The successful integration of almost every rail-connected point into a national system of strategic defense permitted an application on an unprecedented scale of the Napoleonic concept of concentration at the most critical point. Both the civilian and the military leadership of the Confederacy agreed on this, but they disagreed over whether they should apply this system and concept to an offensive. The partisans of the offensive—a group that Thomas L. Connelly and Archer Jones, in *The Politics of Command,* called the "western concentration bloc"—wished to seize the initiative and bring about a surprise offensive convergence against a weak Union line.

P. G. T. Beauregard expressed it in classical form; others, such as the Kentuckians, simply wanted to recover their state. The coincidence of relative Union weakness in central Tennessee enabled all factions to coalesce to form the bloc and unite behind Beauregard's applications of the principle. In the winter and spring of 1863 this brought them into conflict with R. E. Lee, not because he did not understand or had not used the principle to animate his strategy, but because Beauregard's proposal involved weakening Lee's army— and that was something which Lee *never* could see any advantage in! In defending his own army against reduction, Lee was led, temporarily, to repudiate the quite promising principle espoused by the western concentration bloc.

In the Chickamauga campaign of September 1863, the bloc partly succeeded. The long-advocated offensive came only as a counteroffensive, as at Shiloh, to retrieve a loss. Once the Confederates had assembled their troops in the West, their high command, including

R. E. Lee, pushed for offensives in Tennessee long after they had lost the element of surprise and the Union counterconcentration had made such an operation unrealistic. The massing of troops in North Carolina may even have caused Davis and Lee to harbor unrealistic expectations in 1864 about what Joseph E. Johnston and Hood could achieve against Sherman.

But the Confederates used their railways for concentrations at successive points so systematically and efficiently that in his strategy for 1864 Grant included key elements intended to prevent any further repetition of this fundamental rebel strategic theme. In order for this to happen, Richmond would have had to supply good direction and constantly restructure departmental lines to reflect the changing military situation, and this was not adequately done.[3]

Beginning with an array of miniature departments, Davis gradually enlarged them until, in the fall of 1862, he had evolved a complex—if enigmatic—system embracing four regional commands. Disrupted by the Vicksburg campaign, the western region was not restored until the fall of 1864 when Davis placed Beauregard in command of the Military Division of the West. When Sherman began his March to the Sea, Davis also subordinated South Carolina, Georgia, and Florida to this division.

Though more effective under Beauregard than it had been under Johnston, even this large division lacked the resources essential to combating Sherman's Military Division of the Mississippi. The Confederacy's military departmental organization was better structured than the Union's was early in the war, but with Grant's emergence to high prominence following the fall of Vicksburg, Union command structure, on the whole, thenceforth equaled, and eventually surpassed, that of the Confederates.

The collaboration between Davis and Lee proved most fruitful for the Confederacy during Lee's brief term in 1862 as "general commanding" (functioning essentially in the manner of a modern chief of staff, not at that time himself also trying to command an army in the field). Thereafter, though Lee remained a constant and wise

3. It long has been a suspicion of mine that Civil War scholarship has not adequately investigated and described the Confederate military department system. A good historical atlas on this topic is among my many planned, and even already begun, projects.

advisor, his removal from Richmond not only limited his influence, but also on occasion deprived him of the information needed to give well-founded advice to Davis. Equally important, Lee's absorption in his own army, and with the war in Virginia only, deprived him of the perspective needed to formulate broader and more balanced views.

Lee's primary role with respect to grand strategy, then, amounted essentially to that of a brilliant, really unequaled, department and army commander. He grasped the part that his effective defense of his own theater could play in wearing down the enemy's will to win. Though he was a master of the Napoleonic method, Lee's strategy remained essentially defensive, and this was how he fought most of his battles. Still, his strategy often *seemed* offensive, for on four occasions he employed a turning movement to force the enemy back. Three of these—Second Bull Run, Antietam, and Gettysburg—resulted in spectacular battles, but Lee's fundamental purpose had been and remained to keep the enemy at bay and to cover his Virginia supply base. Lee's campaigns compare well with those waged by the masters of the art of war in any age. Probably it is fair that he has been equated with Frederick the Great. But, as Connelly and Jones observed, "he was only a Virginia Frederick."

When Lee departed Richmond to take command of what soon became known as the Army of Northern Virginia, he took with him the staff officers that had constituted an embryonic general staff. While working in Richmond, they were an enormously important experiment in moving toward modernity. But Lee left no one behind to fill the role he had been playing as chief of staff, and no staff as well! This was one of the most egregious of all Confederate blunders. True, Davis in part well employed his war secretaries, especially George W. Randolph and James A. Seddon, in this role; but until Braxton Bragg came to Richmond late in the war, Davis primarily carried the burden of being chief of staff, and he carried too much.

Not only did Davis lack Lincoln's opportunity to reflect upon and refine plans, tasks appropriated in the Confederacy primarily by

Beauregard, but he was also physically and emotionally exhausted by overwork. Davis's improvisation of conducting his headquarters business for so long a time without any chief of staff cost the Confederacy heavily. Not only did headquarters lack sufficient staff, but that weakness also drew the war secretary into the conduct of operations. That the Confederacy could supply Richmond all during the siege of Petersburg, from June 1864 through March 1865, shows, however, that the Southern system could be made to work. But the absorption in the concerns of day-to-day operations by both the president and the secretary of war tended to delay the adequate addressing of problems until they had become crises. This clearly contributed to the failure to apply more than partial and piecemeal solutions to such crucial matters as, for example, railroad control. The long interval without a chief of staff perhaps constituted Davis's major failing as commander in chief. He understood what a proper headquarters needed, but neglected to produce it.

Why? Because Davis was possessed of a misleading overconfidence in himself and his abilities. His West Point and professional army background and outlook, his keen superiority as a military administrator, and, most important of all, his long history of good fortune gave him an unrealistic confidence in his grand military prescriptions. So sure that he could get through every crisis and scrape, as he had done at so many moments in his life previously, Jefferson Davis proved to be a failure as commander in chief because he did not perceive how important it was to see the faults of his friends, and how necessary it was for him to grow with his job, handle pressure, and take decisive action which sometimes would mean *not* relying on his friends, or even going against them.

Davis's shortcomings, though not as clearly exposed during the early months of the conflict as they would be by war's end, nevertheless inflicted serious damage on the Southern cause from the very start. An early and crucial error was to appoint Samuel Cooper to the post of adjutant and inspector general, the highest-ranking position in the Confederate Army. The *idea* for such a position was excellent; but Cooper quickly proved to be a mere paperhound, not at all an able and transcending highest-level wartime assistant, and Davis took no step to relieve or replace him. Had Davis secured a competent officer for this position, he might have avoided some of his later failures.

Second, Davis allowed himself to be blinded by personal feelings. This showed most crucially in his appointment—and retention after demonstrated ineptness—of Leonidas Polk to an important field command. Davis's choice immediately redounded to the detriment of the Confederacy when Polk seized Columbus, Kentucky, alienating the undecided sentiment in that state and destroying whatever chance the Confederacy might have had of gaining Kentucky's allegiance. Even then, Davis failed to correct the mistake and retained Polk in high command—until at last, in 1864, fate intervened, and the bishop-general was mortally wounded.

Third, Davis failed to act quickly and decisively to salvage the situation that Polk had exacerbated in Kentucky. Prominent Kentuckians and Tennesseans told Davis that if he would disclaim Polk's move and order a withdrawal, all was not yet lost. But Davis did nothing of the kind.

Fourth, and most egregiously, the Confederate president overemphasized the importance of the Virginia theater and neglected the crucial needs of the West. There are complex reasons why this was so, especially early in the war: Davis exaggerated the abilities of and placed unrealistic reliance in his old friend Albert Sidney Johnston; this, coupled with Davis's poor judgment under pressures that were created by the Confederacy's inadequate means and materiel of war, led him to allow a grossly malapportioned share of men and materiel to the wrong places.

Alas, as the war progressed, instead of getting better (as Lincoln assuredly did) Davis's interaction with his generals became vastly more complex and problematical. Davis failed to make peace, or come to terms, with Beauregard, from whom he had early become alienated. Hence he failed to get anything near the contribution that that intelligent—possibly, it is fair to say, brilliant—officer might have made. Davis stuck with Braxton Bragg in field command far too long. That officer had clearly demonstrated the need that he be relieved. There can be no exoneration for Davis's failure, following the Battle of Murfreesboro, to straighten out the mess that had come to exist in the officer corps of the Army of Tennessee. Davis grossly misused the capabilities of Joseph E. Johnston—again, obviously because of a personality clash. Unlike Lincoln, who shone in this ability, Davis could not work with people whom he disliked or whom he knew disliked him. Lastly, the responsibility for the outcome of the Vicksburg campaign can in large measure be laid at Davis's feet.

Having removed Bragg from field command, Davis not only failed to secure a good replacement; he also compounded the matter by bringing the very unpopular Bragg to Richmond as a principal military advisor. So, as the winter months of 1864 unfolded and the North went about preparing to end the war with a final offensive, the Confederate president did little more than argue with Joseph E. Johnston as to whether the South could attempt to take the initiative.

A more resolute and self-reliant commander in chief than Davis might have compelled Johnston to assume an offensive, or immediately replace him. Who knows for sure? Grady McWhiney has suggested that the Confederacy lost because of Davis's physical sickliness. Not only was Davis sickly, he seems also to have been inclined to choose sickly men to lead the Confederacy's armies! And sickliness, to be sure, is a form of weakness.

But whatever the source, there was identifiable weakness in some of Davis's decisions and hesitations. When the final Union offensive commenced, Davis bided his time and watched the ever-retreating Joe Johnston allow the Federals to reach the gates of Atlanta. When Hood at last was put in Johnston's place, it was already too late; he had very little room in which to work, and Atlanta was soon lost. Richard McMurry has rightly opined that if Johnston had been left in command, we could study the amphibious evacuation of Key West. It is not that Johnston should have been retained, it is that he should have been replaced long before he finally was, and it is also that Hood was the wrong man.

So did the South lose the Civil War because of Jefferson Davis's flawed leadership? In the main, yes. Three top-level appointees—Polk, Bragg, and Hood—did enough that was bad to doom the Confederacy. But could the South have won? The weaker side does sometimes prevail. And much combat power still remained in Southern hands at the war's end; I am not a subscriber to the so-called "bled-white" thesis. But could the struggle have been meaningfully continued, as Davis truly believed was possible? I think not. The soldiers were beaten. The guerrilla option, so enticing to many students, was not a viable one in this case. The South did not have the necessary advantageous strongholds. But even more assuredly, the Southern populace was not even close to being up to waging a protracted guerrilla struggle.

To win a war, the victor ultimately has to diminish the loser's will to continue resistance. Sherman's devastating marauding raids did just that to the vast mass of the Southern populace. But it had all previously become moot anyway, in November 1864, with Abraham Lincoln's reelection.

To conclude, I do not believe that the Confederate generals compare significantly unfavorably to the Northern generals. For every nincompoop such as a Theophilus Holmes or a Felix Zollicoffer there is on the other side a Nathaniel Banks or a Benjamin Butler (or a James Ledlie, whom Grady McWhiney described as the Union's worst general), and they cancel each other out. Each side had a share of "great" and "near-great" generals, and it is hairsplitting to an extreme to attribute the war's outcome to some scale-tipping, slightly larger share of greatness on the side of the North. So the Confederate generals as a whole are not to blame for the Confederate defeat—at least not in the conventional sense.[4]

The defeated Confederate armies surrendered, and the soldiers went home for the same reason that many of their former comrades had already deserted: they did not want an independent Confederacy badly enough to pay the necessary price; they placed the welfare of their loved ones ahead of the creation of any new nation. This was true too of the Confederate populace at large: they might early have decided to try to "win the peace," but they *knew* they had lost the war.

4. Nor, as readers know who are familiar with what I and my collaborators tried to prove, and surely did delineate, in *Why the South Lost the Civil War* (1986), do I attribute Confederate defeat to "overwhelming numbers and resources."

Stephen D. Lee and the Guns at Second Manassas

This essay was read at the 1989 Deep Delta Civil War Symposium and appeared in the annual volume that results from the symposium's proceedings; this particular volume was subtitled *Themes in Honor of T. Harry Williams.*

It is now twenty-seven years since I first began investigating the life and career of Stephen D. Lee, and thirteen years since my biography of him initially appeared in print.[1] The book was the first, and I would imagine in all likelihood forever to be the only, full-length biography of this remarkable man to be published, and he was the last Civil War general of his rank to have his biography written. There are a number of reasons that Lee was for so long passed over by scholars, and eventually not even noticed by most students and buffs, and I went into some explanation of these in my book. One of those reasons was *not*, I am sure, that S. D. Lee was the dullest of all the Confederate generals (nor is that even true, although I was tempted to begin my narration with that statement, in a mock opposite to the way that my mentor T. Harry Williams began his colorful work on that most colorful figure, P. G. T. Beauregard). What happened that allowed S. D. Lee to be all but forgotten until my biography was, I honestly think, mainly accidental. That, and the fact that the relevant primary sources were so widely scattered.

This essay appeared in *Leadership during the Civil War: Themes in Honor of T. Harry Williams,* ed. Roman J. Heleniak and Lawrence J. Hewitt (Shippensburg, Pa.: White Mane, 1992).

1. Herman Hattaway, *General Stephen D. Lee* (Jackson: University of Mississippi Press, 1976). It seems pointless to repeat the documentation from the book; hence I have footnoted only the passages that are not specifically documented in the book.

I always have been glad that Professor Williams had an interest in having a graduate student work on S. D. Lee, and that it became my job to do so. Whatever else Lee may have been, and however good a general he was, he certainly has been good for me! His life made an acceptable book, and not only that, it became a book that won the Confederate Memorial Literary Society's Jefferson Davis Award, given at the Museum of the Confederacy, and now—so many years later, and to my tremendous gratification—it has been reissued in a fine paperback edition by the University of Mississippi Press, an edition that the History Book Club featured as an "HBC Classic." I'm especially pleased with my good friend Jack Davis's praise-filled critique which he did for the Club.

Well, I knew some time ago that this book was going to be reissued, so when the good folks here in Louisiana who produce the annual symposium asked me again this year to appear on the program, it seemed that it would be nice and even symbolically appropriate to commemorate the reissue of *General Stephen D. Lee* by taking another look—now, at this more mature point in my own career—at one of the high points of Lee's military career. I wondered if I might now arrive at any different conclusions, or if I could find any fresh material which had eluded me before and that might shed new light on a still-shady element in Lee's story.

S. D. Lee's activities at the Second Battle of Manassas, I always have felt, made his reputation initially, and, in the long period of his not being much noticed by Civil War enthusiasts, if he was recalled for one thing only it usually was for this episode. And I myself had never, until April 8, 1989, gotten around to visiting the battlefield! I know that my dear and respected friends—among them Richard Sommers and Albert Castel—believe it is reprehensible to write about military actions if one has not personally visited the ground where they took place, and indeed I agree with them; it's just that in the old days my wife and I simply did not have enough time or money to afford getting to *everyplace* that S. D. Lee saw action. One of the things that made Lee so fun, but also hard, to study was that he got practically everywhere: from Fort Sumter to the Virginia battlefields, to Mississippi and subsequently all over the western theater, and finally to a corps command in Georgia, Tennessee, and North Carolina. It was just an unfortunate coincidence in my life's travel itinerary that Manassas got short shrift, and I was awfully glad to have the opportunity at last, as a result of my being one of the featured speakers at a meeting there of Jerry Russell's Confederate Historical Institute. It *is* true that visits to the terrain provide insight that can be obtained in no other way, and I profited from my experience.

Stephen Dill Lee was born September 22, 1833. Thus, he was 27½ years of age as the Civil War began and he accepted commission as a Confederate captain and served as P. G. T. Beauregard's aide during the operations against Fort Sumter. Lee had graduated from West Point in 1854, seventeenth in a class of forty-six, and had served for the ensuing seven years as a lieutenant of artillery in the United States Army. He would have been 28 years and 11 months old at Second Manassas—where, he later recalled, he had the first serious religious thought in his life. Before he met and married his wife, late in the war, he never belonged to any church, though he had turned during the conflict from his youthful indifference. At Second Manassas he looked out across the field just before the Yankee hordes charged across it and said: "Well there is hell to pay here, for sure, and . . . nothing but some unseen and superintending power, can tell where this thing is going to end."[2]

Shortly after the capitulation of Fort Sumter, Lee transferred to the Hampton (South Carolina) Legion to be its artillery battery commander, and that unit moved to the vicinity of Manassas to join the Confederate army in Virginia, eventually becoming an element of Maj. Gen. James Longstreet's division. Lee participated conspicuously and well during the various minor episodes of the fall and winter of 1861-1862. Thus, when the Hampton Legion's artillery was reorganized into a two-battery battalion, Lee was named battalion commander, and was promoted to major on November 8, 1861.

Lee and the battalion won Maj. Gen. John Bell Hood's praise for gallant service in support of the latter's brigade during the battle of

2. Partially identified Charleston, South Carolina, newspaper clipping in scrapbooks of Stephen Dill Lee, Lee Museum, Columbus, Mississippi, book 3.

Eltham's Landing on May 7, 1862, and at Hood's urging, Lee was promoted two days later to lieutenant colonel. (Hood, incidentally, was a fellow member of Lee's West Point graduating class.) Lee remained with his battalion within the Hampton Legion for the rest of the Confederate retreat up the Virginia peninsula, but at the end of May, when the Southerners made a defensive stand near Richmond, Lee joined Brig. Gen. William H. C. Whiting's division staff, though retaining command of the battalion. In this new capacity Lee served as liaison officer between Whiting and his division's two brigades. Lee's artillery battalion did not become engaged in the Battle of Fair Oaks (also called Seven Pines) on May 31, 1862, a fateful episode that resulted in the wounding of the army commander, Gen. Joseph E. Johnston, and his ultimate replacement by Gen. Robert E. Lee.

General Lee at once commenced reorganization, renaming his force the Army of Northern Virginia and uniting it with previously detached troops under Maj. Gen. Thomas J. Jackson. He had inherited a cumbersomely construed command composed of quasi-independent divisions, sometimes called "wings." Maj. Gen. Daniel H. Hill had the left, James Longstreet the center, and John B. Magruder the right. Gustavus W. Smith, who had been army second in command, previously had the reserve, but, after initially succeeding Johnston to head the army, had suffered a nervous breakdown.

During early June, Magruder became much impressed with S. D. Lee's performance, and requested his transfer to his wing. General Lee acquiesced, and Magruder named S. D. Lee to be chief of artillery for the right wing.

As wing chief of artillery, Lee exercised a degree of supervision and advisory responsibility over the various batteries that were assigned to brigades, 44 guns served by 815 men, and he personally commanded the reserve, 22 pieces.

S. D. Lee's artillery participated in a number of hard fights during the Seven Days campaign, June 25–July 1, 1862, but Magruder's conduct—and the overall conduct of his wing—was assessed unfavorably at general headquarters. Shortly after the campaign concluded, General Lee accomplished some drastic restructuring and arranged for the transfer of Magruder to the western theater. Indeed, all four of the officers within the Army of Northern Virginia who outranked Longstreet were soon transferred, leaving Long-street the senior major general and second in command.

During August 1862, both the Northern and the Southern armies in Virginia made organizational changes; the Confederates restructured into two corps, a larger one of five divisions under Longstreet and a smaller one of three divisions under Jackson, and made significant changes in artillery distribution. Thenceforth Confederate artillery was to be doled out much less than before to units of brigade or smaller size; now it was more typically to be concentrated—in battalion-sized units—at division or corps level and kept well toward the front, with the exception of an army reserve.

S. D. Lee acquired command of an artillery battalion, a new one still incompletely organized and formed. (Eventually it had six batteries; for Second Manassas it was understrength.) The reorganizations occurred rapidly, and took place only a short time before the Second Manassas campaign began; as a result, the sources are a bit garbled—some are contradictory, and some are surprisingly brief—and I have not been able to determine the precise types or exact numbers of guns that Lee's battalion had for the campaign. Civil War artillery batteries typically had four guns, but they often had as many as six—indeed, it was determined by artillery leaders that this larger number was the wiser one, but logistical limitations usually precluded such an arrangement—and batteries sometimes, because of losses or other circumstances, had fewer than four guns.[3] (A seriously understrength battery likely would soon be reinforced or combined with another.) Numerous sources say Lee's battalion for the Second Manassas campaign had eighteen guns, and Lee himself recalled in 1878 that he had had nine howitzers and nine rifles, but a contemporary news release written by one of the battalion's battery commanders asserted that the battalion consisted of sixteen guns, supplemented for the Second Manassas campaign by four others, two from Norfolk and two from Lynchburg, the supplemental pieces being long-range rifles.[4]

3. Edward Porter Alexander, "Confederate Artillery Service," *Southern Historical Society Papers* 11:99. This collection is hereinafter referred to as *SHSP*.
4. "Most of them long-range rifles," according to Joseph Mills Hanson, *Bull Run Remembers* (Manassas, Va.: National Capitol Publishers, 1953), 124. See also partially identified newspaper clipping dated August 31, 1862, in scrap-

Lee's battalion was the army artillery reserve, and as such he reported directly to General Lee, not to Longstreet, although the battalion moved with an element of Longstreet's corps, Maj. Gen. Richard H. Anderson's division, the army's infantry reserve. Lee's battalion was referred to as "light artillery" and the objective was, obviously, for the army reserve artillery to be highly mobile. Until Lee took over the unit, it briefly had been commanded by its executive officer, Maj. Delaware ("Del") Kemper, and Kemper remained in the battalion thereafter. The unit comprised six batteries:

1. The Bath Battery, or Eubank's (Virginia) Battery, commanded by Capt. John L. Eubank. This well-prepared outfit was one of seventy-five artillery batteries which, between November 1, 1861, and June 1862, were equipped and trained at Camp Lee, a basic training center located on the Hermitage Fair Grounds near Richmond.[5] The unit was armed with four smoothbores.

2. One section of the Portsmouth Battery, or Grimes's (Virginia) Battery, with two Parrotts, under Lt. Thomas J. Oakham.[6] The state furnished this unit's pieces, and later one of them was put on display at the U.S. Navy Yard.[7]

3. Jordan's Battery, or the Bedford (Virginia) Battery, under Capt. Tyler Calhoun Jordan, later an artillery colonel.[8] No source has been found to ascertain what the unit had for armament at Second Manassas. It took four rifles into the 1863 Pennsylvania campaign,[9] but S. D. Lee's Second Manassas report indicated that the unit had at least one howitzer.

4. The Richmond Battery, or Parker's (Virginia) Battery, under Capt. William Wing Parker. A few of the personnel of this later-famous

books of Blewett Lee, Lee Museum; and Robert K. Krick, *Parker's Virginia Battery C.S.A.*, rev. ed. (Wilmington, N.C.: Broadfoot Publishing, 1989), esp. chap. 3.

5. *SHSP* 26:244.

6. *SHSP* 6:250. Oakham's name appears as "Oakum" in *SHSP* 34:148 and 150, and as "Oakhum" in the index to the *SHSP* as well as in S. D. Lee's report in *The War of the Rebellion: A Compilation of the Official Records of the Union and Confederate Armies* (Washington: Government Printing Office, 1880–1901), ser. 1, vol. 12, pt. 2, pp. 577–78. Hereinafter cited as *OR*.

7. *Confederate Veteran* 14: 390.

8. *OR* 1, 51:2, 900.

9. *OR* 1, 25:1, 877.

battery were teenagers, though subsequent myth suggested that almost all of them were. Actually the average age in the battery was 25.2 years, and one of the men was 48.[10] Nevertheless, and not totally without reason, it was called the "Boy Battery" and was at first a source of grief for S. D. Lee, who was angry at having any extremely young men in his battalion and concerned over their total lack of training and experience. The battery joined Lee's battalion only ten or twelve days before the Second Battle of Manassas, and in those days, Lee made himself quite unpopular with the unit by working them extremely hard in forced training.[11] But it paid off and they performed well in the battle, their first combat. Lee mentions in his report of Second Manassas that the unit had two howitzers, and Robert K. Krick, in his careful study of the Parker Battery, not only confirms that but also identifies the rest of the battery's armament at Second Manassas as being two Parrott rifles.[12] Parker later recalled that his battery had four 3-inch rifles, which had been captured from the Federals (doubtless in McClellan's Peninsular Campaign) and this is confirmed by chronologically later notations in the Official Records.

5. Rhett's (South Carolina) Battery, under Lt. William Elliott. Lee's Second Manassas report mentions two of the unit's pieces as being howitzers; an article in *Confederate Military History* implies that the unit had (at least some) short-range guns: at Antietam it fired at short range.[13]

6. Taylor's (Virginia) Battery, under Capt. John Saunders Taylor. This battery is one of the foggier elements in the picture. Jennings Cropper Wise, in *The Long Arm of Lee*, stated that Taylor's unit was not with Lee, but rather that the battalion's sixth battery was the Ashland Battery, under Capt. Pichegru Woolfolk Jr. Wise was wrong; Woolfolk's battery replaced Taylor's, for some reason which I do not know, for the subsequent campaign in Maryland. But what armament did Taylor have? Again, with certainty and specifically for Second Manassas, I do not know, but it probably was the four 12-pounder Napoleons that constituted the unit's armament later in

10. Krick, *Parker's Virginia Battery,* 6–9.
11. *SHSP* 35:103–5.
12. Krick, *Parker's Virginia Battery,* 35.
13. *Confederate Military History* 6:158.

the war.[14] But if this is true, it does not solve the total puzzle, for when Lee wrote about Second Manassas in 1878 he did not recall having had any Napoleons.[15] It seems unlikely that Lee, a professionally trained career artillerist, ever would have referred to Napoleons as howitzers, though both were smoothbores.

So Lee's longest-range guns were Oakham's two Parrotts, probably the smaller 3-inch type that could hurl a $9\frac{1}{2}$-pound projectile approximately 3,000 yards (the larger 20-Parrott—which, of course, they could have been—had about the same range).[16] The 3-inch Ordnance Rifle or the 3-inch Rodman Rifle (whatever Jordan and Parker may have had) could fire 10-pound projectiles approximately 2,800 yards. If any of Lee's smoothbores were Napoleons, they could fire 12-pound projectiles to a range of 1,566 yards.

Some of the smoothbores in the battalion beyond doubt were howitzers; *all* of them may possibly have been. Although howitzers were not always smoothbore, they generally were. Howitzers typically were made of bronze and were manufactured in standard projectile weight classes: 12-, 24-, and 32-pounders. They had short tubes with chambered interiors that allowed a light powder charge to lob a shell on a high trajectory, and thus in employment were similar to mortars—very effective against personnel and in covering "dead spaces" in a field of fire. Basing a best guess on the rapid mobility of Lee's battalion, his howitzers probably were the 12-pounders, which had a maximum range of 1,070 yards.[17]

Other known officers in Lee's battalion included Lt. William H. Kemper, adjutant, and Lieutenants Taylor (I never have been able to learn his first name), Stephen Capers Gilbert, J. T. Brown (apparently

14. *OR* 1, 12:2, 546–51.

15. Gary W. Gallagher, ed., *Fighting for the Confederacy: The Personal Recollections of General Edward Porter Alexander* (Chapel Hill: University of North Carolina Press, 1989), 134. Alexander and Lee had been close friends ever since Lee was cadet lieutenant in Alexander's plebe company at West Point, and later they carried on a chummy correspondence.

16. Krick, *Parker's Virginia Battery*, 50.

17. I have extrapolated my technical data from L. Van Loan Naisawald, *Grape and Canister: The Story of the Field Artillery of the Army of the Potomac, 1861–1865* (New York: Oxford University Press, 1960); Fairfax Downey, *The Guns at Gettysburg* (New York: Collier Books, 1962); and Jennings Cropper Wise, *The Long Arm of Lee,* 2 vols. (Lynchburg, Va.: J. P. Bell, 1915).

J. Thompson Brown Jr., later an artillery battery commander), and W. W. Fickling (also later promoted to captain and given command of a battery). Their names are known because Lee cited them for good conduct in his report of Second Manassas. There may, or may not, have been other officers.

At some point before the Battle of Second Manassas, Lee's battalion was reinforced. Two rifle guns and their crews were detached from one of the batteries in Jackson's corps—probably Capt. W. T. Poague's—and united with Lee's other guns. The general's son, Robert E. Lee Jr.—later a Confederate captain, but now serving in the ranks—was "number one" crewman for one of the pieces, and it is his later published recollections that reveal this little part of the story.[18]

Strategic maneuvers preceded the Second Battle of Manassas.[19] General Lee ordered an advance to commence from Gordonsville on August 20. Longstreet's corps on the right was to cross the Rapidan River at Raccoon Ford; Jackson's, on the left, was to cross at Sommerville Ford. Anderson's division, to which was attached S. D. Lee's battalion, constituted the army reserve.

The short-lived Federal Army of Virginia, 47,000 strong, under Maj. Gen. John Pope, had begun moving on July 14 toward Gordonsville. As the campaign proceeded to unfold, General Lee gained intelligence that Pope soon would be reinforced. To prevent that, and in hopes of "striking a blow," as Lee liked to phrase it, the Army of Northern Virginia effectuated a turning movement, Jackson's corps thrusting ahead and succeeding in getting between Pope's force and Washington.

Jackson concentrated north of the Warrenton Turnpike, just above Groveton, and waited. Pope's forces approached, and on August 28

18. Robert E. Lee Jr., *Recollections and Letters of General Robert E. Lee, by His Son, Captain Robert E. Lee* (New York: Doubleday, Page, 1904), 76.
19. While I was writing this paper, John Hennessy was working on *Return to Bull Run,* his definitive history of the Second Manassas Campaign. During my visit to the battle site in 1989, he related to me the information I use in the paragraphs that follow.

clashed with Jackson's men in a fierce little skirmish called the Battle of Groveton, which lasted until nearly midnight. Assessing the situation, Pope erroneously concluded that Jackson was attempting to withdraw into the valley.

That night the head of Longstreet's columns reached Thoroughfare Gap and the Federal forces previously guarding the gap were ordered to move toward Manassas, for the concentration that Pope believed would spell Jackson's doom. On August 29, Longstreet's troops gradually approached Jackson's position, the first of them contacting Jackson's right flank by 11 A.M. and the bulk of them uniting by midafternoon. S. D. Lee and his artillery still remained in the mountain passes.

Blindly confident of imminent success, Pope ordered his entire force to concentrate for a decisive assault. But Jackson had selected an admirable defensive position behind an unfinished railroad bed. The grades and cuts provided ready-made entrenchments while the ties and rocks afforded cover for the men. Pope conducted a series of piecemeal, uncoordinated frontal assaults, all of which failed. Jackson's men followed up the various repulses by advancing to seize positions forward of the main defensive line.

Night brought a temporary end to the fighting, while the Union troops regrouped into a single mass and the Confederates made some important movements. Jackson's men abandoned the advanced positions they had won, and all returned to the strong defensive line along the unfinished railroad. Longstreet's corps stretched out next to them, at an angle bending to the front so that the Confederate army occupied a four-mile-long line shaped like an open V, facing the enemy to the east.

Lee's artillery battalion, with the last of Longstreet's forces, received orders late in the evening to march toward the front. Lee and his men moved in darkness and, after a tiresome trek, encamped just before dawn on the 30th, not knowing precisely where they were in relation to Jackson's corps, only that they were somewhere on the Warrenton Turnpike. At daybreak Lee discovered that his bivouac occupied some of the positions involved in the fights of the Battle of Groveton two days earlier.

Lee consulted with Major General Hood, one of Longstreet's division commanders and closest to Jackson's corps, and then decided to put his battalion on the same spot that had been occupied the day before by the Washington Artillery of New Orleans. (This fact is important, for later, in determining who should receive credit, and how much, for the great Confederate success, it would be pointed out that the position was obviously an excellent one, and that Lee certainly needed to expend little or no mental energy in selecting it.) In this position, Lee's battalion could fire across Jackson's front, in direct support of Col. Stapleton Crutchfield, Jackson's artillery chief. Lee's artillery, adjacent to Hood's brigades, constituted the exact midpoint of the Confederate lines.

Interestingly, only recently has the National Park Service become aware of the precise location of Lee's guns—and indeed, it knows the gun emplacement spots for only about one-third of them. Only a small part of the Manassas battle area was set aside for commemorative purposes during the nineteenth century; with the passing of time, various additional parcels of land gradually were acquired and added to what is now the Manassas National Battlefield. One day, relic hunters turned up at park headquarters, sheepishly admitting that they had found and opened a Confederate gravesite and quite by accident had also found several concentrations of friction primer remnants—archaeological evidence of the gun emplacements. Before that, park experts had guessed that the location was some twenty-five or more yards forward of where it actually was.

The position hardly could have been better: the guns pointed northeast and were nestled along a commanding ridge about a quarter of a mile long. They may have been situated just behind a stone wall (which of course would have offered cover to the gunners, helping to protect them from any enemy assault upon the position). No sources mention a stone wall, but remnants of one are there to this day. If it was not there at the time of the battle, it would have had to have been leveled before that time or built and subsequently leveled since. No one now knows. Whether the wall was there or not, the gunners overlooked a field of fire embracing some two thousand yards—over a mile to the front! Immediately opposite Jackson's lines stretched an open field, of which Lee's fire could sweep any part. Beyond that, to the east, was farmland with cornfields, orchards, and fences—an inviting expanse for enemy skirmishers—and still farther to the east was timberland, an obvious assembly area for a Union assault force. General Lee himself inspected Colonel Lee's position and declared, "You are just where I wanted you; stay there."

Remembering S. D. Lee's unhampered field of fire, one battalion member recalled that he "had a grand view of the plains of Manassas, reaching as far as Centreville." While no major strike occurred until noon, the first Federal infantry became visible at 7 A.M., some two thousand yards away. Lee's guns opened fire, forcing the enemy, even at that distance, to scurry for cover. The Federals returned the volley with long-range guns.

During the morning, the act was repeated many times. At every appearance of Union infantry, Lee's artillery harassed them. They answered with fire from their own big guns, but did no damage to Lee's emplacements. One of Lee's men recalled that "the enemy had a 36 pounder," certainly a large artillery piece, "but fortunately he did not get our range."[20] Lee himself helped with some of the firing. He sighted a gun for 3,500 yards, aimed at a Federal caisson, and killed the two wheelhorses with his second shot. Meanwhile, the Federals continued preparations for a massive charge.

Throughout the morning Lee's artillery engaged only a far-distant enemy, and some of the other nearby Confederates grew complacent. One regimental commander actually sat in the shade of a persimmon tree to eat his breakfast of dry crackers and boiled bacon, watching Lee direct fire at a line of troops too far away to recognize as soldiers until sunlight glinting off their bayonets betrayed them. Around noon the Federals tested the position with an advance, driving in the few Confederate skirmishers. The artillery drove them back, and then suddenly all firing ceased. An ominous silence prevailed.

At about 3 P.M., a huge concentration of Federals, which had massed behind the timber opposite Lee's position, advanced in heavy force against Jackson's left, "glittering lines of battle in magnificent array," one Southerner recalled. Accompanied by crash after crash of musketry, regiment after regiment of blue-coated soldiers moved toward the extreme left of Jackson's lines. One of the men in Lee's battalion later penned a news release for the *Richmond Dispatch*:

20. Newspaper clipping, August 31, 1862, in scrapbooks of Blewett Lee, Lee Museum.

The shells burst above, around, and [seemingly] beneath us. Every man is at his post, no talking—no ducking of heads now. An intense, silent earnestness. It was an hour big with every man's history. It was a struggle for life. The face of every man was flushed, his eye full, . . . It seemed like the very heavens were in a blaze, or, like two angry clouds surcharged with electricity and wafted by opposing winds, had met terrific in battle.[21]

The Confederates fought back furiously, some quickly running out of ammunition. At intervals, they scrambled out and stripped the dead and wounded of cartridge boxes. At some points along Jackson's front, crouching Federals were huddled so close that some Confederates resorted to throwing rocks at them.

Momentarily fearful of a breakthrough, Jackson sent a desperate message to General Lee, requesting reinforcements. The general immediately ordered Longstreet to send a division; but by the time Longstreet received the order, huge masses of Federal troops, the main assault force, were crossing the field of fire of Colonel Lee's guns, aimed toward Jackson's center. Henry Kyd Douglas, one of Jackson's couriers, later recalled that Longstreet had replied to the request for reinforcements that before any could reach Jackson, "that attack will be broken by artillery."[22] It was about 4 P.M. As one of the men present later phrased it, Lee had "planted artillery so thick . . . that cannoneers almost elbowed each other."

(It is fair, and perhaps important, to observe that Colonel Crutchfield had Jackson's corps artillery emplaced within the lines, and eighteen of those guns helped repulse the assaults. They fired frontally into the attacking troops, supported by the effective enfilade fire that Lee's position allowed.)[23]

The assault force, despite two attempts to rally itself, was thrown back. Douglas, who witnessed it, recalled that the first "assaulting

21. Ibid.

22. Henry Kyd Douglas, *I Rode with Stonewall* (Chapel Hill: University of North Carolina Press, 1940), 140.

23. Monroe F. Cockrell, ed., *Gunner with Stonewall: Reminiscences of William Thomas Poague* (Jackson, Tenn.: McCowat-Mercer Press, 1957), 38; Hanson, *Bull Run Remembers*, 124.

line halted, . . . thrown into confusion, and they fled. In their place came another line, with the same disastrous result. And then again a splendid column of attack, compact and determined, came grandly up to their endeavor." But Lee's artillery stood ready, and "when the blue line was within proper range, these hoarse hounds of war were unleashed and the destruction they did was fearful. Deep rents were torn in the enemy's ranks, their colors went down, one after another." One soldier wrote, "The heavens rocked with the roar of the Confederate batteries," and another recalled "such a blaze of artillery as I never heard." For thirty full minutes, regiment after regiment—thousands of Federal troops—charged into the open. Lee's guns belched an incessant fire. Thousands of reserve troops stood ready to exploit any success by the main assault, but they never moved up, intimidated by Lee's effective fire.

Suffering tremendously from the continuing artillery bursts, three Federal regiments slashed desperately forward, in a futile attempt to assault Lee's guns. The howitzers belched canister, pinpoints of flame jutting forth. All the Federal forces finally were repulsed, some of their dead falling within two hundred yards of Lee's guns.

There is one minor point on which I have been persuaded to change my mind from what I believed when I first published *General Stephen D. Lee.* I said then that in capitalizing on Lee's successful fire, Longstreet ordered up to the position the other batteries that had been attached to his corps, making thirty guns in all which joined in the enfilade fire that wrought the final destruction of the Federal assault, sweeping the last blue waves from the field.[24] Longstreet did order the other guns forward, but they were far to the right of Lee's position, and never got within effective range. At the crucial moment, it was S. D. Lee's show.

Lee had his short-range guns moved to within five hundred yards of their targets, and they did severe damage until finally having to quit firing because the thick smoke created a blinding curtain

24. See Lenoir Chambers, *Stonewall Jackson,* 2 vols. (New York: William Morrow & Co., 1959), 2:170, this being the source I used at the time.

over the battlefield. This smoke also hampered the feeble Federal effort at counterfire. Only two Union batteries fired on Lee, and these overshot their mark.

The Union "charge was turned into a retreat," Douglas recalled, "and they soon broke over the field in a wild rout. The avenging shot and shell scattered the fleeing mass and their flight became a panic." Longstreet's grey host at last counterattacked, inflicting severe punishment on some units of the disorganized Federals, the kind that General Lee had attempted unsuccessfully to achieve all during the Seven Days campaign. The Confederates, who "came on like demons emerging from the earth," one Federal observer said, pushed the demoralized Northerners for more than a mile and a half, well into the old battlefield of First Manassas. One Federal regiment, Duryee's Zouaves from New York, suffered, in killed and wounded, the greatest losses of any regiment on any day in the entire war.[25]

Much credit belonged to S. D. Lee and his guns. In addition to having had a perfect position from which to fire, their performance had been magnificent. In repelling the charges, Lee's men had worked incessantly; six of them sustained wounds, including the executive officer Kemper, who was hurt badly in the arm. For two of the batteries, this was their first battle action. The enormous expenditures of each gun—estimated by one careful student at not less than 150 rounds apiece—made this one of the greatest muzzle-loading artillery conflicts in history. It also made Lee something of a hero. His name was on the lips of every soldier in the army. Some even said, with obvious extravagance, that "never, in the history of war, had one man commanded so much artillery, with so much skill and effect as he did."

In later years many people cited Second Manassas as one of Lee's two or three outstanding Civil War accomplishments. Apparently, however, Lee did not receive as much credit and adulation from his

25. Frank E. Vandiver, *Mighty Stonewall* (New York: McGraw-Hill, 1957), 370–71; inscription on monument to Duryee's Zouaves, at the battlefield.

superiors as he did from his admirers. It is true that General Lee had said to him, the first time they met after the battle, "Young man, come here! I want to thank you for what you did yesterday. You did good work." And the following December, President Jefferson Davis, referring to Lee, said, "I have reason to believe that at the last great conflict on the field of Manassas he served to turn the tide of battle and consummate the victory." But the general gave Lee no special personal credit in his official report. He mentioned only that Lee occupied the same position as Walton's Washington Artillery the day before and that under Lee's "well directed fire, the supporting lines were broken and fell back in confusion." That was all: no high praise.

Longstreet exhibited an even cooler attitude. In his official report, he blandly stated that "Colonel S. D. Lee, with his reserve artillery placed in the position occupied the day previous by Colonel Walton, engaged the enemy in a very severe artillery combat. The result was, as on the day previous, a success."

Years later, in 1877 and 1878, Longstreet and Lee fought a bitter literary debate.[26] Perhaps they always had been cool toward one another, maybe even enemies; it is impossible now to prove one way or the other. We do know that after 1870 Longstreet increasingly came under personal attack, and his enemies tried to besmirch his war reputation. Among several episodes about which he was harried was *his* conduct at Second Manassas. At times, in attempting to defend himself, he was goaded into intemperance.

What Longstreet did with respect to Lee's performance and contribution at Second Manassas was to damn him and it with faint praise: Longstreet did not say anything really negative; he simply did not say much at all, and he grossly exaggerated the importance of the artillery he had moved in the end to Lee's support. As Gary W. Gallagher recently put it, "Lee had much the better of the exchange."[27]

Longstreet's postwar bitterness notwithstanding, it is difficult to assess his and General Lee's apparent restraint at the time concerning

26. See *SHSP* 6:59–70, 215–17, 250–54.
27. Gallagher gives a good explanation of this particular matter in "Scapegoat in Victory: James Longstreet and the Second Battle of Manassas," *Civil War History* 34 (December 1988): 293–307.

S. D. Lee's performance at Second Manassas. Contrasted with many assessments by other writers, both participants at Second Manassas as well as students of the battle, they were remarkably matter-of-fact about Lee's contributions.

To be sure, Lee had good luck! True to his sometime nickname "Pet of Fortune," he wandered by default onto a position that Walton's Washington Artillery already had selected but abandoned because they were too debilitated to continue in action. Indeed, luck may well have been the principal factor in the outcome: luck that Lee's guns stood where they happened to be, and luck that Pope's Federals were hurled in such massive numbers and so persistently into Lee's enfilading fire zone. Yet Second Manassas was a great Confederate victory. Undeniably, Lee's luck and his skill both entered into the picture. Suppose he had not gone to the trouble of trying to train his youthful and inexperienced gunners; suppose they had broken, or been overrun? (One modern expert in infantry assault tactics suggested to me recently that the most obviously desirable way out for Pope's forces was to use cavalry to assault Lee's position and then thrust troops just to the right of it, breaking through the Confederate lines there and rolling laterally into Longstreet's minions.) Lee was the man of the moment. Had there been many more such moments, the outcome of the war might have been different.

⟪⬦⟫ P. G. T. Beauregard

with Michael J. C. Taylor

Michael J. C. Taylor was my third doctoral student. He secured a tenure-track position at Dickinson State University, Dickinson, North Dakota. His dissertation was on the constitutional philosophy of state rights. For his second book-length project, he chose to work on a biography of Zeppo Marx. We were commissioned to do this piece on Beauregard by Jon Wakelyn for a 1998 book of essays he and Charles F. Ritter coedited and dedicated to the memory and work of Thomas Lawrence Connelly. We do not claim to have rendered a completely fresh depiction of the Creole's life, but rather to have done our best to synthesize extant scholarship.

The popular historian Clifford Dowdey, in his 1955 book *The Land They Fought For,* characterized P. G. T. Beauregard as "the Confederacy's first hero." T. Harry Williams began his biography of the same year by declaring his subject was "the most colorful of all the Confederate generals."[1] Indeed, Beauregard was involved in every phase of the conduct of the war, and proved himself a competent commander at a crucial time when the South's command base was diminishing. Though he had defended an agrarian Old South, when defeat came he adapted to realities and, in the process, helped to industrialize a New South.

This essay first appeared in *Leaders of the American Civil War: A Biographical and Historiographical Dictionary,* ed. Charles F. Ritter and Jon L. Wakelyn (Westport, Conn.: Greenwood Press, 1998).

1. Clifford Dowdey, *The History of the Confederacy 1832–1865* (reprint of *The Land They Fought For;* New York: Marlboro Books, 1992), 113; T. Harry Williams, *P. G. T. Beauregard: Napoleon in Gray* (Baton Rouge: Louisiana State University Press, 1955), 1.

Pierre Gustave Toutant Beauregard was born on May 28, 1818, to a Creole family whose French ancestral ties led back to the thirteenth century. The fine Beauregard House near Chalmette, Louisiana—an exurb of New Orleans—sits adjacent to the War of 1812 Battlefield and is open to the public. Though "Pierre" was added to his name at his Roman Catholic baptism, he preferred Gustave or Gus. Young Gus did not speak a word of English until he was twelve years old, when he was sent to boarding school. Of his childhood and adolescence, Williams concedes that "almost nothing is known," because so few records have survived.[2]

At the lad's urging, Beauregard's father—though he was surprised and perhaps a bit disappointed that his son wanted a military career—arranged for him to study at the U.S. Military Academy at West Point. Williams described him as a "grave, reserved, and withdrawn [cadet who] excelled in sports, rode a horse beautifully, and made high marks."[3] He graduated in 1838 second in his class. Among his peers were Irvin McDowell, Jubal A. Early, Richard Ewell, Joseph Hooker, and William Tecumseh Sherman. After finishing his studies, Beauregard received a commission as a second lieutenant in the prestigious corps of engineers.

For the first five years of his military career, Beauregard was a civil engineer; his most significant duty was the supervision of the topographical and hydrographical surveys of Barataria Bay on the Louisiana Gulf. During this tour of duty, in September 1841, he married Marie Laure Villere, the daughter of a wealthy local planter. By all accounts, the young officer was devoted to Marie, and she bore him two sons, René and Henri, to whom he was a dedicated father. In March 1850, Marie died giving birth to a daughter, who was named Laure, for her mother. Though he grieved for his wife, Beauregard was devoted to his daughter, whom he said was "as perfect a human being as I have ever known."[4]

During the Mexican War, Beauregard served with the corps of engineers under Commanding General Winfield Scott. Beauregard's fellow officers included Robert E. Lee, George G. Meade, and Joseph

2. Williams, *Beauregard*, 4.
3. Ibid., 7.
4. Ibid., 325.

E. Johnston. His primary function was to devise topographical surveys for Scott and his subordinate commanders, often with other young officers such as Ulysses S. Grant, Thomas J. Jackson, and Jubal A. Early.

It was the young lieutenant who influenced General Scott's decision to attack at Chapultepec. Scott informed his immediate staff in late August 1847 that he planned to attack the Mexican capital before Santa Anna could raze his exterior line. When the old general asked for suggestions, Captain Lee voiced his support for a plan, to which Beauregard disagreed. The Creole asserted that a victory at Chapultepec would open two of Santa Anna's most traveled causeways into Mexico City. His arguments convinced Brig. Gen. Franklin Pierce, who, in turn, convinced Scott.

In the battle itself, Beauregard demonstrated valor as he rode with Johnston, inspiring the foot soldiers with audacious theatrics even while under fire. He was conspicuous and proud, being one of the first to enter Mexico City, and under a heavy barrage of fire as well. Steven E. Woodworth, in *Jefferson Davis and His Generals*, points out an early evidence of Beauregard's touchiness: "Though serving with distinction and receiving plenty of recognition in Scott's reports, Beauregard fumed that he was not singled out for special praise above the other engineers, particularly Robert E. Lee."[5]

Following the war, Beauregard took a leave of absence because his health had been aggravated by the Mexican climate. Later, he returned to New Orleans and labored in behalf of the Franklin Pierce campaign throughout 1852. For his efforts, he was rewarded by the new president with an appointment as the superintending engineer at New Orleans. The duties of the position did little to satisfy him, however, and, according to Williams, Beauregard "displayed a testy impatience with people, especially politicians, who criticized his work or tried to interfere with him."[6]

Beauregard married for a second time, to Caroline Deslonde, the influential sister-in-law of Louisiana senator John Slidell. According to Williams, though Beauregard was affectionate toward his new

5. Steven E. Woodworth, *Jefferson Davis and His Generals: The Failure of Confederate Command in the West* (Lawrence: University of Kansas Press, 1990), 73.
6. Williams, *Beauregard*, 36.

bride, he "did not love her with the ardor he had devoted to Marie Laure." After three years, Beauregard had tired of his military career, believing he had been maliciously slighted by the War Department for promotions he thought he deserved. Indeed, Woodworth says, "By 1856, Beauregard was so dissatisfied with the army that he considered joining the filibusterer William Walker in his mad adventure at turning Nicaragua into a slave empire."[7] Beauregard ventured into elective politics, running for mayor of New Orleans in 1858. He lost a close race, and remained in the military. His family alliance paid handsome dividends when, in December 1860, Slidell wrangled him an appointment as superintendent of West Point.

Beauregard enjoyed his post only five days. In December 1860, Louisiana seceded from the Union, and, loyal to his state, Beauregard resigned his commission. Though he offered his services to the state without any preconditions, he expected to be named the commanding general of the militia, a position which already had been offered to and accepted by Braxton Bragg. After Beauregard enlisted as a private in a Creole company, Slidell called him to a conference with the newly inaugurated Confederate president, Jefferson Davis, which took place on February 26, 1861. Initially impressed with Beauregard, the president offered him the command of the Confederate forces at Charleston, which he accepted. Beauregard became the Confederacy's first general officer; he received a brigadier generalship in the Provisional Army, C.S.A., to date from March 1, 1861.

The Confederate bombardment of Fort Sumter initiated the most brutal and bloody conflagration in America's history to that time. Beauregard was the first commander of Southern troops to engage in military confrontation with those of the Union. Prior to the shelling of Fort Sumter, a semblance of gentility was maintained between the Confederates and Sumter's defenders, in which the Union commander was allowed to receive comestibles and supplies from Charleston. Upon his arrival, the new Confederate commander found his forces in disarray, ill-prepared to carry out Davis's order to take the fortress in the harbor: "I find a great deal in the way of

7. Ibid.; Woodworth, *Davis and His Generals*, 74.

zeal and energy around me, but little professional knowledge and experience."[8] The general chose his personal staff carefully, among them a captain seven years out of West Point, Stephen D. Lee, the future defender of Vicksburg. Lee's duties were to act as both acting assistant commissary general and acting assistant quartermaster general, and later, acting adjutant general.

Tensions rose between the two forces in early April 1861. President Davis issued a mandate directly ordering Beauregard to force a surrender. In accordance with his instructions, Sumter was also detached from its source of supply. President Lincoln countered with an order to resupply Sumter, and directed Maj. Robert Anderson to hold Sumter by force if necessary. These actions produced a situation which did not sit well with either commander: Anderson, who had been Beauregard's mentor at West Point, now found his former pupil his enemy. Beauregard wrote a personal note urging his former mentor to surrender the garrison, and asked his aides, Col. James Chestnut and Capt. Stephen D. Lee, to deliver it. Anderson refused the request, but added, Lee later wrote, that "if not hacked to pieces by our batteries he would be starved out in a few days."[9] Chestnut and Lee took this statement to mean that the garrison could be taken without a fight.

When negotiations stalled, primarily because Anderson demanded too many concessions, Chestnut and Lee informed Anderson that the shelling would begin in one hour. The assault began in the early morning hours and continued throughout the day, with Anderson beginning return fire at dawn. In the end, Beauregard forced Anderson to surrender. Though bombs, shells, and mortar rounds did little real damage, and though the Union officer soon could have been easily resupplied by sea, Beauregard seized the initiative and gained control. After Fort Sumter, in Williams's words, the general became "the South's first paladin."[10] President Davis described the Creole as "full of talent and of much military

8. *The War of the Rebellion: A Compilation of the Official Records of the Union and Confederate Armies* (Washington: Government Printing Office, 1880–1901), ser. 1, 1:274. Hereinafter cited as *OR.*

9. *OR* 1, 1:18; Stephen D. Lee's diary, Stephen D. Lee Papers, University of North Carolina, Chapel Hill.

10. Williams, *Beauregard,* 61.

experience," and promoted him to the rank of full general in the regular army, to date from July 21, 1861.[11] This made Beauregard fifth in order of seniority, a fact that much rankled the Creole. He would never forgive Davis for this perceived slight, and as events unfolded—as Grady McWhiney correctly pointed out in several publications and speeches, and especially in *Southerners and Other Americans*—he and Davis even came to hate each other.[12]

First Manassas, according to Williams, was "a record of bungled orders, sudden shifts in strategy, and final fortunate Victory."[13] Confederate forces made up in the sheer force of their efforts what deficiencies they had in command infrastructure. The protection of Virginia was of primary importance to the government in Richmond, and two officers were assigned to carry out this directive: Brig. Gen. P. G. T. Beauregard, near the Union capital of Washington, and Gen. Joseph E. Johnston, to the west in the Shenandoah Valley. President Lincoln, believing Beauregard to have upwards of 35,000 men between Washington and Richmond, ordered Gen. Irvin McDowell to divert Johnston and strike Beauregard before Johnston could reinforce.

Beauregard was outnumbered by his West Point classmate McDowell by 10,000 men, but he held control of both Centerville and Manassas and the vital railway artery between them. McDowell planned an envelopment. Beauregard had an advantage over his Union rival. The authors of *Elements of Confederate Defeat* contend that Beauregard's victory was due to one important factor: "The Confederates, with direct connections to Richmond, had employed the telegraph and the railroad to exploit their interior lines and thereby effect a rapid concentration."[14]

It was critical for Johnston to provide reinforcements to Beauregard in a strike against McDowell, but to do so Johnston had to

11. Woodworth, *Davis and His Generals*, 76; Ezra J. Warner, *Generals in Gray: Lives of the Confederate Commanders*, (Baton Rouge: Louisiana State University Press, 1959), 22–23.

12. Grady McWhiney, *Southerners and Other Americans* (New York: Basic Books, 1973).

13. Williams, *Beauregard*, 81.

14. Richard E. Beringer, Herman Hattaway, Archer Jones, and William N. Still Jr., *Elements of Confederate Defeat: Nationalism, War Aims, and Religion* (abridgment of *Why the South Lost the Civil War*; Athens: University of Georgia Press, 1988), 46.

outmaneuver an opponent in the lower Shenandoah Valley. To divert attention, Johnston dispatched cavalry under J. E. B. Stuart to distract the Union army long enough for a larger force to board railway transports to the Manassas line. Once McDowell's flanking column made their move toward Bull Run Creek, the Federals made their attack on Beauregard's army, which quickly retreated. As reinforcements arrived, Beauregard ordered a counterattack, and the Union lines faltered and broke. Beauregard and Johnston proclaimed the First Battle of Manassas "an epoch in the history of liberty." Davis was elated: "Too high praise cannot be bestowed, whether for the skill of the principal officers, or for the gallantry of all the troops."[15]

Experiences in the battle underscored the problem produced by the Confederacy's national flag being so similar to that of the United States: unless a strong wind was blowing, it was hard to tell them apart. The flamboyant and ever-active Beauregard responded by designing the now-familiar Confederate battle flag. He had the three Carry girls (two sisters and a cousin)—who were among the many visitors to be lavishly entertained at his field headquarters—make the first three of these flags, using material from their undergarments. (At least one of these flags still exists, and is on display at the Museum of the Confederacy in New Orleans. The red portions are quite pink. Maybe they always were? Or maybe they just faded over time?)

Beauregard, however, soon began to draw the ire of the Confederate president and most of the War Department through his incessant telegrams complaining about Commissary General Lucius B. Northrop and advocating a large-scale offensive to take Washington and Baltimore. At first the president was benign, smoothing over matters which he viewed as trivial. But when newspapers printed stories, Davis suspected the general had planted them. The last straw came when Beauregard issued public statements questioning the authority of the secretary of war to issue instructions to a full commanding general. Though Davis respected Beauregard as a commander, he wanted him away from the center of power in Richmond.

15. Richard B. Harwell, *The Confederate Reader: How the South Saw the War* (New York: Barnes & Noble, 1992), 41, 43.

Beauregard was assigned to be Albert Sidney Johnston's second-in-command in the western theater. Though irritated by the president's unwillingness to give him a full command, Beauregard later relished the position under Johnston because of the leeway he had in planning and execution. Larry J. Daniel, in his book *Shiloh*, makes a good argument that Johnston and Beauregard harmonized rather well, but that it was "a partnership built upon mutual weaknesses."[16] Beauregard's intelligence network discovered that Grant's forces were in disarray and vulnerable while stationed at Pittsburg Landing, Tennessee. Beauregard proffered his plan to crush Grant before Don Carlos Buell's approaching reinforcements could arrive. Johnston agreed, and Beauregard ordered the commanders of the western forces—Leonidas Polk from Columbus and Earl Van Dorn from Arkansas—to Corinth, Mississippi. Davis ordered Bragg to join Johnston and Beauregard. By late March the forces of the western theater were united and over 40,000 strong.

However, as the march began toward Grant's forces, snarls in the implementation of Beauregard's plan became evident and necessitated the attack being postponed three days. "Such a scheme should never have been tried," Woodworth writes critically, "with a hodge-podge army that had been together less than a week and contained many units that had never made a day's march before, but Beauregard could not resist fancy." Woodworth further observes that "the units were to march on different roads, converging and passing between each other at various intersections according to a rigid schedule, in a scheme that was something like the convolution of a modern-day marching band on a monstrous scale." As it unfolded, the lack of troop discipline and breaches of procedure needed for a sneak attack—such as firing a weapon to see if it would work in a damp environment—were enough to dishearten both Beauregard and Bragg, who urged termination. "There is no chance for surprise," Beauregard wailed, "now they will be entrenched to the eyes." Johnston, however, remained resolute: "I would fight them if they were a million," he said to his aide.[17]

16. Larry J. Daniel, *Shiloh: The Battle That Changed the Civil War* (New York: Simon & Schuster, 1997), 125.
17. Woodworth, *Davis and His Generals*, 96; Herman Hattaway and Archer Jones, *How the North Won: A Military History of the Civil War* (Urbana: University of Illinois Press, 1983), 164; Daniel, *Shiloh*, 128.

At the break of dawn on April 6, 1862, the amassed Confederate forces launched a successful surprise attack on Grant's prostrate army. To their credit, though the Union troops fell back gradually they were potent enough to stagnate a forceful Confederate advance. At an enclave later called "the Hornet's Nest," troops under Brig. Gen. Benjamin Prentis withstood eight Confederate offensives.[18] By the time their line finally broke at 5:30 in the afternoon, Confederate Gen. Albert Sidney Johnston had been mortally wounded and died. In the end, the Battle of Shiloh could be best termed a bloody stalemate, for though both sides had taken the day—the Confederates on the first day and the Union on the second day—they had done so with heavy casualties. In his message to President Davis, the new western commander claimed full victory, but in almost the same breath he demanded that more troops be dispatched. Davis, having scrounged all he could from other areas, was infuriated by Beauregard's request.

Woodworth is hypercritical of Beauregard's battle plan, and, in one of his fiercest strictures, says: "One result of Beauregard's wretched planning was that none of the corps commanders could control his units . . . Men in battle for the first time found themselves being led by officers they did not know." He also claims that Beauregard compounded his errors when, upon assuming command on the death of Johnston, he did not move his troops back to protect the vital railway interchange at Corinth. According to Woodworth, after the second day "the army could take no more and was about to go to pieces."[19]

Following Shiloh, Maj. Gen. Henry Halleck assumed command of Grant and Buell's forces and pressed the Confederates back toward Corinth. Beauregard soon found himself outmanned and outgunned. He deduced that if the Confederates lost the vital railway interchange, "we lose the whole Mississippi Valley and probably our cause." Yet retreat was his only realistic option. What the general had to accomplish, according to Williams, was "to deceive the enemy and prevent demarcation among their own troops."[20] In

---

18. This number is misstated in many accounts, usually being estimated at eleven and sometimes as many as fourteen. Daniel proves the correct number to be eight (*Shiloh*, 215).

19. Woodworth, *Davis and His Generals*, 99, 102.

20. *OR* 1, vol. 10, pt. 2, 403; Williams, *Beauregard*, 153.

this he was successful, implementing a plan which left the Union commanders awaiting an impending attack that never came.

Upon examination, it was a lack of tenacity that caused Beauregard to abandon Corinth. Woodworth asserts: "Robert E. Lee would successfully defend Virginia against overwhelming forces for two years . . . , but Beauregard was not Lee and did not feel up to taking the risks involved."[21] Davis, who was out of patience with the general, was livid at the abandonment of such a vital railway artery without so much as a fight. As if to make matters worse, the general, following his retreat from Corinth, took an unauthorized medical leave, which destroyed any prestige he had within the Confederate government and the Southern press.

Davis summarily dismissed Beauregard and replaced him with Braxton Bragg. Bragg, out of courtesy, sought his predecessor's advice as to how to launch a counteroffensive against the Union in Tennessee. Beauregard suggested a strategy similar to that of First Manassas, making optimal use of the existing railroad. Beauregard's reputation was still a strong one among Union commanders. During his advance on the Williamsburg Road during the Seven Days campaign in late June 1862, Maj. Gen. George McClellan was disturbed by rumors that Beauregard was to lead the defense of Richmond with 200,000 troops; McClellan was ignorant of the truth that Beauregard already had been relieved of command and sat idle over a thousand miles away.

Following his dismissal, General Beauregard was to play no further significant role in the conduct of the war. He spent much of it in command of the defenses of Charleston, South Carolina, where he notably nurtured experimentation and was instrumental in promoting the submarine project which had been moved to that place. He of course kept in touch with events and corresponded with his numerous friends and confidants. Thomas Lawrence Connelly Jr. and Archer Jones, in *The Politics of Command*, assert that the so-called "western concentration bloc" supported Beauregard's grand strategic idea, which in fact was valid and desirable: to stop giving main attention to the war in the East, and instead to concentrate and achieve a decisive victory in the West. The

---

21. Woodworth, *Davis and His Generals*, 104.

strategy, however, was too late adopted and then too halfheart-edly implemented.[22]

Beauregard had one more brush with fame. By May 1864 he was back in Virginia, and probably saved Richmond by discerning and responding to Grant's threat at Petersburg. Grant's plan to force a showdown, Williams says, was "foiled by Beauregard's stubborn defense."[23] With only 2,200 men at his disposal, Beauregard was able to fend off a formidable Union aggression three days in a row, until General Lee was able to get reinforcements into place. In this campaign, Beauregard demonstrated both strength and tenacity by digging in and remaining, despite severe supply deficiencies.

During the war's final stages, General Beauregard was put in command of a newly created Military Division of the West, which comprised two military departments and John Bell Hood's Army of Tennessee. Beauregard did what he could to save the western the-ater, but he misunderstood his authority and ultimately did not do very much, save to facilitate some of the supply arrangements for Hood's ill-fated thrust into Tennessee. Beauregard was met with criticism from Davis. In a letter dated January 8, 1865, to his nephew, Davis stated: "After Sherman started to the South East Genl. Beau-regard thought it impossible to overtake him but that his plans might be frustrated by a rapid advance to Tenn." Though the presi-dent concurred with the initial point of Beauregard's assessment, he dismissed the latter point as "erroneous." After Hood's disastrous failures at Franklin and Nashville, Davis replaced him with Joseph Johnston, rejecting the only other possibility: restoring Beauregard to army command. In a letter dated March 15, 1865, Sen. James Chestnut praised Davis for restoring Johnston: "He seems to pos-sess the confidence of the army, and is certainly better than Genl. Beauregard, whose Star is set."[24]

Following the conclusion of the war, Beauregard did not immedi-ately take the oath of loyalty, determining that it was improper by

22. Thomas Lawrence Connelly and Archer Jones, *The Politics of Command: Factions and Ideas in Confederate Strategy* (Baton Rouge: Louisiana State Uni-versity Press, 1973).

23. Williams, *Beauregard*, 236.

24. Hudson Strode, ed., *Jefferson Davis: Private Letters 1823–1889* (New York: DeCapo Press, 1995), 139, 142.

rules of military protocol to do so until other officers of his rank, primarily S. D. Lee and Joseph Johnston, had done the same. Neither did he ask for an official reprieve from President Andrew Johnson, for, in his own estimation, "it is hard to ask a pardon from an adversary you despise."[25] Yet by September 1865 Beauregard had reversed his position and wrote to the president declaring his allegiance to the United States and asking for a pardon. Three years would pass before clemency was given, and a further eight years until his full rights of citizenship were restored.

Beauregard's request was due, in large part, to his interest in politics. During the 1868 presidential campaign, at the encouragement of General Lee and ex–Confederate Vice President Alexander Stephens, he signed a letter of support for Democrat Horatio Seymour over General Grant, the Republican candidate. In a letter to the 1872 Democratic candidate Horace Greeley, the general called for reconciliation and for Southerners to abandon their animosities toward the North.

During this time, Beauregard was active in the Reform party, a political movement of conservative New Orleans businessmen whose platform recognized civil and political rights of freed blacks. Their primary aim was to incorporate enough black leaders into an alliance with Democrats to oust Radical Republicans in the Louisiana State Legislature. Beauregard was also a prime motivator of the Louisiana Unification movement, a political cause that included both white and black leaders and that sought to oust carpetbag governments and railed against high reconstruction taxes. Although initially the white and black groups cooperated on a bill introduced by Sen. John B. Gordon of Georgia, a former general, rancor between the two groups soon emerged, and what seemed to be a potent political force tore itself apart. The experience so soured Beauregard that he never again sought political office. His only other foray into politics was to support an old friend, Winfield Scott Hancock, for the presidency in 1880 against James Garfield. (Beauregard also had an underlying motive: if Hancock were elected, Beauregard hoped to be appointed to the post of ambassador to France.)

As for earning a living, Beauregard returned to the field he knew

25. Williams, *Beauregard,* 257.

best: civil engineering, primarily with the railroads. At first, he was hired as the chief engineer and general superintendent in charge of rebuilding the New Orleans–Jackson–Great Northern Railroad. After conducting a complete survey of the line, Beauregard threw himself into his task, and within nine months the line had been reestablished between New Orleans and Canton, Mississippi. As revenues soared, Beauregard was named president of the company. After a hostile takeover ousted him, he was asked to do the same type of work for a New Orleans–based city transit company. Through his efforts, the company grew into a profitable enterprise. Yet in less than two years, the general was ousted from his position when the company was bought out by a prosperous tobacco trader; again, Beauregard was out of work, and with many obligations that had to be met.

Members of the New York Lottery syndicate were seeking to establish a new enterprise in an area aloof from the storm of controversy such gambling enterprises had created in other states. Louisiana seemed the perfect place, for, according to Williams, "churches and schools in New Orleans had conducted lotteries since territorial days."[26] Once Louisiana had been chosen, the syndicate's agent, Charles T. Howard, spent $300,000 to pass a charter through the state legislature, and, though the lottery was to be tax-exempt, agreed to subsidize the local charity hospital for $40,000 annually from the proceeds. To maintain public interest, and as a measure to guarantee the lottery's trustworthiness, Howard sought an established Southern icon with an untarnished reputation to be its spokesman.

This practice was not new. Charles Reagan Wilson points out in his book *Baptized in Blood* that liquor companies, railroad interests, and lotteries "frequently hired Confederate generals to give their efforts respectability."[27] Beauregard was approached by Howard in the mid-spring of 1876, following a rash of corruption charges levied against the lottery. The general was leery at first, citing the effect such an association could have on his reputation, but he

---

26. Ibid., 292.

27. Charles Reagan Wilson, *Baptized in Blood: The Religion of the Lost Cause, 1865–1920* (Athens: University of Georgia Press, 1980), 297.

eventually accepted the offer. In fiscal terms, it was a positive step for Beauregard in that it became the basis of his recouping a respectable measure of wealth.

The general's duties were to "sit on the platform and supervise the wheels."[28] He also was given the opportunity to select an associate. Beauregard initially offered the position to Wade Hampton, who turned it down following his election to the governorship of South Carolina. Beauregard's second choice was Jubal Early, the commander of the Washington raids, who immediately agreed. The two Confederates were paid with an handsome annual base salary of $10,000, plus expenses and personal-appearance fees. In return, Beauregard and Early agreed to "supervise" the drawing process at the four largest contests, to publicly defend the lottery against newspaper attacks, and to utilize their influence to achieve the passage of protective legislation. For the next fifteen years, the enterprise proved lucrative, but in the face of growing public sentiment against state-sponsored gambling enterprises and a bill passed in Congress that denied all lottery businesses access to the postal system, the lottery eventually left Louisiana for Honduras.

Within a few years, war memoirs written by the war's leading participants began making their way to the marketplace, and proved popular with the reading public. Soon many others published accounts of their experiences. In 1868, primarily to cash in on this trade, the general started a collection of documents and to scribble notes for his own personal account of the war. Following five years of work on the project, he had little to show for his effort. As more war memoirs were made available, Beauregard found a new reason to write: to defend himself against the attacks from his peers concerning his effectiveness as a commanding officer. He was particularly angered by Joseph Johnston's account and a biography of Albert Sidney Johnston written by his son; both were highly critical of Beauregard's role in the First Manassas and Shiloh campaigns. He believed his reputation had been sullied. He employed a close friend, Alfred Roman, to collaborate with him, and by early 1881 the pair had nearly completed their manuscript.

That same year, Jefferson Davis published his exhaustive history,

28. Williams, *Beauregard*, 297.

The Rise and Fall of the Confederate Government. Davis's account contained scathing criticisms of Beauregard, Joseph Johnston, and others whom the ex-president had deemed less than dedicated to the cause. The work reawakened wartime hostilities in these proud men. Beauregard described Davis's two volumes as "an outrage on truth and history."[29] The general's criticisms were not without merit. Incarcerated at Fort Monroe, Davis wrote his wife Varina: "J. E. Johnston and Beauregard were hopeless as to recruiting their forces from the dispersed men of Lee's army, and equally so as to their ability to check Sherman with the forces they had."[30] Yet according to Davis's published memoirs, the defeat of the Confederacy was due to the poor leadership and strategy of generals such as Johnston and Beauregard and other such field commanders.

What was even more hurtful to the general was that in the five years prior to publication of his book, Davis had consulted Beauregard on specific events of the war in which the latter had participated. Beauregard and his collaborator began a rewrite of their manuscript in which they attacked the Confederate president at every turn, but depersonalized their criticisms by attributing his remarks to "the infirmities of age and the severe trials of his prison life."[31] It took the pair nearly three years to sell the manuscript, and when it was issued, sales were anemic at best.

Although Beauregard was a champion of the "New South" and was among those who wanted the region to assert itself with "the influence it formerly asserted in the Councils of the Nation," he also was active in veterans' affairs.[32] In 1879, when Gen. John Bell Hood

29. Thomas Lawrence Connelly and Barbara Bellows make much of this, suggesting that the statement is exemplary of "the Inner Lost Cause [which] describes a mentality that arose from the ashes of defeat, fought for three decades in print and oratory . . . [by] the people who manned the veterans' organizations, former Rebel generals, such as Beauregard and Joseph Johnston, who more often than not fought among themselves as they gave reasons for Yankee defeat" (*God and General Longstreet: The Lost Cause and the Southern Mind* [Baton Rouge: Louisiana State University Press, 1982], 4). See also Williams, *Beauregard*, 311.

30. Strode, ed., *Jefferson Davis*, 156.

31. Ibid., 313.

32. For much more on this, see Gaines M. Foster, *Ghosts of the Confederacy: Defeat, the Lost Cause, and the Emergence of the New South* (New York: Oxford University Press, 1987).

and his wife died, leaving a large family of small children to care for with but little means, Beauregard utilized his contacts to publish Hood's memoirs, with all of the proceeds to be used for the Hood family. When the cornerstone for a statue of Robert E. Lee was laid in Richmond in 1887, the governor appointed Beauregard as the grand marshal of the festivities. Such affinity for the cause ceased, however, when ex-president Jefferson Davis died in 1889. As one of the few surviving full generals of the Confederacy, Beauregard was given the honor of heading the funeral procession. To this request, the old general flatly refused. He said to his family: "I told them I would not do it. We have always been enemies. I cannot pretend I am sorry he is gone. I am no hypocrite."[33]

During his final years, Beauregard retained the air of a distinguished gentleman. But as personal tragedies befell him, he lessened his public appearances. The death of his beloved daughter Laure following childbirth was a devastating emotional blow from which he never fully recovered. (Perhaps the irony that Laure's mother had died while giving birth to her added to Beauregard's sense of tragedy.) Afterwards, he became quite close to Laure's gentle elder daughter, Lilian, with whom he spent much of his time. The construction of Laure's marble tomb took several months, and on the day she was placed within it, Lilian suddenly died; Beauregard had her buried that same evening with her mother.

In early February 1893, the old general fell ill with what were later described as stomach cramps. Within days, he seemed near death, calling out orders to the troops he had commanded over thirty years before. Within two weeks, however, he rallied, and was taking meals with his family. Late on the night of February 20, General Beauregard died in his sleep. The last surviving full Confederate general, Edmund Kirby Smith, acted as chief mourner as the remains of the hero of Fort Sumter were buried, with full military honors, in the tomb of the Army of Tennessee in Metairie Cemetery. Throughout the service, a statue of Albert Sidney Johnston, Beauregard's superior officer in the western theater, looked down upon the proceedings.

33. Hamilton Basso, *Beauregard, The Great Creole* (New York: Charles Scribner's Sons, 1933), 309–10.

The preeminent work on the general is T. Harry Williams's *P. G. T. Beauregard: Napoleon in Gray*. Williams's prose is clear, concise, and lacks the lyrical varnish that gets in the way of a good tale. This book is not just a narrative of "the enigma of his life," but the story of an intriguing man who adapted to a changing South while his contemporaries wallowed in the mire of defeat. We would recommend this book without hesitation to anyone who either wants to learn more about the American Civil War or who simply wants a good read. T. Michael Parrish is known to be at work on a new biography of Beauregard, and given his already demonstrated talent, it doubtless will transcend Williams's study, as Williams did not exhaust the rich trove of sources known to be extant. Some intriguing delineations of Beauregard's abilities and limitations are also to be found in Larry J. Daniel's book on Shiloh.

General Beauregard possessed both the knowledge and the talent to have been an asset to the Confederacy's command corps. Emory M. Thomas, in *The Confederate Nation*, describes him as "a charismatic personality with a flair for the dramatic," but in the same paragraph notes that Beauregard was "a thoughtful soldier, well versed in the military thinking of his time." Beauregard's reputation rests primarily on the demonstration of his abilities in three crucial confrontations. As the primary commander at Fort Sumter and First Manassas, he was able to achieve victory when his opponent possessed the advantage. To that, Woodworth contends: "Both affairs could easily have turned out differently, but things had gone Beauregard's way, and he became a national hero."[34] At Shiloh, and in the crucial time following Albert Sidney Johnston's death, Beauregard demonstrated a paralyzing reticence that proved his undoing. In the end, the legacy of Gen. P. G. T. Beauregard was that his enormous ego eclipsed his considerable talent.

---

34. Emory M. Thomas, *The Confederate Nation 1861–1865* (New York: Harper & Row, 1979), 110; Woodworth, *Davis and His Generals*, 75.

⊸⬦⊸ MORGAN'S RAID

THE WAR STRIKES HOME

with Michael Gillespie

Michael Gillespie has become an independent writer who lives in Lone Jack, Missouri. He majored in history and secondary education at the University of Missouri–Kansas City and did quite a bit of work with me. He has published articles in *Civil War Times Illustrated, Military History, Encyclopedia U.S.A.,* and various other outlets. We were commissioned to do this piece by the Ohio Historical Society. We wrote it as a "popular piece," aimed at lay readers. It is extrapolated from standard works.

Something was up. Col. Basil W. Duke, commanding a cavalry brigade in Lt. Gen. Braxton Bragg's Army of Tennessee, had sensed it three weeks earlier when he received orders to send "intelligent men" to scout the fords of the Ohio River. Those crossings were well inside enemy lines and far distant from Duke's camp in Alexandria, Tennessee. But the colonel was used to surprises; he and his troopers were "Morgan's men," part of the division of Duke's brother-in-law, Brig. Gen. John Hunt Morgan—the daring raider, the "Thunderbolt of the Confederacy."

Three times in 1862 Morgan's youthful horsemen had swept around the Yankee army and wreaked havoc in Kentucky, destroying bridges, telegraph lines, and supply depots, fighting bluecoats who were never quite able to corner them. Now, in the second week of June 1863, Morgan returned from army headquarters and called together his senior officers. It looked very much like another raid was in the offing.

Morgan greeted his lieutenants with a confident air. The thirty-eight-year-old general, his husky six-foot frame typically adorned by massive cavalry boots and a rakishly plumed hat, was a soldier more by avocation than by training. He had served for a year in the Mexican War and had organized a militia unit a few years before the onset of the Civil War. He was a businessman by profession; his firm manufactured jeans and burlap in Lexington, Kentucky. In nearly two years of war, however, he had established a reputation as a charismatic leader and one of the boldest of Confederate riders.

Presently Morgan outlined the situation. Bragg's army had found its position in middle Tennessee untenable—too weak to defend against an overwhelming and closely maneuvering enemy, yet too hard-pressed to extricate itself safely and retreat beyond the Tennessee River. The army needed a diversion for which the "Thunderbolt" seemed aptly suited: a well-executed raid against the enemy's supply lines to distract the Yankees and delay reinforcements. Accordingly, orders to Morgan directed him to "proceed to Kentucky," destroy railroads and supply depots, and then "return to . . . present position."

Those were the orders as far as they read and as far as his superiors intended them to be construed, but John Morgan had his own ideas about strategy. He argued that such a raid could not possibly fulfill its purpose. The damage it might produce could be easily repaired, and the deception was too obvious to distract the Union army for very long.

With a yearning for independent command, Morgan decided to disregard his orders. From Kentucky he planned to break for the Ohio River and cross into the Old Northwest. He then would ride eastward and possibly join Robert E. Lee's Army of Northern Virginia, then moving toward Pennsylvania; if not, Morgan would recross the upper Ohio and escape through West Virginia. In any event, the raid he envisioned would buy time for the retreating Confederate army, much more so than would any quick dash into Kentucky and back. Not only would it delay Union reinforcements into Tennessee, it also would likely send them on a retrograde chase through their own backyard.

While Colonel Duke and the others looked on, Morgan traced his finger across maps of Indiana and Ohio, noting those areas where he expected the most trouble and explaining how he might react to any given threat. He told his officers that the entire command could be lost, but that the intended gains outweighed the risks. Duke and his fellow officers listened with the inconsistent confidence of men torn between their obedience to general orders and the remarkable genius of the commander they practically worshiped. In the end they were convinced of the merits of the raid. Col. Adam R. "Stovepipe" Johnson, who commanded Morgan's second brigade, later wrote: "I am willing to share any part of the blame. . . . I approved it then and will do so again."

Two hundred and fifty miles away, in Cincinnati, Union Maj. Gen. Ambrose E. Burnside sat amid his paperwork. These were busy times for the genial Burnside. Despite his humiliating defeat at Fredericksburg late in 1862 and his subsequent transfer, he was permitted the still-important task of organizing and training an army for battle.

He reigned as commander of the Department of the Ohio and of its recruit-laden Twenty-third Army Corps—some 41,000 men raised principally within the department area. Plans called for the corps to enter eastern Tennessee through the Cumberland Mountains as soon as possible, and from there to move against Knoxville and Chattanooga. Simultaneously, a much stronger force, Maj. Gen. William S. Rosecrans's Army of the Cumberland, would advance from the vicinity of Nashville. The concerted operation was designed to overwhelm and entrap Confederate forces in middle and eastern Tennessee. In the meantime, while Burnside completed the organization and training of his recruits, one cavalry division— Brig. Gen. Henry M. Judah's 12,000-man force—was sent into Kentucky to guard the vital supply lines stretching from the Ohio River into Tennessee.

On June 11 John Morgan swept his hat before him and bowed to the men of his division as they pounded out of camp on what proved to be their greatest raid—and greatest disaster; 2,460 men divided into two understrength brigades under Colonels Duke and Johnson. Sundry ambulance and forage wagons, four pieces of artillery, and a fair number of personal servants extended the column to over three miles in length.

Delayed by heavy rain, frequent halts, and a Union cavalry raid in the direction of Knoxville that bore watching, they reached the

Cumberland River at Burkesville, Kentucky, three weeks later. The Cumberland then was a boiling, furious stream, swollen by summer storms. Fortunately, the high water also had lulled the Yankees opposite the fords. A portion of Judah's cavalry, patrolling the valley against a rumored Confederate incursion, had drawn off a few miles to the north, never suspecting that any force could get across the swollen river. They learned their lesson too late, as Morgan's men attacked their pickets and chased them into the Union camp.

The Yankees lost twenty men in the melee. Morgan slid past without further resistance, although it took some thirteen hours to ferry everyone over the Cumberland. An embarrassed Judah got off a telegram to Burnside warning of Morgan's presence and overestimating the rebel strength at four thousand men.

From Burkesville the column sloshed on to Columbia. There it brushed against a detachment of Federal cavalry, then went into camp six miles south of the Green River. In Columbia some of the raiders had broken into a store and robbed it. Lt. Col. Robert Alston, Morgan's chief of staff, ordered the plunder returned and commented in his journal that some of the men were not worth a damn. The incident foreshadowed much more looting north of the Ohio.

On July 4 Morgan reached Tebb's Bend on the Green River and found the approach to the bridge blocked by Col. Orlando H. Moore and two hundred men of the Twenty-fifth Michigan Infantry. Using the terrain to his advantage, Moore had fortified, in the words of Colonel Duke, "the strongest natural position I ever saw."

Brigadier General Morgan opened the engagement before dawn, scattering Moore's pickets with artillery fire. Then the raider sent a message to Colonel Moore demanding his surrender. Moore replied, according to Duke, that the Fourth of July was "a bad day for surrenders, and I would rather not."

Morgan, employing his standard tactic for attacking an enemy position, dismounted two regiments—at least five hundred men—and hurled them headlong in a deadly frontal assault. The attackers reached an abatis of felled trees and could get no farther in the face of the Federals' disciplined fire. Finally Morgan called an end to it, sending his division around the determined Yankees and back along the road for Campbellsville and Lebanon.

At Lebanon, on the 5th, Morgan encountered another small but belligerent foe—380 infantrymen from a Unionist Kentucky regiment. Colonel Alston went in under a white flag to demand their surrender and was nearly shot from his horse by overanxious defenders. Shaken but unhurt, Alston delivered his ultimatum to Yankee Lt. Col. Charles S. Hanson. After apologizing to Alston for the breach of military decorum, Hanson replied: "Please take my compliments to General Morgan and tell him that I will never surrender without a struggle."

Thus began a costly house-to-house fight that lasted for six hours. Two of Morgan's brothers, Thomas and Calvin, took part in the final rush on the depot where Hanson's men had barricaded themselves. Tom Morgan was hit and fell dead just moments before the Federals surrendered. Calvin, nearly berserk with grief, seized Hanson by the beard and screamed: "I'll blow your brains out, you damned rascal!" Somehow some men interposed and pulled the officers apart. Morgan's soldiers used the incident as an excuse to ransack the town and burn some twenty buildings.

In taking Lebanon, Morgan captured a supply of arms and ammunition, but he also lost ground to Judah's pursuit, which was now well-organized and crossing the Green River. So the "Thunderbolt" turned to his man of deception: George A. "Lightning" Ellsworth, a telegrapher with an uncanny ability to imitate the "hand" of any other operator. Sharp and keen-witted, he could create convincing though thoroughly fictitious and inaccurate reports. On Morgan's instruction, Ellsworth tapped the Federal telegraph lines, gathered information on the location of the pursuing forces, and scattered them with specious orders.

On July 7 Morgan's advance guard captured the Ohio River steamer *John T. McCombs* as it touched the wharf at Brandenburg, Kentucky. They placed her in the channel, flying a distress signal, and when another passing steamboat, the *Alice Dean,* bore alongside to investigate, the Confederates lunged aboard, capturing her as well.

Union sympathizers in Brandenburg witnessed the hijacking, and some of them crossed the river two miles below to warn Lt. Col. William J. Irwin of the Indiana Legion at Mauckport. Irwin hailed an upbound steamer and ordered the vessel back to Leavenworth, Indiana, where he secured a small cannon mounted on a wagon frame. During the night he assembled the available militia from the area—about three hundred men—and took a position on the shore opposite Brandenburg.

The Confederates arrived in force during a fog on the morning of July 8. They broke open whiskey barrels and poked through private homes while the civilian populace either stood idly by or hid as best they could. Morgan took his ease as the guest of a local resident.

But the peace was soon shattered, as a rifle volley from the Indiana side spattered the surface of the river with spent projectiles. Then a cannon shell whistled over and burst amidst the reclining Confederates. Colonel Duke ran for his field glass and studied the far shore through the mist. Finally he saw them, "a squad of combatants posted behind one or two small houses, a clump of hay stacks, and along the brink of the river."

Now the rebels brought their best artillery to the front—two rifled Parrott cannon. It was no contest; within minutes after the Parrotts opened fire, the frightened Hoosier militiamen turned and fled, leaving their lone cannon behind. Had they trained on the boilers of the captured steamboats, they might have prevented Morgan's crossing.

Determined to secure the opposite shore, Morgan sent two dismounted regiments across immediately. They formed lines in the Indiana bottoms and pressed the defenders into the hills beyond. Then came Morgan's second surprise.

From a broad bend above Brandenburg, a stern-wheel gunboat rounded to. "A bluish-white funnel-shaped cloud spouted out from her left-hand bow," remembered Duke, "and then changing front forward, she snapped a shell at the men on the other side." Duke found himself almost mesmerized by her style of fighting, trying to compare it with anything he had seen on land. Even the gun crews on the Parrotts seemed spellbound by the attack; nearly every shot they fired somehow missed the wooden-armored craft.

The vessel was the U.S.S. *Springfield*, mounting six howitzers within her shield and commanded by Acting Ensign Joseph Watson. Watson held the *Springfield* about a mile above the town while engaging Morgan's artillery pieces. He considered making a dash through the crossfire to ram or shell Morgan's boats, but he knew the steamers could outrun him, and if the *Springfield* were disabled in the attempt, it would fall into the hands of the rebels. After an hour and a half of indecisive firing, Watson withdrew his boat to seek naval reinforcements en route from Louisville.

Fourteen hours later Morgan's division finished the arduous task of ferrying across the river. Federal cavalry had drawn up on the Kentucky shore as the last few raiders crossed the "dead line" into Indiana. The Federals were uniformly confident that the Confederacy's "Thunderbolt" was trapped at last.

For the next four days, Morgan's division trampled across southeastern Indiana, rarely venturing more than thirty miles from the river but changing directions so often that even Indianapolis citizens felt threatened. The first engagement came at Corydon on the afternoon of July 9. Four hundred fifty militiamen armed with repeating rifles threw up a breastwork of logs and fence rails one mile south of town. Their wild but rapid fire compelled Morgan to take the position by both flanks while shelling it from his front. Again, the artillery proved too much for the green defenders and they scattered for the safety of the town. "This was done," wrote one of them later, "not with the best of order . . . , but with excellent speed."

After their subsequent surrender, Morgan paroled the militiamen by swearing them not to take up arms against the Confederacy again, confiscating their weapons, and sending them home under a pledge of honor. Much to everyone's relief, Morgan burned only one farmstead (the occupants of which had fired on his men) and spared the local mills, after officials agreed to pay a $1,400 levy.

Morgan dined that evening in the Kintner Hotel, where he first heard the news of Lee's defeat at Gettysburg. The next day, the division passed through Palmyra and Salem. Along the way, a few small groups of militiamen were easily broken up, and what could have been a dismaying street fight in Salem dissolved after the raiders made a quick dash into the town. Beginning here, the rebels became more inclined to make their Yankee hosts "feel the war."

The Confederates demanded food at each successive farm and cottage, and they often stole household goods and trinkets. Many Hoosier men had rushed to fill the militia ranks, leaving their families at home. "The men have all gone to the 'rally,'" one emboldened wife proclaimed to the passing raiders. "You'll see 'em soon."

The column rested overnight near Vienna. In the darkness, here and elsewhere, unsuspecting residents saw campfires and assumed they were celebrations of the Gettysburg victory. But others, whose homes were the object of rebel curiosity, knew different. "The citizens seemed frightened almost to death," recalled one of Morgan's colonels. "Federal papers have published the wildest tales about us."

Past Vienna, Morgan rode east to Lexington, then struck north for Vernon, Dupont, and Versailles. He simply rode around a strong force at Vernon, tearing up a good deal of railroad in the process. "He baffled all our calculations . . . , sending off flying columns in a dozen directions at a time," wrote a Federal officer who participated in the pursuit. Swift movements left the raiders exhilarated by their own progress. "Like an irresistible avalanche we are sweeping over this country," penned Maj. James B. McCreary in his diary.

As the raid moved eastward, the 65,000 Indiana militiamen now in the field turned toward home, while a pursuing force of 2,500 Federal cavalry continued its trek, at times coming within rifle range of Morgan's rear guard. On July 13 the raiders entered Ohio.

"This state is in imminent danger of an invasion by an armed force," proclaimed Gov. David Tod as he ordered the mobilization of the militia in thirty-two southern Ohio counties. Troops were told to report "with a good serviceable blanket and tin cup" to Cincinnati, Camp Dennison, Camp Chase, Marietta, and Portsmouth. And they responded in droves, some 55,000 eventually—untrained, poorly disciplined, but doggedly determined to end Morgan's mischief. Morgan himself later admitted that he found "every man, woman, and child my enemy" in Ohio. "Every hilltop was a telegraph and every bush an ambush."

The rebels entered the state at Harrison, "the most beautiful town I have yet seen in the North," Major McCreary remarked. With enemy cavalry close behind, they burned the bridge over the Whitewater River, moved southeast toward Miamitown, then northward toward Hamilton. Cutting the telegraph wires, Morgan then sped off to the east and south, skirting the suburbs of Cincinnati under cover of darkness.

For many of the men, especially those in the rear regiments, that night seemed endless. In the gaps that formed, squads of haggard Southerners lost their way and stopped to light torches. At crossroads they searched for signs—dust or the foamy saliva that fell from the jaws of tiring horses—that would indicate the line of march. Some men fell from their saddles, unable to stave off sleep. One weary lieutenant accidentally stumbled into Camp Dennison and found himself the prisoner of armed convalescents.

The following day Morgan reached Williamsburg, having marched ninety miles in thirty-five hours and, despite the loss of numerous stragglers, confident that the worst was now behind him. He expected a horse race across southern Ohio, with only militia to impede his progress. He planned to recross the Ohio River at Buffington Island ford, about thirty-five miles downstream from Parkersburg, West Virginia. Until then, it was simply a matter of obtaining guides to show him the best roads and staying one move ahead of the Federal pursuit led by Judah and Brig. Gen. Edward H. Hobson. Morgan would rely on his proven ploys: burning bridges, disrupting telegraphs, scattering his men through a score of tiny villages, and routinely sweeping aside militia.

The command crossed the Scioto River at Piketon on July 16. They found the roads obstructed by felled trees, and they made a point of adding axes to their list of plunder. They were making good their intention to bring war to the North. Losses later claimed by civilians in Morgan's path included food, horses, medicine, guns, books, clothing, ice skates, calico, silk stockings, a set of false teeth, and a birdcage.

Food topped the list. Colonel Duke found that the good residents of southern Ohio had taken to baking pies and leaving them fresh and hot on the tables as a sort of offering against destruction of their homes. According to Duke:

> The first time that I witnessed this sort of hospitality was when I rode up to a house where a party of my men were standing around a table . . . eyeing the pies hungrily, but showing no disposition to touch them. . . . They feared the pies might be poisoned. I have always been fond of pie . . . and proceeded to eat. . . . The men watched me vigilantly for two or three minutes, and then, as I seemed much better after my repast, they took hold ravenously.

Morgan's business in horse trading was keenly described by Brig. Gen. James M. Shackelford, another of the Union cavalry commanders in pursuit. "His system of horse-stealing was perfect," opined Shackelford in his report. "He would dispatch men from the head of each regiment, on each side of the road, to go five miles into the country, seizing every horse, and then fall in at the rear of the column. In this way he swept the country for ten miles of all the horses."

In their wake, they simply abandoned their own worn-out animals. Four men from Sharonville tried to make money by rounding up the discarded horses and offering them for sale. But they wandered too close to Morgan's camp one night, and were taken prisoner, robbed, paroled, and sent home to less enterprising endeavors.

By one count 2,261 horses were taken in Ohio by Morgan's men. Some of the rebel raiders required at least eight different mounts during the foray; others, like Morgan himself, never changed mounts. The Federals too, were forced to exchange horses during the chase, sometimes remounting the very animals left by Morgan's men. Little wonder that the woods and hollows were filled with livestock secreted there by their owners.

Through Jackson, Winchester, and Ewington, the race continued. The rebels camped near Pomeroy on the night of July 17. Not far behind, Brigadier General Hobson had selected the best of his men, with two pieces of artillery, to make a "supreme effort . . . to bring Morgan to bay and compel him to fight before he could ford the Ohio River." The handpicked men tightened their saddle girths and commenced their sixteenth consecutive all-night ride.

On July 18 Morgan crept forward to Chester. Ten miles of hills and uncertain roads lay between him and Buffington Island. But Hobson's men were peppering his rear guard, and he knew that whole regiments of Federal cavalry were moving around him. He halted in the late afternoon to secure a guide and to close up his straggling column.

After losing more than an hour, the raiders at last managed to cross over the hills and down to the mile-long plain in front of the ford. It was nearly dark when the advance element came to a sudden halt. Ahead, a line of earthworks guarded the crossing; the Confederates could see movements of enemy soldiers behind the works, and the outline of a cannon. In a few minutes, all was lost in the blackness of night. Morgan made a fateful decision to hold steady until dawn.

At first light, in a heavy fog, two regiments of Duke's brigade charged the earthworks. Lunging over the top, they found the works completely abandoned. Then they discovered too late that the position had been occupied by a mere force of militia, who in their own fright had precipitously fled into the night.

Duke informed his men of the situation and swept southward, parallel to the river, looking for enemy pickets. Behind him, soldiers and wagons began to move toward the open ford. Just then, Duke's dismounted regiments stumbled into a Federal battle line that had been concealed by the fog.

There was a brief exchange of fire, then a sudden roar of musketry and artillery. The raiders tore back to their horses and made an effort to regroup.

Within minutes, a second battlefront developed, on a ridge leading back to Chester. Hobson's volunteers now poured out of the hills and pushed "Stovepipe" Johnson's brigade back into the path of Duke's retreating cavalrymen. Together the two Confederate brigades faced south and west, and found themselves in a punishing crossfire.

Then came gunboats, churning into range as if on cue. The whole scene was a symphony of perfect timing by the Federal forces, but orchestrated primarily by mere chance. Lt. Cmdr. LeRoy Fitch wedged his gunboat, the U.S.S. *Moose,* into a narrow chute on the near side of Buffington Island. "I saw a portion of Morgan's force coming down the river just on the edge of the bank," he wrote in his report. "I at once opened fire . . . [and] they wheeled and took back up the river."

Farther up, Fitch spotted a large portion of Morgan's men assembled at the ford. The *Moose* fired her six heavy cannon, and Fitch marveled as "they broke in the greatest confusion, threw away their arms, abandoned their booty, and leaving buggies, carriages, and two pieces of artillery standing on the beach, took to the woods."

Everywhere the rebel lines were crumbling. "Shells and minnie balls were ricocheting and exploding in every direction," wrote McCreary. "Cavalry were charging, and infantry . . . moved upon us. It seemed as if our comparatively small command would be swallowed up by the innumerable horde."

Yet somehow in the sudden and confusing rout, Morgan found an exit—a narrow funnel of land wedged between the ridge and the river at the north end of the Buffington bottoms. It was too rough and narrow for the wagons, but more than sufficient for the hard-riding raiders. They poured through it like water—eleven hundred men in all, including Morgan. Colonel Duke held back the Union assault as long as he could, and then surrendered his seven hundred exhausted troopers.

With his remaining force, Morgan retreated northward along the river. Commander Fitch took up the chase in his gunboat and caught up with the rebels a few hours later at Reedsville. Four hundred raiders were crossing the Ohio when the *Moose* and her escort rounded the bend. Fitch immediately opened fire. Horses and men thrashed and kicked in wild bedlam among spray, smoke, and gasping screams. Morgan had nearly gained the West Virginia shore but wheeled and returned to his men still stranded on the Ohio side. It was all over quickly. Three hundred Confederates had managed to make good their escape, but Morgan and seven hundred more turned back into the Ohio interior; one hundred had perished in the water.

For the next six days, Morgan's diminished command roamed through eastern Ohio while the general feverishly tried to devise some plan of escape. On the first night, the force was nearly surrounded by a group of Yankees that apparently had elected to wait for daylight to attack. The weary Confederates built campfires to deceive them and slipped away along the dark hillsides.

The raiders circled round their former route to Buffington Island and tried crossing the river once again, this time at Cheshire. They were uncertain of the ford, and as one trooper rode into the stream, the towboat *Condor* appeared, brandishing the Pomeroy militia and one very old cannon. Morgan mistook it for a navy gunboat and chose to turn his men around and head north.

In Cincinnati, Major General Burnside studied each incoming telegram, trying to unravel the mystery of Morgan's whereabouts. To his superiors in Washington, he sent carefully worded messages, confidently predicting an end to the raid "within the next twenty-four hours." But to Governor Tod, Burnside admitted that Morgan's men were moving "to some point where they can cross the Ohio too high up for the gun-boats to reach." He guessed they would cross the Miskingum River at Zanesville and warned the governor that the army had no means to protect that town if Morgan moved too quickly.

For a time the raid again took on its former aspect. Militia guarded the small towns and threw timber across the roads; another cavalry force rode close on Morgan's heels, this time under Brigadier General Shackelford; civilians left their homes and hid with their livestock. No one knew where to expect Morgan next.

But Morgan was running out of options, and his men were growing dispirited. Five raiders fell prisoner to ax-swinging farmers, and snipers made the trek a continuous nightmare. In retaliation, the rebels sometimes fired at anyone standing in the distance, man or woman. Wounded raiders lay where they fell. One dead Confederate later was found in a hollow, with a pillow under his head.

Shackelford struck Morgan's rear guard in Guernsey County, while a new squadron under Maj. George W. Rue used the railroads to take up a position between the raiders and the river. The end was fast approaching. On Sunday, July 26, Morgan's faltering column limped into Monroeville and collared a young man just home from the war on a medical discharge. They asked him if he knew any nearby town that was still free of Yankee troops; the youth pointed toward Salineville. The column moved in that direction, straight into a trap.

During the early morning hours, Rue had placed four hundred cavalrymen on the outskirts of Salineville. Morgan's skirmishers sighted them, halted, and tried to flee back. At the same time, Shackelford attacked from the rebel rear.

Fighting at both ends, the harried column swung west, then north, trying to circumvent Rue's force. In the process they surprised a small band of armed men from Lisbon. Morgan approached the leader, James Burbick, and promised him that if he would guide the rebels to the river, they would not disturb any property. Burbick agreed and as the column turned east, Morgan could see the dust raised by Rue's force, which was now converging on them from a distant road.

For a time it seemed that Morgan might beat Rue through the intersection, but Rue's freshly mounted horsemen had dropped off the road, galloped down a dry creek bed and across an open field, and suddenly stood squarely between the rebels and the river.

According to Burbick, Morgan turned to him and offered to surrender, provided that the "Thunderbolt" and his men be paroled. Burbick replied that he did not understand technicalities. Morgan grew irritated, asserted that he could surrender on terms to anyone he pleased at any time, and demanded an answer at once: yes or no? Burbick, a civilian from Columbiana County, accepted Morgan's surrender.

Thus ended the great raid, forty-six days after its inception. Morgan and his officers, however, instead of enjoying parole, soon found themselves in the state penitentiary at Columbus. Burnside reviewed the terms of the surrender and declared them void. In November Morgan managed a dramatic escape from the prison and eventually made his way back to Tennessee, but was killed there ten months later by a private in the Thirteenth Tennessee Cavalry.

Most of Morgan's contemporaries assessed his raid as a failure. In it the Confederacy lost nearly two brigades of seasoned cavalry without inflicting truly serious damage in their wake. Yet the raid most definitely delayed the movement of the Twenty-third Army Corps into eastern Tennessee. And that, in turn, prevented reinforcement of the Army of the Cumberland, which met defeat at Chickamauga. The raid also demonstrated that despite the dreadful outcomes of the Vicksburg and Gettysburg campaigns, the Confederates still had fighting power and the war was far from over. Perhaps most important, the raid gave to the people of the Old Northwest a taste of what one resident called "the miseries of the South," the sobering spectacle of war on one's own homeland and hearthside. Fortunately for the residents of Indiana and Ohio, the Confederates never returned.

✥ SOLDIER OF CONSCIENCE, GEORGE H. THOMAS

A VIRGINIAN FIGHTS FOR THE UNION

with Michael Gillespie

"During the war I permitted the National authorities to do what they pleased with me," wrote an aging George Henry Thomas to President Andrew Johnson. For once in Thomas's life his pen flowed freely, unencumbered by his usual shy and reticent manner. "The life of the nation was then at stake, and it was not proper to press questions of rank," he continued, "but now that the war is over and the nation saved, I demand a command suited to my rank, or I do not want any."

These were not easy words for Thomas, but neither had his treatment at the hands of his superiors been easy to endure for this Virginian who served in the Federal army during the Civil War. He had a heavy burden to bear for his loyalty to the Union and for making a choice of conscience. It had meant banishment from his family and home, and distrust from many of his fellow commanders in the North.

Thomas was born on July 31, 1816, to John and Elizabeth Rochelle Thomas. Theirs was a comfortable home in Southampton County, Virginia. They owned a substantial farm planted in cotton, corn, and tobacco, and ample slaves to work the land and maintain the house. Young George grew up amidst a family of three sisters and two brothers, largely content with his station and with the firm discipline practiced by his parents.

Reprinted with permission from *Virginia Cavalcade* 34:2 (Autumn 1984), © 1984 The Library of Virginia.

He soon displayed a predisposition for quiet observation. A studious introvert, he once built his own saddle after carefully watching the intricate steps taken by a saddle maker, then mastered the art of furniture making. His remarkable drive inclined him to take a keen interest in the children of his father's slaves. Indignant at the laws that forbade their being educated, and defiant of his family's wishes, Thomas secretly conducted instruction sessions, at the end of each day repeating his lessons to his black playmates.

In the summer of Thomas's fifteenth year, the nightmare of the slaveholding class came to fruition in Southampton County. An errant slave, Nat Turner, believing himself to be a prophet, led a small group of bondsmen in a killing orgy during the night of August 21, 1831. By the next morning Turner's band had grown to several dozen slaves, and the murders continued as they roamed from farm to farm. As word of the massacre spread, many whites fled to the county seat. George Thomas drove his family in a wild carriage flight, just ahead of the marauders. As their pursuers gained on them, the Thomases abandoned the vehicle to seek safety in a dense thicket. Their slaves had taken no part in the rebellion and were placed into protective custody until the uprising had settled. The revolt came to a quick end when local veterans formed a militia and struck out after the renegades. Turner fled, but was captured six weeks later and hanged.

The severe reprisals taken by the militiamen reinforced Thomas's personal distaste for slavery. Years later, on the eve of the Civil War, he tried to manumit his wife's servant, but the girl refused to go. She remained in the Thomas family throughout the war, and afterwards she and her husband continued serving the family.

In his late teens Thomas entered the local finishing school, Southampton Academy, where he developed an interest in botany. At nineteen, he began studying law under an uncle who worked as a circuit court clerk. Thomas's personality hardly fit the assertiveness appropriate to the legal profession, but his father's death in 1829 had left the family finances depleted, and Thomas dutifully if mechanically pursued the vocation. Listlessness on his part may have induced a family friend, Cong. John Y. Mason, to suggest that the young man attend the United States Military Academy. Thomas passed the entrance examinations and soon was on his way to West Point, with a warning from Mason not to show his face again if he failed.

The plebe class of 1836 contained a sprinkling of talent, but none of the new cadets revealed more potential than Thomas's room-mate, William Tecumseh "Cump" Sherman. Outgoing, fun-loving, and prone to breaking rules, Sherman was almost the alter ego of the reserved Thomas. Their room often abounded with surplus potatoes, bread, vegetables, and butter spirited from the mess hall. The two cadets became famous for their late-night stewpot and after-lights-out conviviality. When an upperclassman discovered one of the clandestine meetings, Thomas handled the matter skillfully. "Old Tom, as we always called him," remarked one of Thomas's chums, "stepped up to him and said, 'Leave this room immediately or I will throw you through the window.'" Drawn up to full height, Thomas's six-foot, two-hundred-pound frame pre-sented a formidable challenge. There were no more attempts at hazing.

Despite the high attrition rate, Thomas managed to do well at the academy. He graduated twelfth out of forty-two in the class of 1840, and received a commission as a second lieutenant in the artillery. After several months at Fort Columbus, New York, he sailed to Fort Lauderdale, Florida, with the Third Artillery Regiment for duty in the Seminole War. Thomas found the campaigning less exciting than he had hoped. The army fought few stand-up battles, only a series of quick skirmishes against an elusive foe. While the greater part of his regiment took to the field, Thomas found himself in the rear areas. "I have been left behind to take care of this infernal place in consequence of being commissary, etc." he wrote to a friend in July 1841. "This will be the only opportunity I shall have of distin-guishing myself, and not to be able to avail myself of it is too bad." But he did get his chance in November as part of an expedition that captured seventy Seminoles. For "gallantry and good conduct," Thomas received a brevet promotion to first lieutenant.

Thomas subsequently served at Charleston, South Carolina, with Sherman and another friend, Braxton Bragg. Often quarrelsome, even to the point of dueling, Bragg nevertheless got along well with

Sherman and Thomas. They seemed to share a distaste for politics, although Sherman and Thomas, unlike Bragg, never hedged in their support for a perpetual union as the secession debate grew heated during the antebellum years.

Several army officers noted Thomas's Southern origins and his empathy for the region, but he did not fit an easy pattern. Erasmus D. Keyes, his company commander, pronounced Thomas and Robert E. Lee to be the only reasonable Southern men among the hundreds he had known. He also described Thomas as deliberate and self-possessed, "without being arrogant," a man who "did his duty and kept all his appointments precisely."

Thomas's military career began to soar when the United States became involved in war with Mexico. On June 28, 1845, the Third Artillery received orders for duty in Texas. After nearly a year stationed along the Mexican border, Thomas joined in an active campaign under Zachary Taylor. The American column marched on Monterrey and assaulted that city for three days, September 21–23, 1846. Thomas's two-gun section was in the thickest part of the fighting. His show of spirit and calm under pressure won him a brevet captaincy.

On February 23, 1847, Thomas's section fought in the battle of Buena Vista. At one point, late in the action, his guns and men won distinction by holding a difficult position while American infantry and cavalry pulled back. Despite orders to retire, Thomas held firm until Col. Jefferson Davis and his Mississippi Rifles hurled themselves in a counterassault that threw back the Mexican advance. The counterassault became legendary, having allegedly saved the day. There was some controversy as to just who deserved the real credit, and Davis had employed an unorthodox V formation that captivated the public imagination. At least some of the credit for the victory went to Old Reliable Thomas, as his gunners now called him, for the army breveted him once more—this time to major. At home, the proud residents of Southampton County struck a gold-and-silver saber in his honor. "I shall always regard it as the result of tenderness of heart and a friendliness of feeling," Thomas wrote.

Thomas spent the remainder of the Mexican War as a commissary officer in northern Mexico, returning east again for duty in Florida and garrison service in Massachusetts. During these years he studiously read all he could about military science, the self-instruction serving as good preparation for an assignment to teach at West Point. Beginning in April 1851 he taught artillery and cavalry tactics to prankish cadets who found the mature Thomas to be somewhat of a bore and nicknamed him Slow Trot Thomas, partly in jest at the deliberate, heavy gait his massive frame imposed. "A cold, phlegmatic, unimpressionable man," wrote one of him, "but a born soldier." Some of his students thought he graded indifferently, giving high marks for mediocre recitations. Others, like Michael R. Morgan, a future general, remembered Thomas for his sensitivity. Thomas once reported him for neglecting his studies, yet when the two met years later, Morgan recalled Thomas's expression of "deep sorrow at being compelled to take notice of such neglect, and hoped I would forgive and forget it."

In his personal life Thomas had some pleasant experiences at West Point. He shared a close friendship with Robert E. Lee, who became the superintendent at the military academy in 1852. The two Virginians had much in common, though Lee enjoyed a higher social standing. Thomas's days at the academy were also enriched by romance. At age thirty-six he met and fell in love with Frances Lucretia Kellogg, of Troy, New York. They married on November 17, 1852.

Scarcely a year and a half later the army imposed on the couple their first separation when Thomas left for duty at Fort Yuma, in the desert Southwest. There he fought boredom by collecting minerals and plant specimens, forwarding the rarer articles to the Smithsonian Institution.

A year later the army sent Thomas to Jefferson Barracks, Missouri, to join the newly formed Second Cavalry Regiment. Staffed in the main by Southerners—R. E. Lee was its executive officer—the command operated out of several small forts in Texas, whence Thomas occasionally led patrols against marauding Comanche Indians. On one of the expeditions an arrow struck his chin and pinned his jowls to his chest, inflicting a painful though not serious wound—the only combat injury he ever received.

In November 1860 Thomas began a long-awaited one-year fur-lough. He intended to travel by train to New York, but on the way the train stopped in Norfolk, Virginia, where he stepped off to stretch his legs. Missing his step, he fell sprawling into a ditch. For six weeks he remained in Virginia recuperating from a severely sprained back, which bothered him for the remainder of his life.

In January, Thomas reached Washington, D.C., where he reported to General in Chief Winfield Scott on the behavior of David E. Twiggs. Twiggs, a Georgian whose loyalty to the Union had come under suspicion during the late antebellum years, commanded the Department of Texas. Based on Thomas's evaluations and the state-ments of other observers who had noted Twiggs's pro-Southern sentiments, Scott decided to remove Twiggs. But he moved too slowly. In February, before Scott issued the order, Twiggs surren-dered the U.S. forces in Texas to the newly formed Confederate States of America.

Meanwhile, Thomas left Washington for New York to continue his vacation and there to spend the winter of 1860–1861 with his wife. By now he feared that his back injury would result in the end of his active military career, so he wrote to the superintendent of the Virginia Military Institute, seeking a faculty post. To a fellow officer passing through New York on his way south to join the Confederate army, Thomas casually commented "that he too intended to resign and follow."

But Thomas did not submit his resignation. The War Department canceled his leave in April 1861 and promoted him to lieutenant colonel, ordering him to meet remnants of the Second Cavalry—those men from Twiggs's command released by the Texas Con-federates—arriving in New York by steamship. Thomas conducted the troops to Carlisle Barracks, Pennsylvania, where he heard about the firing on Fort Sumter. Virginia had not yet seceded, but in a sud-den burst of patriotism, Thomas sought out a local judge who agreed to administer an oath of allegiance to certify Thomas's loyalty to the Federal government. He then wrote a letter to his sisters in Southampton, telling them of his renewed commitment. The women, themselves sympathetic to the South and in favor of Virginia's secession, turned Thomas's picture to the wall and forbade his name ever again to be spoken in the home.

On April 21, 1861, four days after Virginia withdrew from the Union, Secretary of War Simon Cameron, then in charge of rail transportation in Maryland and Pennsylvania, summoned Thomas to his office. He wanted to assign Thomas to protect a vital rail line on the border, but grew concerned when Thomas seemed to hesitate. "Thomas argued against the war," Cameron reported, "taking the ground that the trouble had been brought upon the country by the abolitionists in the North, and that . . . the South had just cause for complaint. I do not say Thomas refused to obey his orders, but I do say he hesitated and would much prefer that the duty had [d]evolved upon another."

Thomas seemed motivated—and torn—by his sworn allegiance to the federal government. As a combat soldier he could not comprehend enduring the dangers of battle without total adherence to his oath, and he saw nothing now to change his commitment to that oath. He hesitated, perhaps, but only to reaffirm and strengthen his own belief in light of what might lie ahead.

The Cameron episode had done nothing to reassure Thomas's superiors of his loyalty, yet by June 1 they nonetheless had promoted him to full colonel and placed him in command of a cavalry brigade composed mostly of Pennsylvania militiamen. A month later this unit marched into Virginia. At dawn on July 2, near Martinsburg, it encountered enemy fire. More of an accident than a battle, the contest lasted in fits and rushes the whole day. The Confederates finally broke and ran, leaving Thomas with the distinction of having defeated a force under the then-unknown colonel Thomas J. Jackson.

By late summer Thomas found himself in Maryland. The Northern army was attempting to reorganize after its July defeat at Manassas, a battle in which Thomas's brigade had taken no part. Unknown to him, President Abraham Lincoln had considered and rejected a proposal to promote Thomas to brigadier general. As a Virginian, Lincoln supposedly had said, Thomas was still under suspicion; any promotion could wait.

But William T. Sherman, who had won a brigadiership himself, now vouched for Thomas and subsequently secured the promotion. Sherman personally took the news to Thomas, telling him about the concern over his loyalty. Sherman gasped in disbelief when Thomas interrupted and said, "Billy, I am going South." Thomas's face lit up at his friend's reaction, and his eyes twinkled as he continued, "I am going South, but at the head of my men."

Brigadier General Thomas left for Kentucky in November 1861 to organize the First Division, Army of the Ohio. On January 19, 1862, he led four thousand men in a muddy foray against an entrenched Confederate position near Mill Springs. The Confederates were nearly equal in number, but instead of exploiting their defensive advantage, the secessionists sallied out in a driving rainstorm to meet Thomas's careful advance. Thomas's men scored an easy victory, forcing the Southerners back in disarray. True, the Confederates had made all the wrong moves, but Thomas had possessed the good sense and timely judgment to capitalize on their mistakes. The Northern press was elated by this early victory. In glowing terms they wrote about Thomas, his loyalty no longer in question.

By April Thomas's men had maneuvered into Tennessee to operate against enemy forces there. For his superior work, especially for his careful attention to maintaining supply lines and his continued advances, Thomas won promotion to major general of volunteers. It was not, however, a commission in the regular army, and Thomas, the consummate professional soldier, was so insulted that he refused to wear the second star.

Later, in the fall, Thomas was ordered back to Kentucky to supersede Don Carlos Buell as commander of the Army of the Ohio after its retreat from Tennessee. On arriving at Buell's headquarters, he learned that Buell already had ordered an offensive. Unwilling to relieve the commander at the beginning of a campaign, Thomas protested and was given a command position under Buell. Buell succeeded in defeating the Confederates at Perryville, but the War Department relieved him anyway, naming William S. Rosecrans to the command.

Thomas took offense at the appointment because Rosecrans was junior to him in rank. Still smarting under the earlier uncertainty about his loyalty, Thomas also considered Rosecrans's promotion a reflection upon his own "Southern" taint, and wrote bitterly to Washington, saying, "I have made my last protest while the war lasts; you may hereafter put a stick over me if you choose to do so."

Rosecrans led the army to Nashville, Tennessee, and on December 31, 1862, engaged the Confederates at Stones River. During a late-night conference after the first day of fighting, the somewhat unnerved commanding general asked Thomas if he could cover a Union retreat. "This army can't retreat!" Thomas insisted. Perhaps bolstered by Thomas's confidence, Rosecrans acquiesced and decided to stand firm. As it turned out, on the second day of the battle the Federals emerged victorious.

Thomas consequently acquired command of the Fourteenth Corps, part of Rosecrans's Army of the Cumberland. He served reasonably well as a corps commander, though he encountered no opportunities for spectacular performance until September 1863, when the Union and Confederate armies clashed at Chickamauga Creek in Georgia.

In disjointed fighting which lasted throughout the day of September 19, the Federal troops gradually were forced rearward about one mile. The next day, a gap opened in the Union lines, the result of a faulty order, and the Confederate divisions poured through. The Federals were routed and overwhelmed, thrown back in great disorder and confusion.

With a determination that saved Rosecrans's force from a crushing defeat, Thomas's corps tenaciously held Snodgrass Hill, on the right side of the Union lines. Thomas's staunch resistance formed a welcome shield that protected the rest of the blue-clad force, most of it, including Rosecrans's headquarters, fleeing in an uncontrolled retreat. Thomas's men stubbornly maintained their position—like a rock against the tide, someone described them.

The Federal army escaped to Chattanooga, and Thomas, emerging from the battle with the new nickname Rock of Chickamauga, superseded the disgraced Rosecrans and inherited the besieged army. Government officials feared, however, that Thomas might be forced to capitulate before Ulysses S. Grant could bring up sufficient reinforcements to ensure Chattanooga's safety. But Thomas understood the absolute necessity of holding out and wired the War Department that he would starve before surrendering. For two months he held the city, until Grant and Sherman wedged in new troops and supplies.

Grant directed a breakout from Chattanooga on November 24–25. Initially Sherman tried to turn the Confederate flank. When he failed, Thomas's men attacked the advance guard of enemy troops, which were entrenched in rifle pits at the base of Missionary Ridge (the main force was atop the ridge). The Northerners were supposed to stop after securing the ridge base, but on their own initiative they continued pushing forward and upward, storming a crest that had seemed unassailable to their superiors. Grant, fearful of defeat, turned angrily to Thomas and demanded an explanation, but the corps commander had none to give. Grant could find little fault with Thomas, though, after his men succeeded in pushing relentlessly all the way up the slope to route the Confederate defenders.

With the battle concluded and victory in Federal hands, Thomas pointed out to a chaplain a suitable place for a military cemetery. The chaplain asked if he should bury the dead by state or origin. "No, no. Mix them up; mix them up," Thomas quickly answered. "I am tired of state-rights."

During Sherman's advance on Atlanta, which began in May 1864, Thomas's army comprised one of the three prongs with which Sherman planned to crush Gen. Joseph E. Johnston's western Confederate army. On this extended mission, the old friends did not work together smoothly. Thomas's movements seemed too slow to Sherman. "A fresh furrow in a plowed field will stop the whole column," complained Sherman about Thomas's apparent quickness to abandon offense and take the defensive, "and all begin to entrench." By the time Sherman's struggle for Atlanta proved successful four months later, he had at last managed to adjust to Thomas's slowness, which resulted from careful planning rather than from timidity. By then Thomas's men had developed a keen appreciation for their commander's caution, affectionately calling him Pap Thomas.

After Atlanta fell, the Confederates decided to disengage from Sherman's front, the formidable Army of Tennessee under Gen. John B. Hood swinging around to try to recapture Nashville. From there, Hood, an impetuous, aggressive fighter, hoped to reoccupy Kentucky and march to R. E. Lee's aid in Virginia. Sherman dispatched Thomas with his command to defend Tennessee.

This order brought Thomas's most trying times, as well as what proved to be his second great military triumph. Lacking adequate transportation and cohesion, Thomas worked tirelessly to put his force into the proper fighting trim. In November he sent Maj. Gen. John M. Schofield's corps to delay the enemy at Franklin, Tennessee, while he planned the minute details of the battle he expected to ensue. But in place of gratitude for his efforts, Thomas got instead a steady stream of ridicule for taking too long to assault the enemy.

Concerned complaints from Grant and from the War Department—even some from Sherman—crammed the telegraph wires. Thomas was visibly affected by the criticism and lamented of being treated "like a boy," but he patiently explained the critical need to wait for reinforcements to arrive from Chattanooga and the futility of attacking until a thaw alleviated the dangerously icy weather conditions that struck Tennessee during the early weeks of December.

Hundreds of miles away in Virginia, Grant grew more and more inclined to order Thomas's relief. Orders to that effect at last were dispatched on December 15, but, fortuitously, never reached Thomas because Maj. Thomas T. Eckert, head of the military telegraph office in Washington and a man who sympathized with Thomas, delayed sending them.

Before his intended successor, Maj. Gen. John A. Logan, reached Nashville, Thomas met and crushed the Confederates there, just as he had planned. Yet even after this stunning victory, the War Department insisted on dismantling Thomas's "ill-assorted" army and sent the troops elsewhere. Thomas's critics labeled him "selfish" and claimed that only his promotion to permanent major general in the regular army on March 3, 1865, and the thanks of Congress kept him from a vituperative explosion of personal feeling.

When the war ended a month later, Thomas was commanding a military district comprising Tennessee, Kentucky, and parts of Georgia, Alabama, and Mississippi. Unlike the other victorious Northern generals, Thomas could not go home: Southampton would have none of him. Some of his relatives even asked that he change his name. Only a brother living in Mississippi would still speak to him. But the numerous Unionists in Tennessee "adopted" him, and Andrew Johnson, now president of the United States, counted him among his favorites. In 1868 Thomas turned down a brevet promotion to full general, claiming it was politically motivated; he loved the Union but despised its politics.

In 1869 Thomas was ordered to San Francisco to assume command of the Military Division of the Pacific. When he left, a number of individuals assailed him in the press, probably because they were unhappy friends of John M. Schofield and felt that Schofield and not Thomas should have received the glory for the Battle of Nashville. The *New York Tribune* carried one such letter on March 12, 1870, from an anonymous critic who called himself "One Who Fought at Nashville." While Thomas sat penning a detailed and pained reply to the criticisms, he was suddenly paralyzed by a blood clot in his brain. He died on March 28.

If not a man of great prestige, Thomas was a man of profound honor. Even more than he believed in the Union, he believed in his obligations as an army officer. On the battlefield he never committed his men to rash and useless assaults and his soldiers understood that. The day he succeeded Rosecrans in army command, his men broke ranks and swarmed around him. They knew then what historians are only now beginning to recognize: that George H. Thomas deserves to be rated as one of the most thoroughly professional and competent commanders of the Civil War.

◈ LINCOLN'S PRESIDENTIAL EXAMPLE IN DEALING WITH THE MILITARY

Much of this paper was originally written, and delivered, as a speech for the 1986 meeting of the Abraham Lincoln Association in Springfield, Illinois. I was quite involved in working with Archer Jones at the time, researching and writing what became *Why the South Lost the Civil War,* and I am sure that he helped me with this piece too, if only in shaping my thoughts on military strategy, his special forte. The Association eventually published my speech in *Papers of the Abraham Lincoln Association.* Footnotes were cobbled together for the printed version, but all of the quotations are from rather standard and well-known sources (well-known to scholars and specialists in the field, at least). I have therefore opted to present it here much as it originally was—a paper in speech format—though I have retained a few footnotes that might be of interest. I have also added some passages from "Lincoln as Military Strategist," an essay I wrote with Jones that covers some of the same ground.

We ask, and expect, a great deal of our presidents. While we demand they be civilians—at least while they are serving as president—they must also be commander in chief of all the armed forces of the United States. This has great significance and importance because the civilian president actually is part—indeed, he is at the top—of what the military calls the chain of command. He issues orders, salutes and is saluted, and makes ultimate military decisions. He either himself formulates—with any help he can exploit—or must approve of whatever strategy is employed. He is responsible for approving the selection of all the top generals and admirals.

Portions of this essay are excerpted from "Lincoln as Military Strategist," which first appeared in *Civil War History* 26:4 (1980) and is reprinted by permission of the Kent State University Press.

He must work well with a multitude of people, sometimes with individuals whose personalities clash or are disharmonious with his own. And all the while that he is accomplishing this he must also inspire the troops as well as lead the people at home. According to Thomas A. Bailey in his study *Presidential Greatness,* "The American people admire a chieftain who can command their allegiance, unite the sections, placate factions in Congress, inspire them to greater patriotism, and arouse them with a challenge that will appeal to their better selves." All of this Abraham Lincoln did to an exemplary degree.

When Lincoln became president, he was but a rank amateur in military affairs; however, the crisis of the Civil War made it crucial that he learn about such things. And to his great credit, this he did, efficiently and well. After the secession of Virginia and the relocation of the Confederate capital to Richmond, the president initially endorsed proposals to move upon the rebel capital in one swift movement. He believed, somewhat naively, that the sheer weight of Union numbers so early in the war would gain for the North a decisive victory. His hopes were dashed in the panicked flight at Manassas in July 1861.

Lincoln eventually mastered conventional nineteenth-century military strategy. He came to understand and learned how to interact with the better thinking of West Point–trained officers. He and these generals insightfully analyzed operations, believed—correctly—in the superiority of the defensive over the offensive, and saw in turning movements the only way to overcome the power of the rifle-strengthened defensive. Lincoln shouldered full responsibility for making and seeing to the execution of strategic plans sufficient to bring victory. He derived his ideas primarily from his generals, but also from his prescient observations of military realities as exhibited in the course of the war. His military ideas were realistic and workable.

Lincoln was a keen student and, with the early aid of Maj. Gen. George B. McClellan and other officers, he came to be fully at home with his generals' military conceptions. To the question of why "the North with her great armies" so often faced the South in battle "with inferiority of numbers," the president perceptively explained that "the enemy hold the interior, and we the exterior lines." Along with understanding lines of operations, he came to grasp the logistics of field armies and the significance of entrenchments and learned to attach great importance to the turning movement or to any chance "to get in the enemy's rear" or to "intercept the enemy's retreat." The president was early indoctrinated by McClellan with the concept of the power of the defense when, in January 1862, the general in chief explained that the "history of every former war" had "conclusively shown the great advantages which are possessed by an army acting on the defensive and occupying strong positions."

McClellan had found at the beginning of the war that "but few civilians in our country, and indeed not all military men of rank, had a just appreciation of that fact." If "veteran troops frequently falter and are repulsed with loss," then "new levies . . . cannot be expected to advance without cover" against the "murderous fire" of entrenched defenders. He would solve this problem by turning the enemy, for "the effect of this movement" to the enemy's rear "will be to reverse the advantages of position. They will have to seek us in our own works, as we sought them at Manassas." The strength of the defense meant that offensive battles against an enemy with his back to his communications implied a victory which "produces no final results, & may require years of warfare & expenditure to follow up."[1]

Again, in the opening months of 1862, Lincoln agreed to another campaign against Richmond, although for different reasons this time. By then, he had come to a better understanding of military tactics. McClellan had convinced the president that a frontal assault on Richmond, regardless of size or timing, probably would not destroy the enemy's army. In order to inflict actual damage on Confederate forces, the Union army would have to turn the enemy out of his fortified position by entrenching in his rear, threatening his communications, and forcing him to come out and fight over ground selected by the North. That the plan failed was due more to impatience by Lincoln's political associates and McClellan's growing distrust of the administration than to flaws in the grand scheme of the campaign.

1. For Field Marshal Count Helmuth von Moltke's comparable analysis of tactical power of the defense and his similar reliance on turning movements in 1870, see Michael Howard, *The Franco-Prussian War* (New York: Macmillan, 1961), 7.

After the failure of the second drive on Richmond in May and June of 1862, Lincoln's military advisors worked in vain to formulate yet another plan to invest the city. But Richmond's extensive system of defensive works and its well-protected communications, consisting of three trunk-line railroads and a canal, rendered further offensive efforts implausible. Without interdicting Richmond's communications and thereby depriving the city of ample reinforcements, every attack would be futile; yet no turning movement could take place quickly enough to offset the advantage of reinforcements via the South's interior lines. Only through simultaneous advances over a broad front could Lincoln hope to reduce available Confederate reinforcements and eventually carry the city. Therefore, he directed that emphasis be placed on containing the army of Robert E. Lee while Union forces elsewhere made inroads into the Confederacy's vulnerable regions.

The military sophistication that Lincoln acquired in less than a year and a half extended to a clear understanding of the significance of battles and an appreciation of the limited degree to which the Confederates had defeated McClellan at the Seven Days Battles (June 25 through July 1, 1862). Grasping that "the moral effect was the worst" aspect of these battles, he thought it probable that, "in men and material, the enemy suffered more than we in that series of conflicts; while it is certain that he is less able to bear it." Lincoln wrote that he saw the psychological "importance to us, for its bearing upon Europe, that we should achieve military successes; and the same is true for us at home as well as abroad." Yet, comparing the spring 1862 western triumphs at Fort Donelson, Shiloh, and Corinth with the popular fixation on the East, Lincoln felt that "it seems unreasonable that a series of successes extending through half-a-year, and clearing more than a hundred thousand square miles of country, should help us so little, while a half-defeat" at the Seven Days Battles "should hurt us so much in morale."

Often criticized for an exaggerated fear for the safety of Washington, Lincoln had realized that "[Thomas J.] Jackson's game" in the Valley Campaign (May 6–June 9, 1862) had been to "keep three or four times as many of our troops away from Richmond as his own force amounts to." During the Seven Days Battles, Lincoln again showed his firm grasp of the significance of lines of operations when he wrote McClellan that "we protected Washington and the enemy concentrated on you; had we stripped Washington, he would have been upon us before the troops sent could have got to you . . . it is the nature of the case."

By now Lincoln saw that individual battles were unlikely to be decisive and that the means of victory lay in occupying the enemy's territory and breaking lines of communication. Early on, Lincoln explained that his "general idea of the war" was that

> we have the greater numbers, and the enemy has the greater fa-cility of concentrating forces upon the points of collision; that we must fail unless we can find some way of making our advantage an overmatch for his; and that this can be done by menacing him with superior forces at different points, at the same time; so that we can safely attack one, or both, if he makes no change, and if he weakens one to strengthen the other, forebear to attack the strengthened one, but seize, and hold the weakened one, gaining so much.

Modern students of military history have termed this "the principle of simultaneous advance."

To illustrate the simultaneous advance, which ultimately became a controlling idea in Union strategy, Lincoln cited the August 1861 campaign of First Bull Run, where the Confederates used their inte-rior lines to move troops from Winchester to Manassas. "Suppose," Lincoln wrote, "when the Confederates at Winchester ran away to re-enforce Manassas, we had forebode to attack Manassas, but had seized and held Winchester." This was the concept upon which Lincoln based the policy that had abortively begun with his early 1862 order for all armies to advance on Washington's birthday. There followed three simultaneous Union advances: Henry W. Halleck and McClellan in the spring of 1862; Ulysses S. Grant, William S. Rose-crans, and Ambrose E. Burnside in the fall; and Grant and Joseph Hooker in the spring of 1863.

President Lincoln's attention was still riveted upon operations in Virginia when Lee crossed the Potomac on September 4, 1862, in what Halleck, Lincoln's new general in chief, correctly termed a raid. Rather than being alarmed by any possible threat that Lee's raid might pose, Lincoln perceived it as an opportunity to circumvent the power of the defense and have a battle where the enemy's rear was not toward his communications. The optimistic Lincoln not only did not see Philadelphia as "in any danger," but he even explained lines of operations to the anxious governor of Pennsylvania. If half of McClellan's army moved to Harrisburg, "the enemy will turn upon," wrote Lincoln, "and beat the remaining half, and then reach Harrisburg before the part going there, and beat it too."

More significant for Lincoln than the absence of any real threat from the raiders was that the situation presented a golden opportunity for the concentrated forces under McClellan. In their flank position northwest of Washington, McClellan's men precluded an enemy advance northward, because Lee "dares not leave them in his rear." Perceiving Lee to be in a potentially serious predicament, Lincoln urged McClellan not to "let him get off without being hurt," and to "destroy the rebel army if possible." His belief in a chance for hurting the enemy rested on his hope that Lee would raid farther north and McClellan could get in his rear.

After the disappointing Battle of Antietam on September 17, 1862, Lincoln again showed his understanding of the strategy of maneuvering an army to turn the enemy from his position. Writing McClellan, the president, quoting Jomini, reminded the general of "one of the standard maxims of war, . . . 'to operate upon the enemy's communications as much as possible without exposing your own.'"[2] McClellan, Lincoln said, acted "as if this applies against you, but cannot apply in your favor."

Before explaining the vulnerability of Lee's position, Lincoln pointed out that McClellan should not "dread his [Lee's] going into Pennsylvania." If he did, he would give up his communications and the Army of the Potomac would "have nothing to do but follow and

2. See Antoine Henri de Jomini, *The Art of War*, trans. G. H. Mendell and W. P. Craighill (1862; reprint, Westport, Conn.: Greenwood Press, 1971), 80. Here Jomini is himself quoting from chap. 14 of his *Traites des Grandes Operations Militaire*. Jomini did not use the term *turning movement*, treating it instead under the concept of base of operations. Lincoln's exposition here and the situation itself are perhaps more consistent with Jomini's base-of-operations approach than with the turning movement; see *Art of War*, 77–84.

ruin him." Lee, on the other hand, could easily be turned because the Union army was "nearer Richmond by the route you can, and he must take." The president asked McClellan, "why can you not reach there before him" when Lee's route would be the "arc of a circle" and McClellan's the chord? Logistics would be no problem on this march, for "the facility of supplying them from the side away from the enemy is remarkable—as it were, by the different spokes extending from the hub towards the rim."

Reminding McClellan of his own point about the importance of not trying to tackle the enemy in entrenchments, the president emphasized that not only was beating the enemy "easier near to us than far away," but also "if we cannot beat the enemy where he now is, we never can, he being within the entrenchments of Richmond."

Thus did Lincoln analyze the problem posed by the well-demonstrated primacy of the defensive. Unless there were to be a stalemate, with the Union army sitting in futility before the entrenchments of Richmond, something must be accomplished at a distance from those entrenchments. Lincoln did not subscribe to the thesis that Richmond, like Sebastopol, would fall if besieged. Nor did he have any high expectations of what might be accomplished away from entrenchments. But he hoped that his army would fight if a "favorable opportunity" presented itself.

As Lincoln was evolving a doctrine for dealing with the stalemate in Virginia, he was also maturing a strategy for the operations of the western armies. Despite the vast area of the western theater, the military goals there were comparatively straightforward and unchanging. Lincoln's policy centered on territorial and logistical objectives: seeking to control the Mississippi River, eventually to dominate Arkansas and occupy East Tennessee, and to cut the western extension of the Confederacy's strategically vital East Tennessee and Virginia Railroad. By late fall, in collaboration with General in Chief Halleck, Lincoln had assigned first priority to opening the Mississippi River and second to cutting the railroad. "To take and hold the Railroad at, or East of Cleveland in East Tennessee, I think fully as important as taking and holding Richmond," Lincoln wrote. The strategic importance of that railroad had impressed Lincoln early and this conviction intensified because of the belief that Beauregard had reinforced Lee for the Seven Days Battles.

In the new Union priorities, the indecisive Virginia theater ranked third, ahead only of Missouri and Arkansas. In the fall of 1862 Lincoln and Halleck limited their expectations in Virginia to the hope that Burnside's army could advance and "occupy the rebel army south of the Rappahannock." The objective, explained Halleck, was to enable the Army of the Potomac to detach sufficient forces "to place the opening of the Mississippi beyond a doubt." Burnside's failure to push Lee's army far enough "from the vicinity of Washington and the upper Potomac" meant that Lincoln and Halleck could spare no troops from Virginia for the Mississippi campaign. Even so, two divisions under Burnside were sent to strengthen Kentucky in March 1863. Thus Lincoln and Halleck stressed the West and accepted a stalemate in Virginia. Major advances to secure their goals would be made in synchronization with each other and the movements against Lee in Virginia.

Embracing the early design of Maj. Gen. Winfield Scott, Lincoln also ordered the naval blockade of Southern ports. Intended to isolate the South from European aid, the blockade resulted in no immediate occupation of enemy territory but it did serve the important dual purpose of supporting operations against the rebel coastline and rivers.

Pursuing the opposite policy in the East that he did in the West, the president avoided seeking to capture or besiege the rebel capital. Instead he wished to aim at Lee's army, albeit with the feeble blows befitting a tertiary objective. Why was Lincoln apparently so inconsistent in his object for the Army of the Potomac? The principal reason was the tremendous difficulty of taking Richmond. The keys to this problem were in the power of the entrenched defense and the obstacle presented by Richmond's elaborate communications system of three trunk-line railroads and a canal.

Even before the defeat at Fredericksburg on December 13, 1862, and the essential failure of the fall 1862 campaign, Lincoln had come fully to realize the ascendancy of the defense and the relative indecisiveness of military operations. In late November he had explained: "I certainly have been dissatisfied with the slowness of Buell and McClellan, but before I relieved them I had great fears I should not find successors to them, who would be better; and I am sorry to add, that I have seen little since to relieve those fears."

Pointing out that this situation really inhered in the constraints of logistics and the strength of the defensive, he indicated: "I do not clearly see the prospect of any more rapid movements. I fear we shall at last find out that the difficulty is in our case rather than in particular generals."

None of the many plans to take the Confederate capital presented a plausible means of interdicting Richmond's communications. The consequences of such a failure were particularly evident to Halleck, an engineer who had published on fortifications. He was aware that the Crimean city of Sebastopol had, like Richmond, been largely defended by field, rather than permanent, fortifications and he knew how long it had held out against the experienced, professional forces of the combined armies and navies of Britain, France, Sardinia, and the Ottoman Empire. If Sebastopol could hold for more than a year against such a formidable attack, there was no hope that Union troops could conquer Richmond sooner, and probably little that they could capture it at all. Halleck also knew that defensive fortifications so economized on men that one man in fortifications equaled six in the attack. Such a favorable ratio for the defenders of fortifications in a siege would enable the rebels actually to reduce their forces in the Richmond vicinity.

If, as the operations in 1862 had indicated, the enemy could not be beaten in the field, it was clear, as Lincoln had pointed out early in the fall, that it surely could not be beaten "within the entrenchments of Richmond." Lincoln and Halleck adopted the obvious solution: avoid a siege. The alternative to a siege, as explained by the general in chief and endorsed by the president, was to abandon Richmond as an objective. The "first object" of a Virginia campaign was no longer to besiege Richmond "but the defeat or scattering of Lee's army, which threatened Washington and the line of the Upper Potomac." Halleck ordered the Army of the Potomac "to turn the enemy's works, or to threaten their wings or communications; in other words, to keep the enemy occupied till a favorable opportunity to strike a decisive blow." Other measures against Lee's army were to use "cavalry and light artillery upon his communications, and attempt to cut off his supplies and engage him at an advantage."

The ideas Halleck expressed harmonized with and in truth merely extended those expressed by Lincoln in September and October 1862. Lincoln had "confidently believed last September that we could end the war by allowing the enemy to go to Harrisburg and Philadelphia, only that we could not keep down mutiny, and utter demoralization among the Pennsylvanians." Just as he had tried to trap Jackson with Fremont's and McDowell's forces the previous May, so also had he yearned to be able to allow Lee to go too far and block his retreat from Pennsylvania. He had hoped that the Antietam campaign would at least present an opportunity to "hurt" Lee.

Having thus decided on concentration in the West and settled on the futility of attempting to reach and besiege Richmond, Lincoln and Halleck sought to guide the commander of the Army of the Potomac to adopt the unconventional and unpromising objective assigned him.

On January 26, 1863, the new commander, Joseph Hooker, received from the president a general charge to seek "military success" but to "beware of rashness. Beware of rashness, but with energy and sleepless vigilance go forward and give us victories." Lincoln was in a sense echoing his earlier instructions to Burnside to "be cautious," and, though victories were needed, he may well have meant for Hooker, like Burnside, to know that he was not to "understand that the government, or the country, is driving you" to seek these victories rashly. Halleck's instructions were more explicit in that he sent Hooker a copy of his last instructions to Burnside, which made clear that the "first object was, not Richmond, but the defeat or scattering of Lee's army." Hooker was directed "to keep the enemy occupied till a favorable opportunity offered to strike a decisive blow." Keeping the enemy occupied had another significance, for the "great object" was "to occupy the enemy, to prevent his making large detachments or distant raids, and to injure him all you can with the least injury to yourself." In spite of strong words about "the defeat or scattering of Lee's army," Halleck's instructions were well tempered with realism, Hooker being told only "to act against the enemy when circumstances will permit."

Later Lincoln would reiterate these points when he explained to Hooker that there was "*no* eligible route for us into Richmond; and consequently a question of preference between the Rappahannock route, and the James River route is a contest about nothing." Since it was futile to attempt to take the rebel capital, what was to be the mission of the Army of the Potomac? Lincoln explained: "Hence our prime object is the enemies' army in front of us," and against him there was a definite advantage: "Our communications are shorter and safer than are those of the enemy. For this reason, we can with equal powers fret him more than he can us. . . . While he remains intact, I do not think we should take the disadvantage of attacking him in his entrenchments; but we should continually harass and menace him, so that he shall have no leisure in sending away detachments. If he weakens himself, then pitch into him."

When, in June 1863, Lee began an advance, Hooker thought it might present him with an opportunity to take Richmond. Lincoln strongly dissented and pointed out to Hooker: "If you had Richmond invested to-day, you would not be able to take it in twenty days; meanwhile, your communications, and with them, your army would be ruined. I think Lee's Army, and not Richmond, is your true objective point." Seeing in Lee's movement the Antietam campaign opportunity reappearing, Lincoln wrote Hooker: "I believe you are aware that since you took command of the army I have not believed that you had any chance to effect anything until now." Hooker, understanding that he was to seize any chance to strike Lee's army in the open, proposed to attack Lee's rear units, entrenched near Fredericksburg. To this Lincoln promptly objected, pointing out that Lee's detachment "would fight in entrenchments, and have you at a disadvantage, and so, man for man, worst you at that point, while his main force would in some way be getting an advantage of you Northward."

The best way to exploit the situation, wrote Halleck, was "to fight his movable column first instead of first attacking his entrenchments." As Lee advanced, Lincoln explained, "follow on his flank, and on the inside track, shortening your lines, whilst he lengthens his." Then, the general in chief advised, when Lee left "part of his forces in Fredericksburg, while the head of his column, he moves . . . toward the Potomac," there would be an opportunity "to cut him in two, and fight his divided forces." The president, deploring that Hooker's later plan looked "like defensive merely," echoed Halleck's earlier point: if the head of Lee's column was near the Potomac and the tail near Fredericksburg, "the animal must be very slim somewhere. Could you not break him?"

Though the public in the Northeast panicked at Lee's advance and Lincoln called out one hundred thousand militia, the president nevertheless remained calm, reassuring his wife that he did "not think the raid into Pennsylvania amounts to anything at all." Rather than a menace, Lincoln perceived the Confederate raid, like Lee's previous advance to Antietam, as an opportunity to strike the enemy when vulnerable and far from their base, "the best opportunity we have had since the war began."

It must have been with reluctance that Lincoln had adopted such a pessimistic evaluation of military realities on the Virginia front as to abandon hope of taking the rebel capital. But realizing the defensive power of fortifications and the virtual impossibility of interdicting Richmond's communications, he and Halleck had concluded that there should be no siege of Richmond. Such an operation would simply confer on the rebels all the advantages of the use of fortifications in the defense, not only making their army as well as their capital invulnerable to attack, but permitting them to so to economize on troops in their defense that they might well be able to spare reinforcements for their other armies. The best Union strategy in Virginia was, therefore, to keep away from Richmond and concentrate on Lee's army rather than on the counterproductive objective of the rebel capital. This unconventional assessment, soundly based in both military history and engineering, did not promise success in Virginia, because a well-led, veteran army is a most unpromising objective. Yet the alternative was clearly fruitless and the concept was to count on superior numbers and wait for the audacious Lee to make a mistake.

The second conclusion reached by Lincoln and Halleck was that there should be no major operations from southeast of Richmond in spite of the vast superiority of the communications there and the advantage that the rivers offered for turning the enemy's defensive positions. Not only was this line of operations interdicted for striking at Lee's army, it was equally prohibited in the event there was a siege, perhaps imposed by Lee's withdrawal to the defenses of Richmond. Any siege must be carried out from the north side of the city for the same reason that the southeast line of operations was interdicted. The defensive efficiency of the fortifications of Richmond was such that, in the event of a siege from the southeast, the rebels would be able to reduce the troops defending their capital to a very low level and suddenly concentrate the bulk of their forces on the northern Virginia line of operations.

Thus Lincoln's strategy for Virginia differed fundamentally from his strategy for the other theaters. There has long been a tendency, however, to generalize from the Virginia theater in formulating interpretations of Lincoln and his generals. Conscious and unconscious partisans of what might be called the peninsular school have interpreted Lincoln as interfering with field commanders who knew better how to conduct the war in Virginia and have generalized from this to cover Lincoln's conduct of operations in all theaters.

Conscious and unconscious opponents of the peninsular school have taken McClellan's weakness in execution as evidence that his strategy was faulty. Lincoln's stress upon the enemy army as an objective seems orthodox and modern, whereas a preoccupation with territory and a place, the enemy capital, seems to reflect that the field commanders had a less sophisticated understanding of strategy than did Lincoln, one that even smacked of archaic, pre-Napoleonic ideas. Many of the opponents of this point of view wrote after World War II when military operations seemed decisive and armies vulnerable. Some of these post–World War II critics blamed Jomini for the West Point generals' faulty strategy and praised Lincoln for seeing the flaws.

Like the peninsular school, the proponents of Lincoln also have difficulty generalizing their interpretation to the other theaters of the war. Nowhere else did Lincoln advocate the enemy army as an objective. His objectives in other theaters were not armies, the Tennessee railroad and the Mississippi River being the most obvious examples.

The interpretation here proposed has the opposite difficulty in that, featuring a generalized explanation for all operations outside of Virginia, it must also include the special case of Virginia, where Lincoln was apparently inconsistent with the strategy he advocated elsewhere, for he did not advocate an attack on Lee's army in other theaters. Lincoln's emerging feeling that lack of success was not due to the generals but to the "case"—that is, the military realities—and his subsequent reactions to the operations of Hooker and Meade indicate that he shared the generals' skepticism about the annihilation or even the defeat of the enemy army. What Lincoln believed, then, seems to be that action against Lee in the field was preferable to the futility of a siege against a well-fortified enemy in a city whose communications could not be interdicted. Of course, he hoped for a blunder by Lee that would provide an opportunity to hurt the rebel army.

Lincoln's mature strategy, taking both theaters simultaneously into account, was thus a somewhat more sophisticated version of Major General Scott's Anaconda Plan. Two other measures were also part of his overall strategy. In late 1863 his policy of amnesty and reconstruction sought to lure rebels away from their Confederate allegiance, and he hoped, by a combination of political and military action, to reconstruct all of the peripheral areas of the Confederacy.

Before Lincoln implemented his mature political strategy he moved to adopt a measure that was an extension and logical consequence of his Emancipation Proclamation. He announced that blacks freed by the proclamation would "be received into the armed service of the United States to garrison forts, positions, stations, and other places." Skepticism as to whether blacks could be adequate soldiers did not extend to their manning rear-area fortified points or guarding railways, thus "leaving the white forces now necessary at those places, to be employed elsewhere." In this way Lincoln planned for manpower difficulties to be significantly eased by tapping a new source of soldiers, "the great available and as yet unavailed of, force for the restoration of the Union."[3] Arming Southern blacks most effectively harmonized with the basic Anaconda strategy; Lincoln saw that it worked "doubly, weakening the enemy and strengthening us," because it took "so much labor from the insurgent cause, and supplying the places which otherwise must be filled with so many white men."

But Lincoln correctly believed the program weakened the enemy in another way—psychologically. He thought that "the bare sight of fifty thousand armed, and drilled black soldiers on the banks of the Mississippi, would end the rebellion at once." He did not believe

---

3. For Lincoln learning of the role of blacks as soldiers in the Revolution, see Benjamin Quarles, *Lincoln and the Negro* (New York: Oxford University Press, 1962), 155.

that the rebellion could survive if such a black military force could "take shape, and grow, and thrive, in the South." As the recruiting went forward during the spring and summer of 1863, Lincoln, by then envisioning one hundred thousand black troops, believed that they were a "resource which, if vigorously applied now, will soon end the contest."

Hence Lincoln as a strategist was orthodox militarily, relying on professional military advice. In his arguments with McClellan and his successor, George G. Meade, Lincoln had the advice and full agreement of Major General Halleck, leader of the western group of generals who ultimately dominated the Union high command. Like his professional advisors, Lincoln understood the power of the defense and the futility of trying to destroy an enemy army in the open field. That Grant failed for so long to take Richmond, even as the Confederacy perceptively declined, fully vindicated the pessimistic assessment that Lincoln had made in late 1862. That Lee's army remained intact in spite of Grant's direct assaults upon it further confirmed the assumption of the president and his generals about the superiority of the defense.

After some groping and false starts the president settled on Scott's western offensive. The greatest key of all to explain Lincoln as strategist is his desire to achieve simultaneous advances. But he added to this purely military strategy a significant political-logistical aspect in his policy of arming Southern blacks. In his active role and military orthodoxy Lincoln resembles Franklin Roosevelt; in his political warfare he is far closer to the Fourteen Points than to unconditional surrender.

Perhaps no president has suffered more at the hands of his own advisors and generals than Lincoln. He was often judged harshly for inconsequential reasons, such as his awkward appearance and his western mannerisms. He was insulted, ridiculed, and humiliated, yet he tolerated the transgressions because he realized his choice of cabinet members and commanding generals had to be based on professional competence rather than personal preference. Indeed, in Lincoln's wartime administration, personnel decisions mattered as highly toward the war's eventual outcome as did the choice of strategy.

Secretary of War Edwin M. Stanton became the first serious Lincoln detractor, and for what might be called personal vanity. Stanton had met Lincoln as a fellow lawyer in 1855 and had rudely avoided him throughout the case on which they were to have worked together. Stanton had cruelly asked, within Lincoln's hearing, "Where did that long-armed creature come from?" Lincoln was deeply mortified, but five years later, as president, he surprised Stanton by asking him to serve in his cabinet, despite Stanton's virulent condemnation of Lincoln for early war reverses. Stanton had made no apology for calling Lincoln "a low, cunning clown," "that giraffe," and "the original gorilla." Even George McClellan, no friend of Lincoln himself, wrote that he "was often shocked" by the secretary's abuse of Lincoln. But the president's evenhanded dealing with Stanton, his approval of the secretary's job performance, and a striking similarity in family tragedies in time bonded Lincoln and Stanton in close friendship.

Not nearly as amicably resolved, yet possibly even more important to the nation's well-being, was the conflict between the president and Major General McClellan. Twice the commander of the Army of the Potomac and the man who helped frame Lincoln's understanding of military precepts, McClellan constantly ignored the president's political concerns over the war's conduct and dealt with him in a high-handed and condescending manner. Yet Lincoln kept McClellan in high command as long as he seemed to be the best available man for the job, and he never let McClellan's arrogance prevent him from making wise decisions.

Nothing better illustrates that arrogance than an occurrence in the fall of 1861: The president and the secretary of state went to McClellan's house one evening, and, finding him out, waited an hour for his return. Eventually McClellan "came in and, without paying any particular attention to the porter who told him the President was waiting to see him, went up-stairs, passing the door of the room where the President and Secretary of State were seated." After waiting another half hour for McClellan to come down to see them, the president and the secretary sent "a servant to tell the General that they were there, and the answer coolly came that the

General had gone to bed." The president put up with "this unparalleled insolence of epaulettes" not only because he still was trying to learn from McClellan about military matters but also because he realized that it was important to shield McClellan from the already rising popular dissatisfaction with the general.

In McClellan's defense, the quotations above were penned by an obvious enemy, Stephen W. Sears. My second doctoral graduate, Ethan Rafuse, in his dissertation noted with sound underpinning that McClellan had been through an extraordinarily hard day and that, in fact, he was suffering from malaria. But many persons at the time were horrified. When Republican senator Benjamin Wade insisted that Lincoln replace McClellan, the president asked irritably, "With whom could [I] replace him?" "Anybody!" cried Wade. Lincoln shook his head; "anybody" might do for Wade, but he must have "somebody." And for a crucial period of time, that somebody, by virtue of his obvious organizational abilities, simply had to be McClellan.

McClellan, however, never repaid the president's professional trust. During the Peninsular Campaign, the general wrote that the government "cannot hold me responsible for the result" of the campaign, and he told Stanton that he owed "no thanks to you or any other persons in Washington" for saving the army from disaster.

When Lincoln decided that Joe Hooker was the right man for a top command, he did so despite knowing about Hooker's brash bravado and thinly veiled self-seeking tendencies, which, more than any conviction, doubtless had prompted the general's famous remark that Lincoln and the administration were imbeciles and nothing would proceed properly until the Union installed a military dictator. Knowing Hooker well, Lincoln, upon his appointment, sent him a meticulous letter containing this remarkable statement:

> There are some things in regard to which, I am not quite satisfied with you. I believe you to be a brave and skillful soldier, which, of course, I like. I also believe you do not mix politics with your profession, in which you are right. You have confidence in yourself, which is valuable, if not an indispensable quality. You are ambitious, which, within reasonable bounds, does good rather than

harm. But I think that during Gen. Burnside's command of the Army, you have taken counsel of your ambition, and thwarted him as much as you could, in which you did a great wrong to the country, and to a most meritorious brother officer. I hear, in such a way as to believe it, of your recently saying that both the Army and the Government needed a Dictator. Of course it was not for this, but in spite of it, that I have given you the command. Only those generals who gain successes can set up dictators. What I now ask of you is military success, and I will risk the dictatorship.

As commander in chief Lincoln was far from perfect. At times he allowed his generals too much discretion in putting their plans into action and he did nothing when they chose to casually ignore his directives. Caving in to political pressure, he often meddled at the wrong times or failed to do so when the situation required positive leadership. His tolerance for the abuses heaped upon him might have easily been taken as undue meekness or vacillation. There were also instances when individual cabinet members seemed to have the upper hand.

But Lincoln's quick grasp of military knowledge helped to sustain him even in his errors. He never lost sight of the fact that, once at war, the ultimate solution rests in military success. That Lincoln was able not only to seek correct military advice but also to formulate it himself made him, in the true sense of the title, a most able commander in chief.

PART 2
SOCIETY IN WARTIME

☞ The War inside the Church

with Lloyd A. Hunter

The Reverend Lloyd Hunter was pastoring a church in the
Kansas City area when he earned a master's degree under my
direction. He subsequently received a Ph.D. from St. Louis
University and then landed a professorship at Franklin College,
in Indiana. Upon his invitation, I delivered the first version of
this paper as a lecture at a convocation on the Franklin campus.
We then together revised the piece and published it in the
January 1988 issue of *Civil War Times Illustrated*. It made rather a
hit with many scholars and was reprinted in several anthologies,
mainly for use as a collateral reading in survey courses. I continued my interest in, and work on, this topic, and the version here
is a revision of the one we published in 1988.

Decades before the first shots of the Civil War thundered over
Fort Sumter, South Carolina, an equally ominous sound echoed
through America. In churches across the land, hands hammered on
pulpits, and impassioned preachers roared for the purification of
God's favored nation. In the North, this fiery call seared the South
for its sinful ways. In the South, it scathed the wayward North.
Eventually, the call helped crack America's delicate Union in two.

This crack, this great schism between Christians of North and
South, began during the 1830s and the 1840s. So bitter was the division that the Methodist, Baptist, Presbyterian, and Congregational
churches split into separate Northern and Southern denominations.
Still other churches, most notably the Episcopalian, were on the
verge of tearing apart at the Mason–Dixon Line. When Civil War
did come, the Episcopalians divided in a de facto sense: the Confederates published and used a Southern-oriented version of *The Book
of Common Prayer.*

Only recently have scholars begun to probe deeply into the origins of these schisms. The breakups had much more than simply slavery underpinning them. In a brilliant little study Samuel S. Hill demonstrated that even as early as the American Revolution the Northern and Southern churches were more like first cousins than brothers and sisters.[1] On into the antebellum period, before the official divisions, they were more like third cousins. Investigations by other scholars show that religious belief and influences dramatically affected the South's decision to secede. Religion influenced the way Northerners and Southerners conducted the Civil War, and it affected the way people adjusted to life in the postwar South.

The breach in American Christendom came at a time when the issue of slavery was one of the foremost national issues. For reasons ranging from moral concerns to political pragmatism, there were attempts to regulate slavery by refusing to admit any more slave states to the Union, or by admitting such states only when a free state could be admitted simultaneously. Against such attempts, and against the endless stream of abolition petitions from the Northern public, legislators from slave states fought bitterly. Slavery was the most volatile topic of debate in Congress, and there was talk of Southern secession in the 1830s.

At the state level, several Southern slaveholding states passed laws in the 1830s forbidding the dissemination of abolitionist propaganda. Grave penalties—in some cases, death—were prescribed for violators of these codes. There was a fear in the South that abolitionists, who sought the end of slavery and sometimes worked for their goal by helping slaves escape, would bring on violent slave revolts.

For the churches, too, slavery was a heated issue. Northern Christians tended to view bondage as immoral. (At least, that is, they did so after slavery had proved to be relatively unprofitable within *their* borders: all thirteen of the original British colonies had slavery until the time of the Revolution.) They eventually struggled over whether they could tolerate the "peculiar institution" with a clear conscience.

---

1. Hill's 1966 study, *Southern Churches in Crisis,* was reprinted with new introductory material as *Southern Churches in Crisis Revisited* (Tuscaloosa: University of Alabama Press, 1999).

Ultimately, although it took many years to coalesce, the general Northern consensus was a firm no. Slavery quite simply had to be eradicated.

In the South, the churches responded to the North's condemnation of slavery by returning the anathema—the Northern interpretation of Christianity was incorrect, they charged. What resulted was a great schism, but it was easier to bear because of the many other theological and church-government differences that gradually had been emerging. Slavery was merely the trigger that sparked the formal divisions. But the divisions of the churches had great significance. C. C. Goen has argued that dividing the churches was a major development, and that those divisions made dividing the nation more thinkable.[2] Northern believers cried "Unclean!" at the South, and Southern faithful returned the accusation in kind. A controversy that had begun as a moral and theological debate quickly deteriorated into a battle of sectional politics. The true faith was more and more defined by geography, and entire regions were suddenly on the side of right or wrong.

The chasm between the churches of North and South had a profound destructive impact on America's already turbulent political life. Dividing the churches subsequently impacted the divisions of the mainline political parties. This was yet another step toward paving the way for the breaking apart of the nation. The Whig party faded out of existence in the 1850s. Its replacement, the Republican party, was a coalition of western and eastern states, with the South the odd man out; among its other platform planks, it was opposed to further expansion of slavery. The Democratic party divided in 1860 into two hopelessly irreconcilable sections, one predominantly Northern and the other predominantly Southern. That produced a Republican victory, despite the fact that the party's candidate, Abraham Lincoln, garnered only 40 percent of the popular vote. Southerners were convinced by their leaders and manipulators that the Republican victory was enough to induce secession: seven states announced separation before Lincoln's inauguration. Four more formally seceded after the firing on Fort Sumter

2. C. C. Goen, *Broken Churches, Broken Nation: Denominational Schisms and the Coming of the American Civil War* (Macon, Ga.: Mercer University Press, 1985).

and Lincoln's subsequent call for 75,000 volunteers to put down the incipient rebellion.

That religious disputes could lead citizens to take up arms and fight a civil war is not surprising when seen in the context of the nineteenth-century vision of the United States. American nationalism had a religious base, and that base was much more influential than it is now. Much of the populace believed theirs was a nation blessed by God, endowed with a divine mission to be an example of right living to the rest of the world. This perception was largely the result of evangelical Christianity, an interdenominational Protestant movement ablaze with militant, crusading zeal. Evangelicalism, which emphasized good, lengthy sermons rather than ceremony and ritual, spread its message rapidly through ardent preachers. The movement suffused its religious nationalism throughout both North and South during the early antebellum period.

At first, the notion that America was God's chosen country helped nurture national unity. And spectacular numbers of conversions gave mainline denominations—especially the Baptists, Methodists, and Presbyterians, and to a lesser extent the Congregationalists and Episcopalians—a strong voice in the nation's social and political spheres. But with the idea of a "chosen" America came a deep sense of national responsibility to God. When Americans failed to do their duty by following the will and laws of the Almighty, it was a serious matter, a mark on the soul of the Republic. And so, to many Northerners, the Southerners' justification or tolerance of slavery was more than an ethical problem requiring change—it was a violation of America's sacred mission, and had to be stopped at once, even if by radical means.

In the sectional dispute that grew out of this urgent matter of conscience, Northern and Southern Christians turned on each other with the same zeal that had won so many souls. Each side viewed the other as transgressor, as the sinner sullying God's Republic with moral abominations. So intense were these convictions that both sides perceived and portrayed the controversy in cosmic terms. They would come to regard the Civil War as "Armageddon," the ultimate struggle of eternal right against eternal wrong prophesied in the Bible's Book of Revelation (16:16).

If the church leaders of North and South, laymen and clerics alike, had molded different solutions to the moral problems they believed were besmirching America, the war itself might have been avoided. Instead, they watched the breakup of the nation, seeing in it the vindication of their schisms. The secession of the South had confirmed their beliefs that one region was morally right, the other morally wrong. With their dramatic interpretation of events, the churches not only became catalysts in breaking the nation, they also became intimately involved with the war effort, because they saw it as a holy crusade.

Thanks to the fresh scholarship of recent years, we have a new picture of how religion affected the thinking and fighting spirit of the Civil War's combatants. The churches, more than any other institution, seem to have been the underpinning of Civil War morale, at times buoying it, at times eroding it. One of the most inspiring religious concepts in the mind of Civil War–era Northerners seems to have been the doctrine of millenarianism—the belief that the Devil would be restrained and Jesus Christ would come again to establish his kingdom on earth for a thousand years, but that there was a specific list of things that first needed to be achieved and accomplished. Church historian James H. Moorhead has found a striking degree of "post-millenialist" thought in "the four mainline Protestant denominations in the North." With rather more skimpy evidence, he has noted just the opposite in the South: either *pre*-millenarianism— which is fatalistic—or no millenarianism at all.[3] In sum, a vast number of Northern church people believed that the Civil War was Armageddon.

Southerners had a different religious mind-set. While fatalistic, there was assuredly no lack of religious fervor in them. Southerners believed God had a plan, a divine will to which it was crucial to adhere. If people followed God's will, He would bless them and things would go well. If they did not, things would go badly. The problem, of course, was trying to discern the divine plan.

These particular aspects of Southern Protestant thought had no

3. James H. Moorhead, *American Apocalypse: Yankee Protestants and the Civil War, 1860–1869* (New Haven: Yale University Press, 1978); James H. Moorhead, "Millennialism," in *Encyclopedia of Religion in the South,* ed. Samuel S. Hill (Macon, Ga.: Mercer University Press, 1984), 477–79.

denominational boundaries. Indeed, there was a great blurring of denominational differences in the region. Southerners were religious in a cultural way more than in a theological or liturgical way. When a person changed denomination, it was usually for social, cultural, or class reasons rather than as a matter of faith.

Northern Christians could not understand this sort of religious attitude. They took denominational differences more seriously, and were very much more evangelical. As time passed, Northern churchmen increasingly came to view the South not as differently "churched," but quite simply "unchurched." After the war, typical Northerners perceived the South as a great, fertile field for proselytization and reform, and Northern missionaries traveled south to spread Christianity among the heathen. One Northern Methodist minister chortled during the Civil War that events were crushing the "Dagon god of the South" (Dagon was an idol worshiped in Old Testament times by the Philistines).

White Southerners deeply resented these efforts at conversion. Many black Southern Christians felt the same way, if for different reasons. A good example: the African Methodist Episcopal Church and the separate African Methodist Episcopal Church–Zion were both starkly Northern in orientation, outlook, and leadership. After the war this led to the formation of the Southern-based Colored Methodist Episcopal Church, still in existence but with its name changed to Christian Methodist Episcopal Church.

Religious historians have added a new answer to the weighty question, "Why did the South lose the war?" Religion's impact on the outcome of the conflict was dramatic. As the war progressed, Northerners were impelled more and more to push on to victory, because they believed that by doing so they were hastening the coming of the Lord's kingdom. But Southerners, as they looked at the ongoing tragedies and mounting casualty lists, with no future victory apparent, came to feel they had veered away from the will of God. Slowly, and despite their indisputable and awesome sacrifices in the war effort, they began to feel their best recourse was to give up. Other factors contributed to the erosion and ultimate collapse of Southern will, but religion played a vital role.

The South's spirits had fallen far since the war's outset. In 1861, both sides were confident God was on their side. If they made the proper sacrifices, they believed, victory would be theirs. As a Confederate soldier wrote his wife in early 1862, "when we lay *all* upon the altar of our country, the God of Nations will give us a permanent happy existence. How near akin is patriotism to religion."

This unknown soldier could not have known it, but his words underscored a religious element in the American experience that was altered and intensified by the Civil War. Known as "civil religion," something not taken seriously by most scholars until recently, this dimension of America's faith centered upon the nation itself. Much like the religious nationalism of the evangelicals, with which it was clearly infused, it viewed the United States as a redeemer nation, its citizens as a chosen people. It interpreted America's meaning and destiny in light of God's activity among the nations.

Though remarkably similar to evangelical beliefs, civil religion had its differences. As one of its foremost students, Robert N. Bellah, explains, civil religion "actually exists alongside of and rather clearly differentiated from the churches," but it uses biblical symbols and themes as vehicles for the nation's self-understanding. Like all religions, says Bellah, it "has its own prophets and its own martyrs, its own social events and sacred places, its own solemn spirituals," such as presidential inaugurations and, not so long ago, the rededication of the Statue of Liberty.[4]

While it blossomed during the Civil War, American civil religion existed much earlier. In 1630, Puritan John Winthrop told his fellow English colonists aboard the *Arbella* that their new "plantation" at Massachusetts Bay must be God's "City upon a Hill," to which all humankind would look for guidance. From then on, Americans—Northerners and Southerners alike—infused their history with religious meaning. An example is Julia Ward Howe, author of the most famous war poem set to music, who saw "the glory of the coming of the Lord" in the marching ranks of the Union Army of the Potomac. But the same trumpet call easily could have been sounded in Dixie. The renowned "fire-eater" or radical secessionist Benjamin Morgan Palmer, a Presbyterian minister in New Orleans, proposed the

4. Robert N. Bellah, *Broken Covenant: American Civil Religion in Time of Trial* (New York: Seabury Press, 1975). These themes are underscored throughout the work, which deserves reading in full, but see esp. pp. 2–3, 88, 103, 143.

Confederacy was "the cause of God Himself." With this firm conviction, Palmer echoed Howe's "Battle Hymn of the Republic," vowing he would "never call retreat." Civil religion became a way to make sense of the Civil War, of its triumphs and tragedies, and of its outcome.

The Christian theme of sacrifice, death, and rebirth became a permanent ingredient of American civil religion, receiving ritual expression in another outgrowth of the Civil War: Memorial Day. But the theme of sacrifice was most tragically symbolized in the assassination of President Abraham Lincoln on Good Friday, 1865. On the Easter Sunday that followed, Americans immediately proclaimed the fallen president a Christ symbol in the national religion. Lincoln became the perfect human who had willingly sacrificed himself for the ultimate good, the Union's preservation.

It was perceived that Lincoln's was the final blood offering to purify America and to purchase its resurrection to holiness. Yet, for many, he was more than a martyr. Most of all, he had become a much-needed prophet of the civic faith. Indeed, he had been that throughout his presidency, and that was a significant factor in the North's achievement of victory. Interestingly, Lincoln struggled continually to understand the meaning of the war in light of God's purpose. Ever cognizant of divine judgment, Lincoln labeled his countrymen God's "*almost* chosen people." And in his marvelous second inaugural address (possibly even better than his well-known Gettysburg Address) he touched at some length on the topic of God's will and the strong tendency of Americans to identify national goals with that divine will, even when the identification is false.

While Lincoln and others added new dimensions to the old civil religion, Southerners created an entirely new one. Speaking to Confederate veterans in Joplin, Missouri, in autumn 1906, Lawrence M. Griffith, a state official of the Sons of Confederate Veterans, commented that when Dixie's soldiers returned "to find their homes despoiled, their families hungry, and their estates dissipated, there was born in the South a new religion." This regional faith focused, as religious historian Charles Reagan Wilson phrased it, on "a Redeemer Nation that Died."[5] An amalgam of the South's fervent

5. Charles Reagan Wilson, *Baptized in Blood: The Religion of the Lost Cause, 1865–1920* (Athens: University of Georgia Press, 1980), 1.

Protestantism and the powerful myth of the Lost Cause, Southern postwar civil religion elevated the old Confederacy, with its symbols and story, to sacred significance, and commemorated it in periodic rituals.

This religion of the Lost Cause took institutional form in a host of memorial and veterans groups, notably the United Confederate Veterans and the United Daughters of the Confederacy. Southern clergy, many of whom were themselves Civil War veterans, lent zealous support. Like its Northern counterpart, Southern civil religion stressed the sacrifices made by the warriors in gray that the Confederate nation might be cleansed through "the baptism of blood." Wherever Southern veterans and their ladies gathered to share in a reunion, decorate graves, or dedicate a monument—all of which they did countless numbers of times—they recalled their heroes and the sacred ideals for which they had offered their lives. Before them were the symbols of the cause: the gray jacket, the melodic and stirring "Dixie," and the battle flag, itself immortalized in the poetry of Father Abram J. Ryan, "poet priest of the Confederacy": "Furl that banner! softly, slowly, / Treat it gently— it is holy . . ." Father Ryan himself, incidentally, became one of the "saints" in this civil religion: he is memorialized in a stained-glass window at the Confederate Memorial Hall in New Orleans.

There were other saints in Southern civil religion, the spiritual giants of the Confederacy. There was Gen. Robert E. Lee, who, like Christ in Gethsemane, grappled with an agonizing dilemma when he chose to fight for his beloved Virginia. Then, too, there was President Jefferson Davis. The late historian Thomas Lawrence Connelly suggested humorously that one of the requirements for "Confederatesmanship" was that you had to "hate Jefferson Davis."[6] That is, since the perfect R. E. Lee was blameless for the Southern defeat, *somebody* had to be the scapegoat, and who more likely than Davis? But probably a vast majority of Southerners viewed Davis as having suffered symbolic crucifixion, and there was much sympathy for him during his two-year postwar imprisonment without trial. And there was the Moses-like Lt. Gen. Thomas J. "Stonewall" Jackson,

6. Thomas Lawrence Connelly, *Will Success Spoil Jeff Davis?* (New York: McGraw-Hill, 1962). The idea of Lee as a "Christ-like figure" is delineated in various writings by Connelly, especially *The Marble Man: Robert E. Lee and His Image in American History* (New York: Random House, 1977).

whose piety was perhaps the most notorious among all Civil War soldiers but who never reached the "Promised Land" of a victorious Confederacy because he died of wounds sustained in combat. Surely, declared the devotees of the Lost Cause, a nation with such holy symbols could never know final defeat.

The South had been brought low by "overwhelming numbers and resources," as Lee conceded in his farewell to the defeated Army of Northern Virginia. But Southern civil religion taught that in God's own time, the Confederacy, like Israel of old, would be vindicated and, in a transcendent sense, ultimately victorious. And so the South, like the North, was cast as an instrument of God. As such, it too contributed to the civil religion of a people "on the road," not only on the road to reunification of the nation, but also to the pervasive belief articulated by historian and U.S. Senator Albert J. Beveridge that God "has marked the American people as His chosen nation to finally lead in the redemption of the world."

The religion of Northern and Southern Protestant Christians had urged America into war, carried it through the struggle, and helped it deal with the end, whether bitter or joyous. Through its contributions to the nation's civil religion, Civil War spirituality left its legacy, a lasting mark on the way America viewed itself. But there was yet another great spiritual legacy that came from the Civil War: the modern American black churches, which continue even today as essentially racially defined Christian institutions.

Union forces had occupied Richmond only four days when more than a thousand blacks, some sporting the blue jackets they had worn as Federal soldiers, packed into the First African Church to celebrate their new day of freedom. As they had in the days of slavery, they vented their heartfelt sentiments in exuberant and deeply emotional song. As their voices grew louder and their joy peaked, they reached the lines that best expressed their keenest feeling at that moment: "I'm going to join in this army; / I'm going to join in this army of the Lord."

In every state of the former Confederacy, newly freed Negroes echoed these sentiments. In the language of these former bondsmen, the fall of Richmond had been "de Lawd's work." God had acted through "Massa Lincoln's army" to bring about the deliverance he had promised for so long. This was the only way some blacks could understand the recent dramatic events, for they, like almost all Americans, were deeply religious. The freedmen believed in a God who, like the Old Testament Yahweh, intervened in the affairs of the world, and on the side of the oppressed. Ironically, they had learned this message from the very people who had used it to sustain enslavement: the white preachers who had endlessly invoked the apostle Paul's injunction, "Servants, obey your masters."

Blacks rejected the slaveholders' interpretation of this scripture, but clung passionately to Christianity's gospel of liberation, mixing it with remnants of African beliefs. Even in the days of slavery, blacks would often steal away to a hollow or some other secluded spot and indulge in their own churching—what Albert J. Raboteau has called their "invisible institution."[7] There they would "shout" and sing of freedom: "O my Lord delivered Daniel / O why not deliver me too?"

In this way, Negroes established their own brand of Christianity even before the Civil War. But in the war's aftermath, the religious culture of the former slaves changed dramatically. It came into the open, and soon became the very foundation for the black community in freedom. The informal congregations of freed slaves joined themselves to the already extant black churches, and together became, according to church historian Martin Marty, "the most powerful and durable of black institutions in the century."

But despite the emergence of their powerful religious tradition and their newfound freedom, blacks in the postwar years faced a new day that was not always hallmarked by the joy felt at the war's end. The Civil War, besides ensuring freedom for former slaves, also demolished whatever order and stability had existed in the Old South. The old, paternalistic ecclesiastical system, in which blacks worshipped under the eyes of white preachers and in white congregations, had broken down. Its demise was traumatic, for both whites and blacks.

---

7. Albert J. Raboteau, *Slave Religion: The Invisible Institution in the Antebellum South* (New York: Oxford University Press, 1978).

In Charleston, South Carolina, one educated mulatto cleric observed: "There was no one to baptize their children, to perform marriages, or to bury the dead. A ministry had to be created at once—created out of the material at hand." And so, being free, and preferring Negro leadership in their spiritual life, the former bondsmen not only launched a gigantic "black exodus" from the white congregations, they also began rapidly spawning their own clergy. Assisted by Northern missionaries, the black churches molded themselves after the antebellum Protestant denominations of the North, but added their own cultural leaven to become unique.

So, the Civil War's chief legacy to slavery's children, the black church, made the "invisible institution" visible. And as this new church took on structure, it became the social center of the Negro experience. Whether Baptist, Methodist, or Presbyterian, the Afro-American denominations provided their people not only with spiritual interaction and fellowship, but also with economic and educational development. It was through the exemplary work of numerous black preachers and Northern supporters from the American Missionary Association and other benevolent groups that blacks were helped to adjust to life as free men and women.

The black churches' social mission was not limited to the period immediately after the war. In years to come, these spiritual communities would serve as platforms for political life. This function proved particularly crucial when, as Reconstruction failed to fulfill the federal government's goal of equality, white supremacy eventually prevailed again. Then, only the black church gave Southern Negroes the faith and strength to persevere, never despairing that their people might "overcome someday." It is surely no coincidence that the Reverend Dr. Martin Luther King Jr.'s dream of a Dixie that would "be transformed into an oasis of freedom and justice" emerged from institutions founded by those blacks who rejoiced that April day in 1865 when Richmond collapsed.

⮞❖⮜ STATE RIGHTS AND LOCAL DEFENSE

THE CRUX OF FRANK L. OWSLEY'S
STATE-RIGHTS THESIS REEXAMINED

This piece was originally done as a paper that was read at the
Mid-America Conference on History in September 1983. I and
my collaborators had already entered into an agreement to work
on *Why the South Lost the Civil War* and we needed the investigation for that book. I present it here slightly revised from its
original speech format.

In *The Rebel Shore,* James M. Merrill suggested that the early naval
attacks on the Atlantic coast brought fear to the hearts of Southerners, who came to know that Yankee sea power "could strike
swiftly, mercilessly, and without warning against Confederate
shores." Confederate civilians fled to the interior and pleaded for
better defense of their coasts. Merrill wrote: "The theory that state
rights were responsible for the ultimate collapse of the Confederacy
began when Southern governors balked at dispatching men, arms,
and ammunition to the Virginia firing line in order to protect their
own seacoasts." This, he pointed out, set up internal conflict, for
Confederate officials were forced to choose between moving troops
from the main fronts and exposing the coasts. The latter choice
could lead to competition with state governors for men and supplies, for the governors were pressured by citizens to place local defense above the needs of the entire Confederacy.[1]
Certainly it would be an oversimplification to attribute the

1. James M. Merrill, *The Rebel Shore: The Story of Union Sea Power in the Civil
War* (Boston: Little, Brown, 1957), vi, 13–14; see also pp. 25, 52–53.

Confederate state-rights movement solely to the early successes of the Union navy, nor did Merrill intend to suggest that. Yet his remark reminds us that local defense did involve questions of resource and manpower allocation, and that not all local defense issues were generated by incursions into the Confederate interior.

Probably without meaning to do so, Merrill drew our attention to the work of Frank L. Owsley, the historian most responsible for the interpretation that asserts the would-be Confederate nation "died of state rights," and who began his famous book *State Rights in the Confederacy* with a long chapter on local defense.[2]

Although the state-rights interpretation is still prominent in some circles, in recent years there has been less and less substantive discussion of it. At the time of the Civil War centennial, the most prominent collection of essays that attempted to explain the reasons for the Union victory contained no essay directly supporting the "died of state rights" theory; although there was an historiographical reference to Owsley's work, the tone was more that of listing a curiosity than of presenting an underpinning.[3] With the rapidly developing sophistication of historical study, the question of state rights became transformed into one of nationalism, will power, Southern ideology, and the natural tendency of a people under stress to clutch at any weapon. The result has been "to put the Confederacy on the couch"[4] and to see state rights more as a symptom rather than as the fatal disease itself. Equally important is that historians have become more skeptical of Owsley's explanation than his contemporaries had been.

To put it bluntly, as one historian in the late 1970s or early 1980s informally remarked to a group of his peers, who nodded agreement, as far as Owsley's state-rights thesis is concerned, "nobody believes that anymore." But no one has yet bothered to produce a full and formal refutation, as I will endeavor to do here.

2. Frank L. Owsley, *State Rights in the Confederacy* (Chicago: University of Chicago Press, 1925), 1. This influential book was reissued in 1931 and again reprinted by Peter Smith in 1961.

3. David Donald, ed., *Why the North Won the Civil War* (Baton Rouge: Louisiana State University Press, 1960), xi.

4. I owe this phrase to a discussion with the historian and recent biographer of Jefferson Davis, William Cooper Jr.

Owsley, a native Southerner, was born in 1890. *State Rights in the Confederacy* had been his doctoral dissertation and was also his first book, published in 1925. In it Owsley perceived that he was investigating what he called "the seamy side" of Confederate history.[5] Two of Owsley's books, this one as well as *King Cotton Diplomacy*, were considered revolutionary in their time. And Owsley has been revered ever since as an undeniably important historian. But despite much publicity, his state-rights thesis was never universally and uncritically accepted. *State Rights in the Confederacy* was scathingly reviewed by the careful and perceptive scholar Charles W. Ramsdell in the June 1927 issue of the *Mississippi Valley Historical Review*. Ramsdell quite correctly delineated many of the book's more notable faults.

But Owsley *had* taken a fresh tack. Rather than attributing the outcome of the war to Northern military superiority, he asserted, according to Ramsdell, that "state rights jealousy and particularism so weakened the general government that defeat, which otherwise would have been almost impossible, became inevitable." Ramsdell agreed that it is not at all difficult to find evidence that state authorities frequently hampered the Confederate government, but cogently remarked that Owsley "has tried to prove too much and has laid his book open to severe criticism in . . . the handling of evidence." Ramsdell observed that Owsley "has accepted isolated and casual statements as bases for sweeping declarations; he has read into some of his sources statements that are not there even by implication; and he has ignored evidence that tends to disprove or to qualify materially portions of his general thesis."[6]

I will focus upon Owsley's first chapter, which is by far his most important: "Local Defense." I shall consider some of Owsley's explicit arguments and then look at his sources. Time and again, my comparisons suggest that, as Ramsdell observed in 1927, "[p]ossibly the author became over-enamored of this thesis and, like other lovers, lost something of his critical powers."[7]

---

5. Owsley, *State Rights*, vii.
6. Charles W. Ramsdell, review of *State Rights in the Confederacy*, by Frank L. Owsley, *Mississippi Valley Historical Review* 14 (June 1927): 107–8.
7. Ibid., 108. Harriett Chappell Owsley, in the memorial volume to her husband that she edited, included the "Local Defense" chapter as the most representative part of *State Rights*, changing its title to "Local Defense and the

As Ramsdell said, Owsley's "rogues' gallery is crowded with governors." Specifically, according to Owsley, the various governors—especially those of Georgia and North Carolina, but all of them surely—interfered with the war's prosecution in the name of local interests and decentralization, prevented the Confederacy from achieving victory during the first year (when it could decisively have done so), and then for three more years, as the conflict ground to its bitter end, directly contributed to defeat through cantankerous resistance and individual consideration. But—and again, as Ramsdell pointed out—Owsley ignored many things that the governors did to support the war effort, even in some cases going "beyond their constitutional powers in extending aid to the Confederacy." Owsley underplayed the substantial contributions that Govs. Joseph E. Brown and Zebulon Vance's states made to the Confederate war effort. The *Official Records* indicate, for example, that Georgia and North Carolina together contributed 42 percent of the conscripts and volunteers from east of the Mississippi River after the passage of the original conscript law in April 1862.[8]

There was, Owsley stated, a "veritable tug of war between the central and local governments." He believed that "if the individual states had immediately placed the arms in their possession in the hands of the Confederate armies, . . . the Confederate government would have been able to put a much larger army in the field in 1861." In this conjecture, Owsley ignored problems of organizing, training, feeding, and moving the host, implying that the job might have been done in one fell swoop. But even Owsley admitted that "the states did transfer the arms and munitions captured with the United States arsenals," though "in actual practice the several governors each disposed of a large part of these arms according to the interests of their respective states or according to his own individual

Downfall of the Confederacy: A Study in State Rights" (*The South: Old and New Frontiers; Selected Essays of Frank Lawrence Owsley* [Athens: University of Georgia Press, 1969]). My citations to "Local Defense" are to that republication rather than Owsley's original book, because Mrs. Owsley's footnotes are in a less archaic format.

8. Ramsdell, review, 110, 109; John S. Preston to J. C. Breckenridge, February 1865, tabulations A and B, *The War of the Rebellion: A Compilation of the Official Records of the Union and Confederate Armies* (Washington: Government Printing Office, 1880–1901), ser. 4, 3:1101. Hereinafter cited as *OR*.

judgment." This statement admits that new troops *were* organized and given arms. Owsley ridiculed Gov. Thomas Moore of Louisiana for refusing in July 1861 to give the arms for five or six regiments in Confederate service because "it would take all the guns in the arsenal" and because, as Moore said, "We may expect an invasion ourselves in the fall."[9] His estimate was off by only a few months.

The situation in North Carolina became a special bone of contention for Owsley. Gov. Zebulon Vance stands as Owsley's favorite villain, the man who in the end "had on hand in warehouses 92,000 uniforms, thousands of blankets, shoes, and tents. But at the same time Lee's men in Virginia were bare-footed, almost without blankets, tents, and clothing. Vance had enough uniforms to give every man in Lee's army two apiece."[10]

Now, Owsley uncritically accepted what might be called the "ragged rebel myth." The idea that Lee's poor boys shivered in the trenches at Petersburg, and finally had to gingerly pick their way toward Appomattox grossly lacking in clothing and footwear, is an enduring one. What little clothing these wretches got was either sent from home or taken off dead Yankees, the story goes—one that has been accepted by numerous scholars, most notably Bell I. Wiley. But all of this is part of the larger "myth of the Lost Cause." As Leslie D. Jensen points out, the "ragged rebel myth" was created *after* the war both to enhance the glory of the Southern soldiers' achievements and to explain their ultimate defeat.[11]

Lee himself considered lack of food a far more serious problem than lack of clothing as late as March 1865. Even then, the real problem was inadequate distribution and not unavailability of supply. But the real point—contrary to Owsley—is that none of this was Governor Vance's or anyone else in North Carolina's fault. In fact, owing to the disproportionately large percentage of Lee's army that was from that state, what Vance did helped far more than it hurt. As

9. Owsley, "Local Defense," 65, 66; *OR* 4, 1:422.

10. Owsley, *State Rights,* 276–77.

11. Leslie D. Jensen, "A Survey of Confederate Central Government Quartermaster Issue Jackets," *Military Collector and Historian* 46 (1989): 109–22, 162–71. For Bell I. Wiley's acceptance of the "ragged rebel myth," see *The Life of Johnny Reb: The Common Soldier of the Confederacy* (Indianapolis: Bobbs-Merrill, 1943), 113–22.

Marc W. Kruman explains, "It really does not require much knowledge of conditions in North Carolina and of Vance himself to see the injustice" of Owsley's view.[12]

Kruman asserts that historians such as Owsley and his supporters and elaborators—most notably Albert Burton Moore, who extended Owsley's themes of disaffection to conscription, and Georgia Lee Tatum, who more deeply probed the effects of disloyalty—"dwell upon the *symptoms* of dissent in the Confederacy but overlook the underlying causes."[13] The point ultimately is that Owsley and the historians who accepted his argument did not see the forest for the trees: they placed entirely too much credence in the results *supposedly* wreaked by the manifestation of otherwise quite understandable phenomena.

Governor Vance faced a difficult problem in maintaining war morale. Individual liberty occupied a deep-seated place in the minds of white North Carolinians. Kruman writes:

> They believed that a white man deprived of his liberties was just as much a slave as the black bondsman. Black slavery was only the most extreme example of slavery. . . .
>
> If checks were not placed on the power of the rulers, they would concentrate power in their hands and use it to destroy the liberties of the people. Therefore, the people needed specific safeguards for their liberties. A strong state government, [North Carolinians believed, was] the second safeguard of the people's liberties. It could serve as a buffer.[14]

Kruman notes that North Carolinians resisted conscription because they rightly believed that their state already had provided more than its share of soldiers. But "more important . . . was the fear that conscription represented the first step toward military

---

12. Robert E. Lee to John C. Breckinridge, March 9, 1865, *OR* 1, vol. 46, pt. 2, 1295–96; Richard D. Goff, *Confederate Supply* (Durham, N.C.: Duke University Press, 1969), 67–68, 212–13, 220–22, 247–48; Marc W. Kruman, "Dissent in the Confederacy: The North Carolina Experience," *Civil War History* 27 (December 1981): 292–313.

13. Albert Burton Moore, *Conscription and Conflict in the Confederacy* (New York: Macmillan, 1924); Georgia Lee Tatum, *Disloyalty in the Confederacy* (Chapel Hill: University of North Carolina Press, 1934); Kruman, "Dissent," 293–94.

14. Kruman, "Dissent," 297–99.

despotism," a fear that was also aroused when the Confederate Congress authorized the suspension of habeas corpus. When North Carolinians were subsequently arrested, Tarheels also developed "apprehension about the independence of the state's judiciary."[15]

These fears, plus the cumbersome and unpopular substitute laws, contributed to a growing uneasiness that led many Tarheels to issue calls for a convention to allow the state to "act in her sovereign capacity to defend herself." But Kruman's case is that historians have been incorrect in seeing the movements as an effort to achieve a reconstruction of the Union. The evidence, he says, indicates the contrary, that "many Conservatives were trying to extricate themselves from an almost inextricable situation. They wanted to protect their freedom and seek an honorable peace, *but in the Confederacy.*" Vance and others worked against the calling of a convention "because they believed that it would lead to reconstruction rather than to an honorable peace," and they did so by trying to find *other* ways "to preserve the rights and liberties" of the citizenry.[16]

Kruman concludes: "The anxieties of North Carolinians and other white Southerners were paralleled in the North, yet the contours of dissent in the two regions differed."[17] One might justly add: so too did the response of officials who tried to counter or to cater to that dissent, because Northern discontent was tempered considerably by the existence of a quite viable opposition in the form of the Democratic party. President Lincoln had to take account of a powerful, organized opposition; Gov. Horatio Seymour of New York is only one outstanding example.

The significance of this important political difference between the problems of Lincoln and Jefferson Davis is pointed out by David M. Potter. Assuming that long years in a sectional minority protecting slavery with "legalistic safeguard . . . may have impaired the capacity for affirmative and imaginative action on the part of the Southern leaders in general," Potter suggests "that the Confederacy may have suffered real and direct damage from the fact that its political organization lacked a two-party system" to give legitimacy to opposition. Without such a system, the Confederacy lacked a legitimate,

15. Ibid., 299–301.
16. Ibid. 306–8.
17. Ibid., 311.

institutionalized way to influence policy from outside the government.[18] Arthur Schlesinger Sr. pointed out long ago that the notion of state sovereignty had been used at one time or another as a political shelter by almost every state in an effort to protect its interests, but he nevertheless believed the argument "artificial," somewhat like the shelter "that a Western pioneer seeks . . . when a tornado is raging." Lewis O. Saum points out that "as is the case with aspirin for a headache, a state rights position is taken at need, and a shelter makes sense when a tornado threatens."[19] In the same way, state rights made sense to Vance and others like him.

It is significant, in this regard, that not only did Davis not have parties to contend with, but also that Vance in North Carolina *did*; for there, Union Democrats and Whigs had coalesced into the Conservative party, opposing a Confederate party made up of the remaining Democrats and a few Whigs.[20] "North Carolina Conservatives," Kruman observes, "were . . . left with two unsatisfying choices. A small portion moved unwittingly in the direction of disloyalty to the Confederacy and reconstruction of the Union; the larger portion was left to complain bitterly and impotently of the threat to their freedom."[21]

This needs to be emphasized lest we fall into the trap of going along too closely with Owsley's line of argument: time and again, objections to violations of state-rights principles were overruled by the Confederate government; if the states had been getting their way, they would not have had so much complaint to voice. The frequency of complaints did not mark disruption, but rather frustration. For example, except for the coastal areas, North Carolina enjoyed a relatively safe and undisturbed status for most of the war. By the

18. David M. Potter, "Jefferson Davis and the Political Factors in Confederate Defeat," in Donald, ed., *Why the North Won*, 111; Thomas B. Alexander and Richard E. Beringer, *The Anatomy of the Confederate Congress* (Nashville: Vanderbilt University Press, 1972), 342.

19. Lewis O. Saum, "Schlesinger and 'The State Rights Fetish': A Note," *Civil War History* 24 (December 1978): 357–59.

20. Hugh T. Lefler and Albert R. Newsome, *The History of a Southern State: North Carolina*, rev. ed. (Chapel Hill: University of North Carolina Press, 1963), 437–38; Horace W. Raper, "William W. Holden and the Peace Movement in North Carolina," *North Carolina Historical Review* 31 (October 1954): 495–96; Clement Eaton, *A History of the Southern Confederacy* (1954; reprint, New York: Free Press, 1965), 258.

21. Kruman, "Dissent," 311–12.

same token, however, it "was more susceptible to the demands of the Confederate government than other states." Thus, "North Carolina and two other states paid about two-thirds of the total produce collected under the tax-in-kind," and made other contributions in like measure. But Owsley unconsciously deemphasized this positive contribution, because he sought instead evidence to support his own, contrary, thesis.[22]

Governor Vance is a good example of the positive aspects of state rights. He interposed himself between the state and central governments in an effort to mitigate the more direct recalcitrance that might otherwise have resulted in North Carolina. This popular, originally pro-Union, politician was elected governor in September 1862 while serving as a colonel in the army. The Confederate party proved unpopular due to early reverses at Hatteras and Roanoke Island and to widespread objections to secession in the first place. Vance was nominated by the Conservatives (mostly ex-Union Whigs) under the leadership of William W. Holden. Holden was a Raleigh newspaper editor who remained a Unionist until the Fort Sumter incident, then became a secessionist, but by 1862 had lost enthusiasm for the cause. He apparently hoped to achieve control of the North Carolina government through Vance, and then move toward a separate peace. But Holden greatly misjudged Vance. To the great surprise of some of his key supporters, Vance not only promised to support the war, but actually did so; the circumstances of his election as a protest candidate, however, plus his contentious nature, caused him to be depicted as an obstructionist through the remainder of the war—and in much of the historiography that followed. To the extent that Vance did not willingly follow President Davis's lead, he was indeed an obstructionist. But, as Clement Eaton has pointed out, Vance—and Georgia's Governor Brown as well—were under tremendous pressure from constituents, most of whom (in Vance's case) at first had not been secessionists, and many of whom were thoroughly tired of the war and the hardships it brought them.[23] If Jefferson Davis—or Frank Owsley—thought

---

22. Ibid., 312.
23. *Dictionary of American Biography* (New York: Scribners, 1928–1937), 19:159, 9:139; Eaton, *Southern Confederacy*, 256; Hugh T. Lefler and Albert R. Newsome, *Zebulon Baird Vance* (Raleigh, N.C.: State Department of Archives and History,

Vance was a problem, he should have paused to consider what Holden or someone like him would have done.

Supported by subversive groups such as the Heroes of America, an anti-Confederate secret society, Holden and his followers wanted North Carolina to call a convention and negotiate a separate peace. Holden got a great deal of attention with his claim that it was a "rich man's war and a poor man's fight," but his following proved significantly smaller than that of Vance.[24] Holden did get into power after the war was over, when President Andrew Johnson appointed him provisional governor.

If Vance served as Owsley's chief villain, Brown of Georgia never lagged far behind (and in truth Owsley mentioned him much more often). Here too, Owsley damns by overstatement and omission. As Ramsdell said: "There seems to be no ground for the assertion (p. 15) that Brown, not content with holding on to the state's arms, was determined 'to get as much more as possible out of the Confederate government.' "[25]

Worse still, Owsley resorted to distortion, innuendo, and misrepresentation of sources. He says, as an aside, that Brown "was successfully attempting to bring under his control the entire management of the coast defense of Georgia." As proof, Owsley cited a letter by Brig. Gen. Alexander R. Lawton, commanding the Department of Georgia, to Secretary of War Judah P. Benjamin, dated November 1, 1861, which says, in part: "Governor Brown has suddenly shown a disposition to exercise a good deal of authority over, and claim much credit for, the coast defense, and his desire now is to make such appointments as will secure the control to him in case of an attack." The letter continues with remarks about two other officers and Brown that lead one to suspect that Lawton was an ambitious busybody who happened not to like nor to get along well with Brown.[26]

1963), 1:xii–xiv; Thomas Miller to Vance, November 10, 1862, ibid., 324; Martha Coletrane to Vance, November 18, 1862, ibid., 374.

24. James Alex Bagget, "Origins of Upper South Scalawag Leadership," *Civil War History* 29 (March 1983): 69.

25. Ramsdell, review, 108.

26. Owsley, "Local Defense," 70; Alexander R. Lawton to Judah P. Benjamin, November 1, 1861, *OR* 1, 6:307.

Owsley's next footnote cites support for his statement that Brown induced Lawton to seize the cargo of a blockade runner and to place the rifles thereon into the hands of local defense troops. The footnote adds that "Brown had shown Lawton a message from Richmond that convinced the latter of an imminent invasion. From the well-known tactics of Brown," Owsley commented, "one can readily understand what that persistent individual was up to." But the passage in the *Official Records* that Owsley cited is from a long letter from Lawton to Benjamin dated October 5, 1861, attempting to justify and explain why Lawton, on his own initiative, had seized the rifles. It indicates that "for several days after the arrival of the *Bermuda* at Savannah it was impossible to ascertain here whether the arms and munitions by the steamer were public or private property. Sorely pressed for the want of arms, and authorized as I was by the War Department . . . I am not aware that I transcended my authority. . . . Was there no emergency to justify my act?" Not only did the governor show Lawton a private dispatch from Richmond warning of an imminent invasion, but the same information also reached Lawton from Howell Cobb and from Secretary Benjamin himself.[27]

Furthermore, Owsley's next clause implies that the whole cargo was kept. The source is a letter by Lawton to Gen. Samuel Cooper, dated September 25, 1861, in which Lawton said: "[T]here are thousands of unarmed men offering to organize for the defense of this coast. . . . Before this letter reaches you most of these arms will probably be placed in the hands of troops actually mustered into the [national] service. . . . I will . . . be happy to direct the shipment of the remainder to such places as may be directed." Owsley concluded his argument concerning the use—or misuse, in his opinion—of arms during the war's first year by stating: "The initial advantages of better trained soldiery and better generals were lost and the popular enthusiasm for war was dissipated: State rights had reaped its first harvest."[28]

The arguments presented in *How the North Won* by Archer Jones and myself show, I believe, that Owsley was mistaken when he

27. "Local Defense," 70 n. 44; Lawton to Benjamin, October 5, 1861, *OR* 4, 1:668; Benjamin to Lawton, September 25, 1861, *OR* 1, 6:283.
28. "Local Defense," 71.

spoke of "initial advantages." But the amusing thing is, Owsley wanted to have it both ways. After some months, the Confederacy did manage to acquire sufficient arms, but then it could not get men.[29] The connection, Owsley thought, was that the Confederacy lacked men because the governors withheld them in order to use them for local defense. He overlooked that many of these men were not only engaged in essential occupations at home, but also were— as Owsley's chapter title implies—involved in local defense. Such troops *helped* the war effort, did they not?

In making his case, Owsley unfortunately betrayed a certain sloppiness in research that led him to make inaccurate assertions. Footnote 76 in "Local Defense" cites material that supposedly supports Owsley's statement that Brigadier General Lawton wrote Secretary Benjamin "that Brown was planning to put General W. H. T. Walker, who had left the Confederate service embittered against the government, in charge of the state defense, and he [Lawton] was so dejected over the prospect that he predicted disaster and asked to be relieved of his place." However, the source that Owsley cited consists of letters written between Lawton and Benjamin in late September 1861, *not* mid-March, the time that Owsley was discussing in this context.[30] There is *some* relevant material in the citation used by Owsley for his footnote 43, however; but it does not say what Owsley indicated it did. Lawton wrote to Benjamin on November 1, 1861:

> It is now well understood that Governor Brown will at once appoint General W. H. T. Walker a major-general. . . . General Walker is an old friend of mine, and under other circumstances I could have no objections whatever to serving under him, as he is several years my senior, but I fear that the feelings with which he has now left the Confederate service, fomented by the temper which Governor Brown has (in the past at least) exhibited toward the War Department, might cause great embarrassment here . . . Besides, after passing through the labor, the anxiety, the alarms,

---

29. Richard E. Beringer, Herman Hattaway, Archer Jones, and William N. Still Jr., *Why the South Lost the Civil War* (Athens: University of Georgia Press, 1986), 443–57; Owsley, "Local Defense," 71.

30. Owsley, "Local Defense," 73. The source Owsley cited was *OR* 1, 1:284.

and complaints of the people on the coast, *I would regret to see the results pass from my control, when we are comparatively in a condition to receive the enemy.* If it must pass into their hands, I would gladly receive an order for service in some other department. [italics mine][31]

This is *not* a statement of dejection!

Part 2 of Owsley's essay on local defense covers the war's next three years. Its point of departure is the rebuilding of the various state military organizations after they had been broken up by the implementation of the conscript law of April 1862. "Nine-tenths of the men in many of the organizations," Owsley asserted, "were subject to general service, which, added to the notorious inefficiency and cowardice of such organizations [a statement for which Owsley cited no source], made it absolutely necessary that the Confederate government should obtain control of them."[32] Beginning a series of descriptions of the process in each state, Owsley directed his first fusillade at Alabama's governor, John Gill Shorter.

Proceeding through a series of steps in his supposed attempt to grasp local power, according to Owsley, "Governor Shorter came out with the bold request that the war department allow him to enlist in the state defense all the conscripts in the counties of Barbour, Pike, Henry, Dale, Coffee, and Covington."[33] The source cited by Owsley is a letter from Assistant Secretary of War John A. Campbell to Shorter, dated January 23, 1863, in which Campbell wrote:

The President consents that the conscripts in the counties . . . may be mustered into service for coast defense. . . . The object of the Department is to meet your views frankly and to give you all that you ask, that with the means thus furnished and others at your command, you may afford effectual aid to the population on the

31. Lawton to Benjamin, November 1, 1861, *OR* 1, 1:306–7.
32. Owsley, "Local Defense," 75.
33. Ibid.

coast in the case of any invasion. The conscripts belonging to these organizations will be held subject to the acts of conscription whenever the demand for service elsewhere becomes more imperious.[34]

An earlier letter, also cited by Owsley, indicates that Shorter was hopeful of getting a new military district organized, and, after consulting with the governors of Georgia and Florida, he had asked President Davis to do this. Writing to James A. Seddon in January 14, 1863, Shorter mentioned some very plausible concerns about vagueness in the geographical responsibility of extant district commands. His interests and considerations seem national, or at the very least, regional, and not at all narrowly local in nature:

> I wish also to call your attention to the condition of a company of sharpshooters now in the service of the State, and employed as a guard to the works being constructed on the Chattahoochee River. This company was raised in the summer of 1862, . . . and tendered to the State as one of the companies forming our State Guard. The members . . . were nearly all exempts, over the age of 35 years, but many of them are not liable to enrollment as conscripts. It is a very efficient organization, and is positively needed in the valley of Chattahoochee. I have therefore to request that this company be allowed to volunteer or to be turned over from the State service into the Confederate service for six months or twelve months.

This hardly seems the voice of a shrill state-righter, nor of a man engaged in attempting a bold seizure of authority. Shorter then touched upon the matter that so concerned Owsley:

> I beg your co-operation also in securing the suspension of the enrollment, and authority for conscripts to join the organization of Col. James H. Clanton for coast defense. . . . West Florida is so thinly populated and the contiguous counties of Alabama so denuded by their contributions to the Army that unless an efficient force is sent to that section a few hundred men will be able to

34. Ibid., n. 83. The source Owsley cites is *OR* 1, vol. 52, pt. 2, 414–15.

sally out from Choctawhatchie Bay and rob and lay waste the country. The country near the coast is the common retreat of deserters from our army, tories, and runaway negroes. Our salt manufactories on the coast . . . are of urgent and great importance.

Shorter's is not the argument of a narrow, locally oriented Alabaman. He concluded by expressing his "hope that . . . the people of West Florida, and Southeastern Alabama, who are advised of my efforts in their behalf . . . may not be disappointed in their and my own reasonable expectations."[35]

Owsley charged that Governor Shorter, "[e]mboldened by this success . . . immediately dispatched Colonel Clanton to Richmond with a personal letter to the War Department asking for all *the rest* of the conscripts in Alabama who showed any reluctance in going into Confederate service" (italics mine).[36] This is an example of Owsley's overstatements, for he had not even established that these men were reluctant to serve, much less any of "the rest of the conscripts in Alabama." Only later did it become apparent that Shorter had a draft-resistance problem to deal with, as Shorter's context (but not Owsley's) shifted from the August 1862–January 1863 period to March 1863. The relevant letter, dated March 5, 1863, is from Shorter to Seddon:

> I am informed credibly, that there is a class of men scattered over the State liable to conscription who are hiding out . . . , but who would join Colonel Clanton's command if allowed to do so. The conscript officers, I am told, recommend that they be allowed. . . .
> I am confident that such a course will be advantageous to the Army. The sooner these stragglers are gathered in the better. . . . If he should be successful enough to raise a larger force than might be found necessary for his field of operations it will put it in the power of the Department to re-enforce Mobile.[37]

35. Shorter to James A. Seddon, January 14, 1863, *OR* 1, 15:946–48. For the importance of "salt manufactories," see Ella Lonn, *Salt as a Factor in the Confederacy* (Tuscaloosa: University of Alabama Press, 1965), 172, and chaps. 1, 11, and 12.

36. Owsley, "Local Defense," 75–76.

37. *OR* 4, 2:419–20.

⊸◈⊶

After completing a superficial recitation of the process in each of the other states whereby "the local defense organizations [had] grown up and multiplied until, like the barnacles on the hulk of a floundering ship, they threatened to drag the Confederacy down to destruction," Owsley returned to Governor Brown. And again, he missed the point. Secretary Seddon proposed that organizations be raised for local defense made up of men above and below the military age, and he subsequently went further: the War Department might, he said, simply call upon each governor in an appropriate levy. Owsley misinterpreted Brown's resistance.[38]

The controversy had to do with Brown's concern that men outside the draft age legally could not be forced to serve: if they did serve, they would have to be *induced* to do so. Brown objected to Confederate agents operating in Georgia and trying to do the job apart from state administration, and said that he sincerely believed he could do it more efficiently. Brown does not appear to have been belligerent, although he may have been somewhat impatient, and he certainly—at least not in any of the passages cited by Owsley—did not "instantly [wash] his hands of the whole affair," as Owsley contended. Brown did request permission to take some of the men between 40 and 45 (which, Brown admitted, were by this time liable to call by the draft) "till the President shall have ordered them to be enrolled as conscripts, when they are to be dropped from these organizations. Many of them would be willing to volunteer, for the time, for home defense and I think it good policy to permit them to do so."[39]

Much the same sort of misinterpretation, although without the loaded words, is found in Owsley's discussion of South Carolina's raising of local defense forces along the lines of Seddon's suggestion. South Carolina already was "possessed of a large force in which there were seven conscripts out of every eight men," wrote Owsley. But his source indicates that "fully seven-eighths of those *liable* to conscription" were members of such organizations (italics mine); there was a difference between being liable to conscription

38. Owsley, "Local Defense," 78 nn. 119–21, 80.
39. Ibid., 80; *OR* 4, 2:592.

(the words used by the commandant of conscripts in South Carolina) and actually being a conscript (the words used by Owsley.)[40]

Next Owsley criticized Brown's request to the secretary of war that after the Battle of Chickamauga the six-months troops be allowed "to go home until another big battle was to be fought, in order that they might attend their crops." Owsley said that in this matter "Brown's wrath knew no bounds."[41] But the source that Owsley cited, a letter from Brown to President Davis of November 13, 1863, is a rational and reasoned argument that is neither nasty nor rude. The fact is, the Confederate government had broken faith with these troops: they had been called out on a temporary basis, but Secretary Seddon decided to keep them in continuous service. Brown wrote:

> We must retain a producing class at home to furnish supplies to the Army, or it becomes a mere question of time when we must submit to the enemy on account of our inability longer to support our armies.
>
> The Home Guards are . . . willing to do military service for short periods in sudden emergencies, but they cannot leave their homes for regular service without ruin to themselves and their country. . . . Their wheat is not yet sowed, and cannot be unless they have furloughs.

Brown concluded with the passage that Owsley cited and misinterpreted: "I again most respectfully and earnestly claim for them the right to return home and attend to their home interests till another exigency calls for their services. They are now organized, and if they were at the end of each emergency permitted to return home, they would at all times be ready to make prompt response to each call." This is hardly the demand of a sour, unreasoning man whom "we may safely assume," Owsley told us, "never ceased night or day in his waking hours—or perhaps in his dreams—to throw obstacles in the path of the Confederacy."[42]

---

40. Owsley, "Local Defense," 79; C. D. Melton to John S. Preston, September 12, 1863, *OR* 4, 2:813.
41. Owsley, "Local Defense," 81.
42. *OR* 4, 2:952–53; Owsley, "Local Defense," 82.

One last element in the local-defense argument relates to the conscription act of February 17, 1864, which included a provision that would nationalize by draft all the state forces, further widening the age span of liability: all men 17 years old or between 45 and 50 would be regimented into Confederate units to be used for state defense.[43] Many Confederates thought that the central government was attempting by this law to deprive the states of sufficient producers at home and to circumvent the states from maintaining any "troops of war" at all. These two concerns had been "of minor importance in all the states except Georgia and North Carolina," Owsley opined, but now they became more pressing. In Georgia, it precipitated "the bitterest controversy of the whole war."[44]

Even if Owsley were correct in his claim that "the greater part of the hostility to conscription developed after the passage of the law of February, 1864," it hardly follows—as he implied—that this was one last major contribution to Confederate defeat. More likely, in this case, especially considering the universal disapproval that came from all the states, the central government *had* resorted to an unwise measure. But "[n]ever once throughout the book," as Ramsdell so insightfully said in his contemporary review, "does the author suggest that any policy or act of the Confederate government or of any high Confederate official could be mistaken."[45]

Let us go back now to that "bitterest controversy of the whole war" which ensued in Georgia. We must remember that we are concerned with the period *after* Confederates had failed miserably to capitalize upon their victory at Chickamauga, had been defeated in the struggle for Chattanooga, and had allowed an invasion route to be opened into Georgia with Chattanooga as a base of operations, along which the Federals began thrusting just three months later. Brown was not satisfied with the efficiency of Confederate resistance and response to the unfolding situation, and it might be persuasively argued that he was correct in his dissatis-

43. *OR* 4, 3:178–81.
44. Owsley, "Local Defense," 82, 87.
45. Ibid., 83; Ramsdell, review, 110.

faction.[46] As Owsley said, "By a proclamation declaring that Georgia was abandoned to her own defense [Brown] drafted into state forces all the Confederate details [and] exempts, unless *he* had exempted them." The governor also drafted men in "the Confederate local-defense companies, and all persons subject to military service but not yet actually under Confederate control."[47]

In fact, Brown mustered a rather impressive force—a division-sized organization—and he committed it to combat, subordinate to the command of the Confederate field general, first Joseph E. Johnston and later John Bell Hood. Now, Owsley stated, with condemnation as well as a touch of assumed incredulity concerning Brown's attitude, "even while Atlanta was falling into the hands of the enemy . . . the Governor praised the troops for their service and gallantry, and told them that it was their due, since the emergency was over, that opportunity be given them to put their homes in order and take a breathing spell." He gave them "a thirty-day furlough, during the most critical moments of the campaign around Atlanta."[48] But this is misleading: the "critical moments" had been over for a week. Atlanta fell during the first two days of September, while Brown ordered the furlough on the 10th. Indeed, Brown's proclamation makes more sense than does Owsley!

"You entered the service for the defense of Atlanta," Brown told the troops. "[T]hat city has for the time fallen into the hands of the enemy. . . . The fall of Atlanta leaves the State exposed to further invasion. The enemy will fortify that place [there Brown proved wrong], accumulate supplies, and prepare for a winter campaign against Macon and other interior points." Brown correctly asserted that the crops badly needed attention. But he additionally ordered

> that all persons over the age of fifty years be detailed . . . to perform necessary patrol duty at home, and to arrest and send forward, when the division returns to the field, all who are subject who do not report. . . . [I]t is very important that the division

46. See, for example, Thomas Lawrence Connelly, *Autumn of Glory: The Army of Tennessee, 1863–1865* (Baton Rouge: Louisiana State University Press, 1971), chaps. 9–15.
47. Owsley, "Local Defense," 87–88.
48. Ibid, 89.

reassemble in its full strength at the time appointed, [and] it is not expected that any will be absent at roll-call. All who are thus absent will be considered deserters.[49]

In none of this does Brown sound like a man who wrote, as Owsley said, "with his pen fairly reeking with gall." Owsley even twisted Brown's words, saying that Brown "regarded [President Davis] as a regular Nero," and when asked by Secretary Seddon for his militia to be given over to regular service, chose to "refuse to gratify the President's ambition . . . and surrender the last vestige of the sovereignty of the state."[50]

It is obvious that Brown was upset when he wrote this long letter to Seddon, but it is not an example of irrational vituperation. Brown thought that things had been done that were unfair to Georgia and to Georgians, and perhaps he was right. What Brown actually wrote was:

> While I refuse to gratify the President's ambition *in this particular* [a requisition for 10,000 militia] and to surrender the last vestige of the sovereignty of the State . . . , I beg to assure you that I shall not hesitate to order them to the front . . . when the enemy is to be met upon the soil of their beloved State. Nor will I withhold them from the temporary command of the Confederate general who controls the army during great emergencies when he needs their aid. [italics mine][51]

Finally, it simply does not add up that, as Owsley concluded, "Altogether, local defense contributed very materially to the defeat of the Confederacy." I would in fact offer a very strong opinion that the opposite was the case. Owsley's conclusion, so plausible at first glance, is based upon faulty logic, loaded words, and misreading of the sources. The most notable instance of this last is the famous

49. Ibid., 162; *OR* 1, vol. 52, pt. 2, 735–36.
50. Owsley, "Local Defense," 89.
51. *OR* 1, vol. 52, pt. 2, 736–40.

conclusion about Governor Vance's 92,000 hoarded uniforms: "enough uniforms to give every man in Lee's army [at war's end] two apiece."[52]

The tracks are harder to trace this time. *State Rights in the Confederacy* cites no source for this oft-repeated statement, which appears in a summary chapter entitled "Conclusion." Owsley's dissertation did not include this summation; when he readied it for publication he took passages from various chapters to create the conclusion, and this line was one of them. The source got lost in the shuffle. In the dissertation, the line appears on page 96. Here Owsley cited two sources.[53]

But a check reveals that the sources refer to a single speech that was twice delivered by Vance—and that *long* after the war was over, despite Owsley's claim that Vance made his infamous boast "at the end of the war."[54] It is quite a stretch to say that a speech delivered on August 18, 1875, and again on February 23, 1885, came "at the end of the war"! These speeches were presented to the Southern Historical Society and to the Maryland Line, respectively. So, at best, the authority for the hoard's alleged existence and its size is a single—though repeated—boast by the governor a decade and more after the war's end. And even then, Owsley did not relate precisely all of what Vance said: "At the surrender . . . the State had on hand, ready-made *and in cloth,* 92,000 suits of uniforms" (italics mine).[55] If Vance did have that much (and perhaps he did not), how many were mere bolts of cloth?

Even if we ignore Owsley's misreading of the sources, we still can reach quite the opposite conclusion than he did about the effect of local defense upon Confederate defeat. I do not find that the records reflect *any* criticism of local defense from regular officers. Every state in the Confederacy had cause for nervousness, those on the coast as well as those on the inland frontier. All needed, and the

52. Owsley, "Local Defense," 91; Owsley, *State Rights,* 266–67.

53. Frank L. Owsley, "State Rights in the Confederacy" (Ph.D. diss., University of Chicago, 1925, no. T11718). The sources Owsley cited on p. 96 are: Walter Clark, ed., *Histories of the Several Regiments and Battalions, from North Carolina in the Great War 1861–65* (Raleigh: University of North Carolina Press, 1901), 1:34–35; and *Southern Historical Society Papers* 14:513.

54. Owsley, *State Rights,* 276.

55. Beringer et al., *Why the South Lost,* 534 n. 38.

Confederacy wanted them to have, what the Germans call *Land-sturm*, that is, last-ditch forces for local defense. It seems probable that, in Owsley's anxiety to prove a doubtful thesis—and to draw attention to a fledgling scholar—he overlooked the implications of some of his sources and simply misread others. Owsley's first book-length work, like many dissertations before and since, bears the earmarks of lingering amateurishness and failure to double-check. It is an example of hasty research in which loaded words were made to carry part of the burden of proof that the sources alone were unable to carry.

Much of the state-Confederate antagonism had its origins in the successful operations of the Union navy on the Confederate coasts. Owsley himself made frequent reference to the coastal defense problem. But the governors took steps to meet the difficulties involved in defending their exposed coasts, and the joint effort of the central government and the states prevented the Union navy from carrying on the same sort of successful operations that it did indeed conduct in the first part of the war.

Quite clearly, the local defense organized by the states helped the Confederacy. True: President Davis grossly underrated its value. But Owsley's easy acceptance of the Davis position is not nearly so surprising as that Owsley's inadequately defended thesis, hastily written and hastily revised for publication, should have remained embedded in accepted Civil War historiography, as it did for two generations.

❦ "WE SHALL CEASE TO BE FRIENDS"

with Michael Gillespie

Henry John Temple, Lord Palmerston, prime minister of England, read the news of Southern secession with unguarded pleasure. The prospect of a Confederacy of cotton-producing states, a new nation dedicated to free trade with Europe, delighted him. The seventy-seven-year-old Palmerston also knew that a divided pair of American countries could never pose the transatlantic threat of a single, united nation, either to the European balance of power or to the Old World aristocracy.

As one member of Parliament vindictively announced, the world now would witness "the bursting of the great republican bubble which had been so often held up to us as the model on which to recast our own English constitution." But with secession in America came the unsettling realization that the provinces of Canada lay open, virtually undefended, should the North decide to invade in retaliation for any British aid to the Confederacy.

As its major physical link to the mother country, Canada relied heavily upon the St. Lawrence River, a tenuous connection at best, for hadn't one Canadian commander described it as "everywhere vulnerable through its whole length"? Adding to this vulnerability was nature itself—aside from the falls, rapids, and shoals that rendered the stream only partially navigable at the best of times, the St. Lawrence regularly froze solid from December to April. The provincial governments had built several bypass canals, but those could handle only shallow-draft wooden vessels.

Despite their prime waterway's limitations, the Canadians never had gotten around to finishing their interprovincial rail line. The

This essay first appeared in the August 1984 issue of *Military History*.

Grand Trunk railway joined Toronto, Kingston, Montreal, and Quebec City, but it terminated in Canada East at Riviere-du-Loup; it ran through to the Atlantic coast via Portland, Maine. Only the Temiscouata road connected Riviere-du-Loup with the port city of St. John, New Brunswick, and for one hundred miles that road skirted the border of Maine.

When the American Civil War erupted in April 1861, Britain assumed that the division of the country would remain permanent and therefore granted belligerent status to the Confederacy and opened its ports to rebel vessels. The British preferred that the South's expected victory result without any additional British aid, but the North's ever-tightening naval blockade of the Confederacy not only deprived the South of its transatlantic trade but worked a heavy hardship upon Britain as well.

British textile mills had grown dependent upon Southern cotton; when the cotton stopped coming, the mills began closing. Britain's minister to Washington, Lord Richard B. P. Lyons, using all his powers of diplomatic persuasion, complained loudly to the Union secretary of state, William H. Seward. After several encounters, Lyons went away with the distinct impression that the United States would recant and lift the blockade. By May 1861, however, it appeared to the British government not only that the U.S. would not recant, but also that Seward might try to bring about his country's reunification by provoking a war with England.

Like the United States, meanwhile, Canada relied upon a military backbone of militia, and—just as in the States—such forces proved little more than paper tigers. By law, every male citizen between sixteen and sixty belonged to provincial militias, and each man was expected to train without pay for one or two weekends per year. The actual training varied according to local mood and perceived national threat. Often as not, in any given year, no one bothered to drill at all.

Generally, each battalion was expected to muster yearly, an occasion that developed over time into a day of horseplay. Armed with everything from shotguns to broomsticks, clad in whatever manner of uniform pleased an individual's taste, the male population turned out in high spirits for the great annual parade. Everyone looked forward to the kegs of whiskey supplied in good-natured appreciation by commanding officers. No surprise, then, that such battalions were known as the "sedentary" militia. Excluding British Columbia and the Northwest Territory, the sedentary militia comprised about 250,000 men.

The government also had commissioned another, somewhat more effective militia, composed of elite volunteers. Their units annually underwent ten to twenty days of paid training, and generally were well armed, clothed, and equipped. Possessed with a high degree of military enthusiasm, they could form a quick-reaction force in time of crisis. Officials hoped, too, that in an emergency, the abler men in the sedentary militia might join the elite volunteers, who by early 1861 numbered about 8,400.

In the spring of 1861, British regulars augmented the Canadian militias—about 4,300 British soldiers garrisoned Canada and Nova Scotia, Lt. Gen. Sir W. Fenwick Williams commanding. Born in Nova Scotia, the sixty-one-year-old Williams had acquired a hero's reputation during the Crimean War. Described as "a very handsome old gentleman, with charming manners," he enjoyed high popularity, with some Canadians even boasting that Williams would eat his own shoe leather before surrendering to American forces.

On the seas, meanwhile, the British navy ruled almost absolutely. More than merely outnumbering the U.S. Navy, Her Majesty's fleet easily outclassed that of the Yankees. The American navy then consisted of forty steam vessels and five sizeable but obsolete sailing ships. In glaring contrast the British listed 856 war vessels, including seven hundred steamers and two nearly completed iron ships. Eighty English vessels were of such armament and size to rate classification as battleships. But—to be sure—this was a navy with many commitments worldwide.

Adm. Sir Alexander Milne commanded the British North American fleet—composed initially of two 90-gun battleships and some twenty steam frigates, sloops, and gunboats. He had about five hundred guns in all, and some 6,500 men. Out of necessity, Milne spread his ships from New Brunswick to his North Atlantic base at Bermuda and thence to Jamaica, Antigua, and Barbados.

Both Lieutenant General Williams and Admiral Milne perceived the mounting tensions between Great Britain and the northern United States and responded accordingly. Milne commenced consolidating his too-thinly scattered fleet, while Williams concentrated his regulars in the larger towns of Canada and set about to improve defense works. And he continually wrote the home government to ask for reinforcements.

The diplomatic situation deteriorated through the summer of 1861. Whenever a Northern warship called at a British port, the crew found a cold reception. In England, three Confederate ministers met unofficially with the British foreign secretary, Lord John Russell, an episode that infuriated the Lincoln cabinet. In addition, the Americans grew irritated at British investors who financed the business of blockade running.

Secretary of State Seward countered with bold talk that upset the British cabinet. "We do not desire . . . foreign interference," he advised a London correspondent, but if it came, the United States would "not hesitate, in case of necessity, to resist it to the uttermost." He also called upon free-willed men of Canada, Mexico, and Central America to foment a "spirit of independence on this continent." As to any British recognition of the Confederacy, Seward laid down something of a threat: if, he asserted, "this act . . . is distinctly performed, we from that hour shall cease to be friends, and become once more, . . . enemies of Great Britain."

In August, yet another diplomatic flap occurred when U.S. Secret Service agents discovered that the British consul in Charleston, South Carolina, had been involved in direct talks with the Confederate government. At the same time, Prime Minister Palmerston requested reinforcements for Canada, while citing the Union's recent defeat at Manassas and suggesting that the Federals might now accept the departure of the Confederacy and grab Canada as compensation.

Although the British cabinet quietly sent ten more vessels to Admiral Milne, it refused Palmerston's call for troops—largely out of concern over desertions. Even as Great Britain and the United States edged toward war, American recruiters often found men in the British regular units who would change sides in order to obtain the bounties offered for enlistment in the Union army. Such American "crimps," as they were called, caused at least one Canadian-based battalion to be relocated farther from the U.S. border. Then, too, the British worried that their Irish and black West Indian regiments might desert to the North en masse.

By autumn, an uncomfortable calm had settled. The Canadian militia units received new arms, and the British regulars already in Canada quietly had garrisoned and secured Toronto, Quebec, and several other cities. In the American South, realization had begun to sink in that the war barely had begun, and another set of Confederate diplomats prepared to sail for Europe in a renewed attempt to secure recognition.

And then came the unexpected.

On November 8, 1861, light seas parted easily before the heavy bow of the screw sloop U.S.S. *San Jacinto* as she plowed across a narrow neck of the Old Bahamas Channel, 240 miles east of Havana, Cuba. On her deck stood Capt. Charles D. Wilkes, erect and attentive, examining an approaching vessel with unusual interest.

Wilkes was bad-tempered and stubbornly independent, so much so that Navy Secretary Gideon Welles once noted that Wilkes was "not himself as obedient as he should be." Added Welles, "He has abilities but not good judgement in all respects." Wilkes had wasted the fall of that year in fruitless, even unauthorized search for Confederate cruisers, but now, at last, he had news of tangible quarry—two Confederate commissioners were aboard the approaching British vessel R.M.S. *Trent*.

Intending to make a name for himself regardless of the risk, Wilkes gathered his officers together and, after placing several under arrest "who were at heart rebels," announced to the remainder that he would stop and board the *Trent*. The boarding task itself would fall to the executive officer, Lt. Donald MacNeil Fairfax. His orders were to make prisoners of James M. Mason, commissioner to Great Britain, and John Slidell, commissioner to France, and their secretaries, and to seize the *Trent* as a prize.

As the approaching vessel steamed closer, she hoisted her Royal Mail Company pennant and a British ensign. The *San Jacinto* responded by raising American colors and sent a shot across the *Trent's* bow. The *Trent* ignored that, but stopped, finally, when a second round—a shell—burst in her path.

Lieutenant Fairfax, with a Marine detachment, rowed over in a cutter, while the British captain, James Moir, shouted out over his trumpet, "What do you mean by heaving my vessel to in this manner?" Fairfax, however, remained calm, mindful "of the great risk of precipitating war." In fact, without informing Wilkes, Fairfax already had decided not to seize the *Trent*, but only to arrest Mason and Slidell.

Upon boarding the *Trent*, Fairfax quickly discovered two disconcerting things: the commissioners would not surrender without token resistance, and certain other passengers intended to make as much as possible out of the incident. One of these, a royal naval commander in charge of the mails, Richard Williams, hid the Confederate dispatch case and coaxed Mason into belligerent responses to Fairfax.

After several minor incidents, which the Marines quelled, the commissioners finally were taken aboard the *San Jacinto* and the *Trent* resumed her journey. Mason and Slidell eventually were delivered to Fort Warren, Massachusetts.

While public opinion in the North rendered Wilkes a hero and his actions just, the news of what had happened reached England on November 27 and struck with the fury of a hurricane. An American in England at the time wrote: "The people are frantic with rage, and were the country polled, I fear 999 men out of 1,000 would declare for immediate war." Upon hearing the news, Lord Palmerston allegedly threw down his hat and shouted, "I don't know whether you are going to stand this, but I'll be damned if I do!"

By December 4, Her Majesty's Government had moved to prohibit the export of arms, ammunition, and military supplies to the Union, and had issued a veiled ultimatum to the Lincoln administration: release the commissioners and apologize to Britain, or face the consequences.

To formulate a plan for making war against the United States, the cabinet consulted various military theoreticians and veteran officers both of the War of 1812 and the Crimea. Canada, the experts declared, was defensible, but only if the authorities acted quickly.

At the immediate onset of hostilities, it was thought, British troops would attack the partially completed Fort Montgomery at Rouse's Point, New York. The fort was situated on Lake Champlain and controlled access to the Richelieu River. The three-acre, stone-walled fortification had been under construction sporadically for twenty-five years and now was defended only by the carpenters and masons who worked there, who had organized themselves into a quasi-military company. The British felt certain that the Americans would by spring mount some sort of offensive in that vicinity. Occupation of Fort Montgomery might also work the advantage of threatening Union communications in upper New York, especially around Ogdensburg. Whoever held that area likely would command Lake Ontario, and certainly would control ingress and egress to all the Great Lakes.

Holding the Welland Canal also rated high on the British-Canadian defensive list. This vital link between Lakes Erie and Ontario circumvented Niagara Falls, but lay only sixteen miles inside Canada at its farthest point and fell entirely in the narrow peninsula between Hamilton and Buffalo. Important, too, was Fort Malden, at Amherstburg, on the southernmost tip of Canada West. It guarded the entrance to the St. Clair River and controlled passage between Lakes Erie and Huron.

The safety of the entire upper Canadian peninsula from Georgian Bay to Lake Ontario hinged on possession of the Welland Canal and Fort Malden. While both of these sites were in Canadian territory, the strategists also planned to seize Fort Niagara, near Buffalo, in order to add a margin of protection to the Welland Canal, and to seize Fort Mackinaw, at the entrance to Lake Michigan. Thus, even the basic plan involved some invasion of American territory, but in addition several staff officers suggested a raid on the arsenal at Sackett's Harbor, New York, where the Yankees had stored thirty tons of black powder and a number of naval guns.

The guns would be of particular value to the Canadians, since they did not have a single gunboat on the Lakes, while the North had a side-wheel steamer, the U.S.S. *Michigan,* the U.S. Navy's first iron-hulled warship. Mounting only a single 18-pound gun and holding a crew of but eighty-eight sailors, she nevertheless would present quite an obstacle to any Canadian craft. Even if the Canadians managed additionally to arm some of their merchantmen, they had no means readily available for rolling and fitting armor. It seemed reasonable that only a first strike against the *Michigan* would ensure the British and their Canadian brethren of success on the Lakes.

Furthermore, the British intended to invade Maine. In so doing, they hoped first to thwart any attempted Union move into Canada, and secondly they needed the Grand Trunk rail line that ran from

Portland to Montreal and beyond. The minimum plan called for employing 7,640 regulars, comprising eight battalions of infantry, three batteries of field artillery, two batteries of garrison artillery, and two engineer companies. A more ambitious plan envisioned augmenting this invasion force with forty thousand militia. But the planners prudently placed little faith in the militia and, after deliberation, tentatively decided either to place the militia in garrisons, freeing more regulars for campaigning, or to attach them to the regulars to "act as the pioneers of the army."

The British troop movement to North America began on December 18, 1861, as 1,800 Grenadier Guards and Scots Fusilier Guards filed aboard two ships in Southampton. Ironically, one of the vessels, the *Adriatic,* only recently had been purchased from an American company; painted on her paddle box were the Stars and Stripes. Over the next two weeks, nine more transports departed for the Canadian provinces, a remarkable feat considering the lack of a general staff to coordinate the transfer.

At the same time, the Canadians mobilized: "War, war; we hear nothing but war," wrote one Canadian woman as she watched the frantic efforts. The Toronto *Globe* reported that "at the corner of every street, you hear the excited discussions as to the Mason and Slidell outrage, the next news from England, the erection of forts, and the probabilities of a fight with the Americans." Students, hunting clubs, and workmen all formed military companies.

Lieutenant General Williams managed to find some sixty instructional cadre to drill the volunteers. He himself crisscrossed the provinces inspecting fortifications, moving about with such determined fury that Canada's governor-general fretted it was "difficult to keep before [Williams] . . . that we are not [already] at war."

The first transports from England arrived on December 26. But the crossing had been nightmarish. Fierce North Atlantic storms had caught part of the fleet, sinking one storeship and forcing another back to England. The logistical problems were rendered even worse because the quartermaster officer, Lt. Col. Garnet J. Wolseley, and his staff had been sent on the fleet's slowest vessel. "The unfortunate and obvious result," wrote Wolseley, "was that the troops reached Canada before we did, for our old tub of a ship took 29 days in getting to Halifax, Nova Scotia." Even then, Wolseley's journey had another, almost comical segment: he and his staff took a Cunard mail steamer for Boston, toured that city as guests of insistent passengers they had met, and then traveled in civilian clothing by rail to Montreal.

Meanwhile, the leading troop transport, the *Persia*, had threaded its way past the St. Lawrence ice floes as far as Bic, in Quebec, where the men disembarked. The *Persia*'s captain then ordered that the ship leave the river, even before the equipment could be unloaded, because thickening ice threatened to crush the vessel. The hapless troops managed to hire local sleighs to take them to the Grand Trunk railhead at Riviere-du-Loup.

None of the other ships entered the near-freezing river at all. The larger steamers sailed for the harbor of St. John, New Brunswick, where the troops staggered off, seasick and cold, in the face of a heavy snowstorm. The local militia gave them some relief by walking guard tours and helping to unload the military stores. In the meantime, some of the smaller ships, carrying low-priority items, docked at Halifax for the winter.

On December 30, the Sixty-second Regiment of Foot arrived at St. Andrews, New Brunswick, a small port city on the Maine border. Beginning on January 1, 1862, they sent forward 153 men per day by rail to Canterbury, where the line ended. There they hired sleighs to take them to Woodstock, from which they expected to secure the Temiscouata road.

They had orders, if war broke out, to take the town of Houlton, Maine. Accordingly, Lt. Col. James Daubeny quietly slipped across the border to scout the place. "The town," he wrote, "consists of scattered houses extending over more than a mile in length and lying at the bottom of a hill. The only garrison in the place were 60 volunteers, whom I saw marching in the Town without arms to the inspiriting air of Yankee Doodle played on a solitary fife." Daubeny anticipated an easy conquest.

The troops at St. John soon began their own winter odyssey. Each morning 160 of them left by sleigh for Riviere-du-Loup, about 250 miles northwest. Each sleigh carried two buffalo robes, while each man wore a greatcoat, sweater, woolen underwear, scarf, and boots stuffed with straw, as well as a bedroll. All the men made it, with only a few suffering from any frostbite or exposure.

In fact, the entire troop deployment took place without serious mishap. The men found their way to Kingston, Toronto, Hamilton, Guelph, New London, and Montreal. Including those previously in garrison, the breakdown looked like this: Canada East and West—eleven battalions of infantry, ten batteries of artillery, three companies of engineers, and two support battalions; Nova Scotia—two battalions of infantry and four batteries; New Brunswick—two battalions of infantry and four batteries; and Newfoundland—one battery. In all, there now were 17,658 regulars in place.

Also during December 1861 and January 1862, the Royal Navy bolstered its North American fleet. Admiral Milne now commanded some forty vessels, with twenty more ready to steam to his assistance. He planned on destroying the Union's fleet blockading Southern ports, then to employ his ships in a blockade of Northern ports. He anticipated no direct cooperation with the Confederate army or navy, but if successful, his actions obviously would free them to wreak havoc of their own. Alternately, he had a plan to use Port Royal, South Carolina, as a base, and to harass Union communications in the Chesapeake, but he feared having to make any direct assaults upon coastal fortifications. He doubtless harbored some respect for the Union navy—which had been swelling rapidly in size and now boasted more than 250 vessels.

As it turned out, the troop deployments and naval preparations were rendered somewhat anticlimactic. On December 26, the Lincoln administration agreed to free Mason and Slidell and offered a token apology. Nonetheless, the troops in Canada remained in readiness under the justification that something else just as threatening as the *Trent* Affair, as it came to be called, might happen and bring the countries to war. The poor treatment of Northern sailors visiting British ports around the world continued. Both sides feared another incident might occur.

If war had erupted, how did the British expect to conduct it? Frankly, they held out little hope for retaining the Great Lakes. But they *were* determined to hold the St. Lawrence line. Williams intended to burn the bridges and block the river at Montreal, but in all probability, nearby Ontario would have been lost; communications with that area ran too close and too far across the American front. Still, with a great deal of effort, portions of Maine and of northern New England could have been occupied.

The British entertained no dream of conquering the North; they knew it was too big and too powerful, even with a two-front war on its hands. Losses in the Great Lakes region would have been a bitter price to pay for the portions of territory seized, but who could know what the future might bring, or when losses might be recouped? The post–Civil War United States certainly would have been less potent, for assuredly, some portion of the Confederacy would have survived. The North's Mississippi Valley Campaign of 1862 doubtless would have ground to a halt, and the remainder of the Civil War might well have been fought in and over possession of the border states.

On the open seas, the British navy clearly would have prevailed. But lifting the blockade might have cost dearly: a Union naval dash for Nassau, or even Bermuda, could have resulted in embarrassment for the Royal Navy. As long as we are playing this "what might have been" game, which professional historians are not supposed to do: *If* the Confederacy had prevailed, or at the very least some significant portion of it, and at the same time *if* the British had seized parts of the Northeast, then Germany would have won World War I, there would not have been a World War II, and Germany and Japan—not Russia and the United States—would have been the great powers.

But back to reality: The chance of war between the United States and Britain ended in the uncomfortable knowledge that the two nations could in fact entertain thoughts of invading each other. The actual end of the Civil War, of course, did not come until April 1865, and, again, on the Canadian border it came in an almost comic context.

Driven by boredom and alcohol, officers of the Sixty-fifth Canadian Volunteers had decided at last to seize Fort Montgomery. They sent Capt. Gustave A. Drolet across the border to reconnoiter. He arrived in the village of Champlain, only to be swept up in a memorial parade for the slain American president, Abraham Lincoln. Following the procession into a church, the slightly hung-over captain suddenly found himself, in the solemnity of the moment, the subject of approving words and gestures by the throng—who mistook him to be an official representative of Her Majesty's Government.

The American officers present subsequently invited him to the fort for dinner and drinks. They toasted the British army and "Old

Vic"—that is, Queen Victoria—to which Drolet took offense and challenged his hosts to a duel. The Americans agreed, playfully, and the "duel" was fought, but with alternate swigs of bourbon as the weapon. Drolet lost, and he returned to his regiment a day later with only a vague recollection of the past twenty-four hours. While ruefully fighting the pounding of a throbbing headache, he advised his fellow officers to cancel the invasion—and thus ended any lingering chance of war.

Part 3
The Art of War

✧ BALLOONS AND THE AMERICAN MILITARY

CIVIL WAR TO WORLD WAR I

Near Houma, Louisiana, where I grew up, there was a huge naval air station, and among my most vivid boyhood memories is having seen many a blimp flying overhead during the Second World War. These sights seared themselves in my mind and induced a lifelong interest in balloons and blimps in military use.

From the Champ-de-Mars, a large parade ground in Paris, France, on a drizzly summer day, August 27, 1783, the world's first hydrogen-filled balloon took to the air. Benjamin Franklin, America's venerable inventor-statesman, was then in Paris, serving as his infant country's minister to France. Captivated, he stood among the spectators, gazing intently, when someone remarked to him, "Interesting, but what use is it?" Franklin replied, "What use is a newborn baby?"

Franklin immediately perceived great military possibilities for the new technology. He wrote to a friend:

> Convincing sovereigns of the folly of wars may perhaps be one effect of it, since it will be impracticable for the most potent of them to guard his dominions. Five thousand balloons, capable of raising two men each, could not cost more than five ships of the line; and where is the prince who could afford so to cover his

This essay first appeared, under the title "Balloons: America's First Air Force," in the June 1984 issue of *American History Illustrated* and is reprinted with the permission of PRIMEDIA Special Interest Publications (History Group), copyright American History Illustrated.

country with troops for its defense as that ten thousand men descending from the clouds might not in many places do an infinite
deal of mischief before a force could be brought together to repel
them?

Franklin accurately forecast several military applications for balloons, "such as elevating an engineer to take a view of an enemy's
army, works, etc., conveying intelligence into or out of a besieged
town, giving signals to distant places, or the like." Franklin hastened to inform his scientific colleagues in London, Vienna, and
Philadelphia of the new invention, stressing to them its military implications.

The first aerial voyage in the United States took place ten years
later, at Philadelphia, on January 9, 1793. President George Washington was among the observers. During the ensuing sixty-seven
years a number of technical developments in ballooning took place,
and elsewhere in the world some military use was made of balloons—notably by the French revolutionary armies—but the American military establishment made no use of balloons until the Civil
War. By the early part of the nineteenth century a certain disen-
chantment with balloons had set in, and it persisted for nearly five
decades. Many authorities viewed balloons as too dangerous, too
uncontrollable, or as little more than playthings.

Thaddeus Sobieski Colincourt Lowe of Jefferson Mills, New Hampshire, emerged as the Civil War's best-known aeronaut. Interested
in ballooning since 1856, Lowe also invented a device for determining one's latitude and longitude quickly without a horizon. He
became a protégé of Professor Joseph Henry of the Smithsonian
Institution, who soon after the outbreak of the war was asked by
Secretary of War Simon Cameron to report on possible military uses
for balloons. Lowe himself was in Washington at the time, having
had the idea of trying to interest authorities in balloons.

On June 17, 1861, Lowe and two telegraphers ascended near
the White House with telegraph lines dangling to the earth. Lowe
sent President Lincoln a message: "Abe: All is Well." Lincoln was

impressed, and named Lowe the chief aeronaut of the Army of the Potomac. Lowe subsequently recruited and managed the North's first balloon squadron—the nation's first air arm.

Lowe's Civil War career had almost died aborning. On April 20, 1861, he had left Cincinnati, Ohio, by balloon, bound on a test flight to the Atlantic coast. After being whisked some nine hundred miles in nine hours, he descended near Pea Ridge, South Carolina, in secessionist territory. An angry and suspicious crowd surrounded him, and believing Lowe to be a Yankee spy, someone suggested that they should lynch him. Fortunately for the balloonist, a man who had witnessed one of Lowe's ascents at Charleston the previous year happened to be present and vouched for him as a scientific investigator not connected with military matters. Lowe's captors put him in a nearby jail for the night but released him the next day. Lowe always claimed thereafter to have been the first prisoner of the Civil War.

Both the North and South employed balloons primarily for observation throughout the war. A sketch made by an observer in Lowe's balloon on December 8, 1861, showing rebel positions near the Virginia-Maryland border, is preserved in the National Air and Space Museum, Smithsonian Institution. Aerial photographs, too, were possible—though quite difficult to produce because of the technical limitations of the time. The photographer William Black had snapped the first aerial photographs taken in America: several panoramas of Boston, in 1860.

On several occasions during the first two years of the Civil War, Lowe and other aeronauts provided useful aerial surveillance for Union generals in the eastern theater. Perhaps the most notable instance was at the Battle of Fair Oaks (or Seven Pines) in May 1862, when—at least according to Lowe—his aerial observations from a captive hydrogen balloon provided vital information that narrowly averted a Federal disaster. In his unpublished memoirs, surviving in the archives of the Institute of Aerospace Sciences in New York, he recorded: "From eleven o'clock, until dark, on the 29th of May, the enemy commenced to concentrate their forces in front of Fair Oaks, moving on roads entirely out of sight of our pickets, and concealing themselves as much as possible in and behind woods where none of their movements could be seen except from the balloon."

Lowe reported this intelligence to Maj. Gen. George B. McClellan, who made redeployments without which, Lowe believed, "it is very evident that our left or that portion of our army behind the Chickahominy would have been driven back and in consequence the whole army routed."

Nor was that all. Lowe wrote:

> On the 31st of May, at noon, I ascended at Mechanicsville and discovered bodies of the enemy and trains of wagons moving from Richmond toward Fair Oaks. I remained in the air watching their movements until nearly two o'clock when I saw the enemy form in line of battle, and cannonading immediately commenced. . . . I saw we were facing a great battle. . . . I made an observation that showed that the Confederates were marching to attack our troops on the right bank of the Chickahominy before the completion of the bridge would permit those on the left bank to join them. This would mean the destruction of our army. I descended immediately and sent off the most important dispatch of any during my whole experience in the military service.

Again McClellan responded, and Lowe's news apparently was a key factor in saving the day. Lowe once again "ascended to a height of a thousand feet and there witnessed the Titanic struggle. The whole scene of action was plainly visible and reports of the progress of the battle were constantly sent till darkness fell upon the grand but terrible spectacle."

Other prominent American balloonists who served the Union cause included John LaMountain, the brothers James and Ezra Allen, and John Wise. Wise probably deserves even more credit than Lowe as one of America's great balloonists. His career in the air spanned more than forty years. Wise's greatest contribution was the invention of the ripping panel, which allowed balloonists to deflate their gasbags instantly upon landing and thus avoid being dragged across the countryside on windy days. As early as the Mexican War, Wise had perceived immense potential for aerial warfare. In 1846 he had proposed the quite feasible idea of dropping bombs and torpedoes upon the Mexican garrison in their fortress at Veracruz. (That Wise's proposal was not acted upon left it to the Austrians three years later, in 1849, to carry out the first air assault in history—against Venice.)

Despite its inherent value, the Union's air squadron eventually languished. Many administrative problems remained unsolved; Lowe encountered much difficulty in persuading officers of the value of aerial observations, and indeed the air corps was expensive. In 1863 Lowe quit his job in exasperation. The air corps itself quietly folded shortly thereafter.

The Confederacy had far fewer resources for making balloons, or anything else for that matter, than did the North, but the rebels often made up for physical deficiencies with superior ingenuity.

The first Confederate balloons were made of varnished cotton, and were inflated with air heated by burning pine knots and turpentine. They were tethered by a half-mile of rope with one end secured to a windlass. Haul-downs through danger zones could be hastened by hitching teams of artillery horses to the windlass and sending the animals galloping down a nearby road.

Military balloons always attracted numerous rubberneckers, and the unwelcome bystanders often caused problems. Once a spectator got caught in the windlass of a Confederate balloon, and his companion freed him by chopping the rope with an ax. Unfortunately for the aeronaut, the rescue attempt loosed the balloon as well. First the vessel drifted over enemy lines, then a lucky change in wind direction brought it back. Both friend and foe alike fired freely upon the hapless pilot's vessel—one side regarding it as an enemy target, and the other viewing it as a friend, though one who needed to be brought down.

The Confederacy's cotton balloons proved unsatisfactory, being unstable and having inadequate lift. But the South later obtained two silk balloons. Capt. Langdon Cheves at Chatham Armory in Savannah, Georgia, constructed the first one from bolts of silk in a variety of patterns, and varnished the sections with guttapercha car springs that had been dissolved in naphtha. Shipped to the capital, where the Richmond Gas Works inflated it with coal gas, the balloon was then towed by locomotive to Lt. Gen. James Longstreet's command. Longstreet was delighted, for as he later wrote: "The Federals had been using balloons in examining our positions, and we watched with envious eyes their beautiful observations as they floated high in the air well out of the range of our guns. While we were longing for the balloons that poverty denied us, a genius arose for the occasion [and] a great patchwork ship . . . was ready for use in the Seven Days' Campaign."

The second Confederate silk balloon was built by Capt. Charles Cevor, a Southern balloonist who had made several ascensions before the Civil War. The balloon was pieced together from old silk frocks donated by patriotic Southern ladies. The Charleston city gasworks filled the silkbag, and it then was hauled north to the Confederate armed tugboat, *Teaser*, on the James River. The Southerners attempted to send the vessel downriver, where they intended to launch the balloon, thus establishing their would-be nation as among the pioneers in naval aviation. But the balloon was captured when *Teaser* ran aground and fell prey to the Union ironclad U.S.S. *Monitor* and her escort, the U.S.S. *Maratanza.*

Some technical innovations that are typically thought of as belonging more to the era of the world wars were foreshadowed during the Civil War; two of these were blackouts and overhead camouflage. On September 2, 1861, Confederate Brig. Gen. P. G. T. Beauregard issued instructions that "every precaution [must be] taken to prevent the enemy from discovering by balloons or other means the numbers of our advanced commands or outposts. No lights should be kept at night except where absolutely necessary, and then under such screens as may conceal the lights from observation. Further, tents, if used, ought to be pitched under the cover of woods and sheltered in all cases as far as possible from accurate computation."

Later Beauregard also advised the use of camouflage for deceiving enemy aerial observers. He wrote in December 1861:

> It may become suddenly important to prevent the enemy's balloon observations from discovering whether or not we have guns in our batteries, or more properly to let them believe that we have, [so] you will have at once the position of each gun protected from aerial vision by a shed of leaves or brushwood, elevated six feet from the ground or the height of the crest, putting in each embrasure a piece of wood of the proper size (blackened) to represent a gun.

These imitation cannon were known as "Quaker guns."

The Confederates also toyed briefly with another innovative though grim idea: dropping poison gas from balloons. Early in the war a scientifically inclined Southerner and volunteer soldier, Isham Walker of Holly Springs, Mississippi, wrote such a proposal to Confederate Secretary of War Leroy P. Walker. (The letter does not suggest that the two Walkers were related.) Apparently no one in the Confederate War Department liked, or believed in, the idea enough to follow up on it, although Private Walker drew detailed plans and offered a plausible course of action. Of course, as events in later wars proved, the proposal was feasible.

Ironically, it was a foreign visitor and military observer, rather than the Americans, who perceived long-term possibilities for the further development of military air power: a young German officer, Count Ferdinand von Zeppelin. He witnessed several of Lowe's ascensions and went up himself once in a noncombat situation. Later, after Zeppelin's retirement from the German army, he became a world leader in aviation and developed the large, rigid airships that are his namesake.

The United States Navy, as well as the army, entered the air age during the Civil War. On August 3, 1861, the U.S.S. *Fanny* became the country's first aircraft carrier. Aeronaut John LaMountain used the ship as his base for a balloon reconnaissance along the Potomac River. Since Washington, D.C., at that particular moment was perhaps the most effectively blockaded city on either side, LaMountain's information greatly raised the spirits of the populace: his reports countered rife, though false, rumors that Confederate forces were closing in.

Lowe later had a "balloon boat" specially fitted out. From that vessel he successfully sent up an observation balloon on November 11, 1861, at New Market Bridge near Fort Monroe, Virginia.

After the Civil War, balloons were not used again by the United States Army until the early 1890s. The Signal Corps reintroduced them, experimenting and developing techniques for their employment. In 1893 the Signal Corps exhibited a military balloon at the

World's Columbian Exposition in Chicago, and in 1896 organized a model balloon train at Fort Logan, Colorado. Army aviation, after this rebirth, continued thereafter without further interruption, as it does to this day.

During the Spanish-American War, the first American balloon to be shot down by enemy fire fell from the air. On July 1, 1898, a captive balloon piloted by Lt. Col. George Derby, accompanied by Maj. Joseph E. Maxfield of the Signal Corps, was hovering above United States troops near Santiago, Cuba, to report on Spanish troop movements. Suddenly, enemy gunfire deflated the envelope. The American ground troops were actually relieved, for the balloon had been drawing too much fire toward them.

Indeed, at a stream crossing on the crowded main trail to San Juan Heights, enemy gunners had scored heavily on the Americans. Anticipating that the Americans would use the trail for their advance, the Spaniards had made careful preparations to rain fire on them. Towed by the Americans along the trail, first by wagon and then, in rougher terrain, by hand, the balloon clearly pinpointed the front of the advancing line.

Maj. Gen. William R. Shafter's aide-de-camp recorded the near-chaotic scene wherein the balloon was hit: "Winding their way among the troops the balloon was soon within a few hundred yards of the Aguadores River. The enemy's musketry fire was already becoming quite spirited, but when the balloon reached this point it was opened upon by a heavy fire from field-guns, and the musketry fire also increased. The third shell or shrapnel fired at the balloon struck it, and the next one tore it so badly that it at once descended."

Stephen Crane—the famous young author of *The Red Badge of Courage*—also was present as a highly paid reporter for the *New York World*. He later wrote that "The front had burst out with a roar like a brushfire. . . . The balloon was dying, dying a gigantic and public death before the eyes of two armies. It quivered, sank, faded into the trees amid the flurry of a battle that was suddenly and tremendously like a storm." Before going down, however, the pilot managed to spot another road crossing the Aguadores River four or five hundred yards farther downstream. He managed to get this information to headquarters, and his newly discovered pathway provided the Americans with a much-needed alternate approach.

In August 1907, the army created an aeronautical division within the Signal Corps to take charge "of all matters pertaining to military ballooning, air machines, and all kindred subjects." In 1909 the division purchased its first airplane from the Wright brothers. Airplanes, of course, were destined to eclipse balloons, but the glory days of military ballooning were not yet quite over.

The United States expended considerable effort on its balloon arm during World War I. At first balloon training took place at Fort Omaha, Nebraska, but winter weather induced moving the balloon school to a new camp named in honor of John Wise, near San Antonio, Texas. Three other balloon schools were soon established: Camp Eustis, Virginia; Fort Sill, Oklahoma; and Ross Field, Arcadia, California. By the end of the war, the army had trained 751 balloon officers and had organized eighty-nine balloon companies, of which thirty-three were sent to Europe. Two others were organized and trained in France.

A typical balloon company consisted of six officers and 150 men equipped with two balloons. A cable connected each balloon to an engine-driven winch. The occupants maintained communications with the ground by telephone, and with high-powered binoculars they could observe enemy operations within a radius of ten or more miles. Their main mission was to regulate artillery fire, locate targets, and report activities within enemy lines.

The balloon companies worked hard. By day they made observations, by night they moved to new locations. Like the infantry, they endured primitive living conditions. And, while infantry units were relieved periodically, some balloon crews were on the front without relief throughout the Chateau-Thierry, St. Mihiel, and Meuse-Argonne campaigns.

Some wag, in what was a slang-infested era, nicknamed America's World War I aeronauts "gas bag men." One of these gas bag men was Everett McKinley Dirksen of Illinois, later a colorful and eminent United States senator. Another of the doughboy balloonists, George Cobb, recalled years later that "we could get a Croix de Guerre and a furlough if we were shot down by the Germans. We all had parachutes, and the Boche would almost never shoot at us as we were descending."

On the other hand, Frank Luke Jr., America's second-ranking air ace during the war, downed fifteen German observation balloons in seventeen days. Known as the "Balloon Buster," he attained a score of twenty-one before he himself was killed when his Spad was shot down in September 1918.

Apparently, some of the aeronauts had a lot of free time on their hands. Cobb recalled:

> Most of those gas bag men were heavy drinkers. I remember these two in particular who were always boasting about all the liquor they could consume. So the French set up a drinking contest between the two. I'll be damned if they didn't bet on the match . . . One of these lushes promptly got sick, while the other calmly went over and poured himself [another] drink. "Le victor," cried a Frenchman and held up the hand of the still-thirsty gas man.

During this war, too, the dirigible came into its own. At the conflict's beginning, England, France, and Germany each possessed small fleets of these rigid, long-range airships, and each nation used them extensively for scouting. The German zeppelins were the largest, fastest, and most efficient of the dirigibles, and by January 1915, that nation had equipped them with bombs.

Throughout the war the dirigibles maintained a lead over airplanes in range and weight-carrying ability, but their large size, limited maneuverability, relatively slow rate of climb, and highly inflammable hydrogen gas contents made them vulnerable when attacked by the rapidly improving airplanes. Once located, dirigibles were easily destroyed. "There really was nothing to it," asserted British air hero Lt. Leefe Robinson, who was the first to shoot down a raiding German airship over English soil. "Once the airship is detected, it's a goner. I only had to climb above it, open fire, and drop hand grenades."

By the end of 1917, bombing raids by dirigibles had stopped, though the airships were still used for submarine scouting and for escorting convoys. And even toward the war's end, trying to capitalize upon the pluses that the era's dirigibles continued to offer, the United States and England cooperated in experiments wherein planes would be carried by dirigibles and launched from the air.

In the end, forty-five American air squadrons and twenty-three balloon companies saw combat service. American fliers were credited with the destruction of 776 enemy planes and 72 enemy balloons, while 290 American planes and 37 balloons were lost to enemy action.

The Americans produced, up to November 1, 1919, some 14,000 planes, 42,000 engines, and 41,000 balloons and airships. When the armistice came, war contracts were abruptly terminated, and the American aviation industry virtually collapsed within a year. Some military use of balloons continued in the postwar period, notably by National Guard aviation units composed of air observation, balloon, and photo crews.

Balloons, and later blimps, reappeared in the American military arsenal—especially in the 1920s, early 1930s, and during World War II—but they were limited to supporting roles in military aviation. Their occasional use, in special situations, continues even to this day.

THE WAR BOARD, THE BASIS OF THE UNITED STATES' FIRST GENERAL STAFF

with Archer Jones

In the slow evolution of the modern general staff, the United States lagged behind the leading European armies. As late as the Civil War the country woefully lacked an adequate staff structure, but during that war the United States Army evolved for its Washington headquarters a very effective model, one that corresponded to that used in contemporary Prussia. But because this superior staff organization was largely informal, it did not last beyond the large-scale military operations that called it into being.

The United States entered the war with a system that melded both special and general staffs but was characterized more by the functions of the former than the latter. In Civil War field armies an officer sometimes enjoyed the unofficial title of chief of staff and sought to coordinate the activities of the army's special staff officers and often the aides-de-camp who helped to perform general-staff duties.[1]

But the War Department staff was even more primitive than that evolved by field armies. The army's staff consisted of special sections whose chiefs reported directly to the secretary of war. Though there was no chief of staff, there was a general in chief, an informal position not provided for in law. However, the special staff did not report to the general in chief; in fact special staff officers in subordinate

This essay first appeared in *Military Affairs* 46:1 (February 1982) and is reprinted by permission of the Society for Military History.

1. See J. D. Hittle, *The Military Staff: Its History and Development* (Harrisburg, Pa.: Military Service Publishing, 1952), 12.

commands reported not to their commanders but to the special staff officers at higher headquarters. Thus the general in chief could not actually exercise command of the army since troops could not be moved or fed without quartermaster or commissary support and neither he nor his subordinate commanders controlled those key staff officers. Operational control of the army was lodged in the civilian secretary of war, and there existed no real general staff at all. The secretary could secure military advice from the general in chief, but neither of them had a general staff to manage military operations.[2]

The deficiencies of this organization were immediately apparent to Abraham Lincoln's energetic new secretary of war, Edwin M. Stanton. Stanton acted on his conviction that "to work an army of five hundred thousand with machinery adapted for peace establishment of twelve thousand" was "no easy task," making it necessary "to bring the War Department up to the standard of times" by providing "time for thought, combination and conference."[3] So, almost immediately, Stanton formed the War Board, an embryonic American version of a general staff, consisting of the heads of the various army bureaus.

On March 7, 1862, Ret. Maj. Gen. Ethan Allen Hitchcock received a telegraphic summons from Secretary of War Stanton for a personal conference in Washington. Hitchcock boarded a train in St. Louis that same day and traveled directly to the secretary's office, arriving "covered with dust." He had had several hemorrhages en route. Stanton whisked the weak, queasy, and unhappy sixty-four-year-old soldier to the president and "sundry other high functionaries of the government."

Hitchcock arrived in Washington just as Lincoln had dismissed

2. T. Harry Williams, *Americans at War: The Development of the American Military System* (Baton Rouge: Louisiana State University Press, 1960), 3–43 passim; Robert F. Stohlman Jr., *The Powerless Position: The Commanding General of the Army of the United States, 1864–1903* (Manhattan, Kan.: Military Affairs, 1975), 1–21; William P. Craighill, *The Army Officer's Pocket Companion: Principally Designed for Staff Officers in the Field* (New York: Van Nostrand, 1862), 257; H. L. Scott, *Military Dictionary: Comprising Technical Definitions; Information on Raising and Keeping Troops; . . .* (New York: Van Nostrand, 1861), 570.

3. Stanton to Charles A. Dana, February 1, 1862, in Charles A. Dana, *Recollections of the Civil War* (New York: Appleton, 1898), 6.

George B. McClellan as general in chief and decided to appoint no successor. Hungry for competent military leaders, Lincoln and Stanton believed that Hitchcock's long military past rendered him extraordinarily capable and they succeeded, after several rebuffs, in persuading him to accept a significant new staff job.[4] This reluctant soldier, grandson of the famous Revolutionary War leader Ethan Allen, had graduated from West Point in 1817 and served in the army until 1855. Now he assumed a dual position as personal advisor to Stanton and as head of the War Board, Stanton's innovative and important creation.

In his reforms, the Northern war secretary attacked the problem of securing unity of command by going outside the formal structure prescribed by law and tradition. The Union reorganization concerned operations, primarily in the implementation of strategy otherwise determined. Even more important, the new War Board facilitated logistics and, as a body, recommended strategy. It did not function as a source of commands or operational directives. Under Stanton's plan these continued to come from the war secretary, to whom the board reported.

To establish the War Board, the secretary gathered together the heads of several bureaus of the army "to effect an informal organization for his own instruction, and in order to bring to bear the whole power of the Government upon the operations of the present war."[5] Unconsciously he began the creation of a general staff. The personnel of the War Board included several brigadier generals: Lorenzo Thomas, adjutant general; Montgomery C. Meigs, quartermaster general; James W. Ripley, chief of ordnance; Joseph G. Totten, chief engineer; and Joseph P. Taylor, commissary general. Major General Hitchcock did not join the board until its third meeting, but

4. Hitchcock to Mrs. Mann, March 15, 1862, Hitchcock Papers, Library of Congress; W. A. Croffut, ed., *Fifty Years in Camp and Field: Diary of Major-General Ethan Allen Hitchcock, U.S.A.* (New York: G. P. Putnam's Sons, 1909), 437. While some scholars have remarked on this assignment, we believe they all have failed to perceive the significance of it and what grew out of it, probably because Hitchcock himself proved so ineffective in the long run and because they did not appreciate the residual informal organizational structure that continued to function after the discontinuation of the staff job's formal existence.

5. Proceedings of the War Board, entry for March 13, 1862, Stanton Papers, Library of Congress.

thereafter he served as its head, the de facto chief of staff, although he participated little in its discussions.

Collectively the board became a body of such significance and importance that the famous military officer and scholar Emory Upton later called it the "Second Aulic Council."[6] That Austrian institution had often controlled military operations, frequently prescribing the strategy of particular campaigns. The comparison did not altogether flatter the War Board, for the Aulic Council stood for overcentralized control.

Though Upton failed adequately to appreciate the War Board, he correctly understood its sub-rosa functioning. The various bureau chiefs undoubtedly brought with them many informal relationships that were not anticipated by the formal organizational structure of the bureaus. Social psychologists call these relationships "informal organizations," and recent research has revealed that a multitude of such informal contacts abound in modern organizations.

In creating the War Board, Stanton consciously or unconsciously mobilized the natural tendencies of the organization to increase coordination among the bureaus and to provide a source of formal advice on operational questions. In bringing the bureau chiefs together in the War Board, he reinforced what very likely preexisted as an informal organization within his department, alongside and in addition to the formal structure.[7]

But Stanton did far more than strengthen and give sanction and impetus to the existing, or at least incipient, organization in which the bureau chiefs had collaborated informally. He gave it a new formal, but extralegal, charter. Charged not merely to work together to coordinate their own staff duties and to help, advise, and regulate one another, the War Board members were to broaden their authority to cover operational concerns, which was normally the province only of the adjutant general and general in chief. Again, Stanton was probably exploiting the natural inclinations of the bureau chiefs.

Placing the emphasis upon the staff rather than the chief, Lincoln

---

6. Emory Upton, *The Military Policy of the United States from 1775* (Washington, 1907), 291–94.

7. Proceedings of the War Board, wide sampling of entries, Stanton Papers.

and Stanton brought the staff into control over operations. But the Union president delegated nothing, and that was just as well, because Hitchcock's infirmities and reluctance to innovate rendered him incapable of functioning like a genuine chief of staff even if he had been endowed with that authority. The War Board, based upon a collegial or committee model, conducted formal meetings during which it dealt with topics that included seacoast defense, ironclad vessels of various types, support for amphibious expeditions, ordnance, officer and enlisted personnel management matters, quartermaster functions, corps branch consolidation proposals, the Military Academy, army strength, staff appointments, and prisoner policies. The board also gave attention to operations. All of these areas, Stanton correctly thought, required the kind of planning and coordination that the board could provide. The War Board brought its logistical control into the service of operational objectives and helped to provide an operations staff by drawing on the administrative resources of all the staff departments. The board took a further important step when, in order to ensure that the Ram Fleet built for the western rivers had sufficient provisions, it established a well-coordinated and greatly expanded supply system.[8]

In the Civil War, as in all wars, supply was crucial, and Montgomery Meigs brilliantly exemplified the traditionally key role of quartermaster in operations. As quartermaster general, Meigs performed tasks that are celebrated in the annals of military history. His successful management of Northern resources made a major contribution to the eventual victory. Naturally mistakes were made, and incompetence, deficiencies, and waste were present, but the abuses of the early months of the war soon disappeared, while more and more the Union soldier became the best-provided-for fighting man in all history. As a member of the War Board, through its formal and then later its informal existence, the able Meigs

8. Hitchcock to Stanton, March 19, 1862, Stanton Papers; Benjamin P. Thomas and Harold M. Hyman, *Stanton: The Life and Times of Lincoln's Secretary of War* (New York: Knopf, 1962), 186, 191.

gained an insight into needs and an influence over operations that significantly enhanced the effectiveness of his department and augmented its contribution. His position on the board, together with the importance of his department, gave him a strong voice in operational decisions.

The chief of ordnance and the commissary general were also significant members of the War Board. They discharged their departmental duties competently, providing well for the armies in the field, but they lacked the broader influence enjoyed by Meigs, the capable former engineer officer.

The War Board came into existence at a critical and exciting moment in the evolution of Union strategy, when McClellan moved to the Peninsula and West Tennessee fell to Halleck's forces. The board was of special value at a time when there was no general in chief. But after Stanton had been in office several months and he and Lincoln had acquired more confidence and experience in conducting operations, the board became less of a formal entity. In large part this fading from formal existence resulted from Hitchcock's failure to emerge as a satisfactory chief of staff. He finally cited ill health as an excuse to resign, but revealed in a long letter to Winfield Scott, on May 28, 1862, that he had quit because he was irked. He had perceived his function to be one of operational control and strategy formulation, and he had grown frustrated that his superiors did not faithfully follow his advice.[9]

Meanwhile, having come under critical fire from certain politicians, especially the radical Republicans, the War Board began to adopt a lower profile. It ceased holding formal meetings as such and stopped recording exact transcriptions of its deliberations. But it did continue in existence, in a formal sense, at least through mid-July 1862, and informally thereafter. Stanton may not have been the least bit disappointed: he had said at the first War Board meeting that he wanted it to be an informal organization. In part he had established it to help learn how the army functioned. After this was accomplished, he no longer felt the need for collective meetings. He

9. Proceedings of the War Board, entries for March 13, 14, 18, and 25, 1862, Stanton Papers; Hitchcock to Stanton, April 28, May 13, and May 26, 1862, and Hitchcock to Scott, May 28, 1862, Hitchcock Papers, Library of Congress.

had instituted a primitive form of general staff, and perhaps he dimly realized that, but he never truly saw the general staff as a necessary and permanent organ.

At this point, a suitable occupant was found for the position of general in chief in Henry Wager Halleck, and Hitchcock was dispensed with, but the board would go on informally. In appointing Halleck, Lincoln placed in command a regular officer with genuine prestige in the army and a record of brilliant successes in the West. The new general in chief was fortunate in the informal structure of the Washington headquarters.

Instead of assuming a powerless position with no control of the staff, Halleck stepped onto a stage created by the War Board, and he effectively played the role in which Hitchcock had been miscast. In addition to the members of the board, the informal general staff included the assistant secretaries of war. Despite their titles, they really functioned as general staff officers, were constantly involved in personnel, intelligence, and supply matters, and even occasionally reported on and evaluated operational recommendations.

The War Board itself had become involved in strategy determination. This was particularly true in regard to Hitchcock's activities, for he always envisioned his primary and proper functions to be within that realm. The members of the board arrived at a crucial decision in this respect when they concurred with Lincoln's apprehension that McClellan had not adequately planned for the security of Washington during the Peninsular Campaign and helped the president to override part of that general's plan.

Generally, however, Stanton and his corps of assistants were seeking to facilitate logistics, not operations. Assistant war secretaries John Tucker and Tom Scott, Gens. Lorenzo Thomas and Meigs, the journalist–assistant war secretary Charles A. Dana, Stanton's military aide Edward R. S. Canby, and even such an unlikely individual as a lieutenant who officially served as Maj. Gen. John C. Fremont's aide all worked as Stanton's special agents. They reported on subjects such as transportation, road construction and repair, cavalry horses, efficiency in filling requisitions, and a multitude of comparable activities. They coordinated the activities of the staff bureaus, supplementing the coordination supplied by the War Board. But the board had linked logistical with operational concerns, aided by

Hitchcock's operational responsibilities. Particularly involved in operations were Q.M. Gen. Meigs and that capable general-purpose officer of the engineers, Brig. Gen. John G. Barnard.[10]

When Halleck became general in chief, he thus, in part, succeeded to Hitchcock's role. Though the War Board ceased to exist formally in 1862, its legacy of interbureau cooperation remained so strong that it continued to have a significant, though informal, existence. Because of Hitchcock's position as chairman, Halleck inherited a measure of informal authority over the bureaus; owing to bureau involvement in operational planning, the theoretically independent special staff sections concerned themselves with and responded more readily to operational requirements. Real staff coordination, in theory reposing only in the civilian secretary of war, therefore permeated a lower level—the professional soldiers.

Though meager, Halleck's staff of twenty-three officers and men added immeasurably to an undermanned headquarters. Conversely, his inadequate staff gained significant augmentation by informal additions from the personnel of the bureaus. Meigs, for example, had accompanied him on a crucial visit to McClellan and had quickly prepared in his own office a creditable and accurate estimate of enemy strength. Halleck's staff—including his able chief, Brig. Gen. George W. Cullum, and his adjutant, Col. John C. Kelton, later adjutant general of the army—integrated logistics, intelligence, and operations. Though the most intimate members of the informal headquarters staff were Meigs and Barnard, others were active, among them Col. Edward D. Townsend, the acting adjutant general of the army. To a greater or lesser degree others, such as Major General Canby and the assistant secretaries, also functioned as part of the informal headquarters staff.[11]

10. Myriad letters exchanged between all of these individuals exist, mostly preserved in *The War of the Rebellion: A Compilation of the Official Records of the Union and Confederate Armies* (Washington: Government Printing Office, 1880–1901). Hereinafter cited as *OR*.

11. For an excellent brief treatment of the informal organization and a bibliography, see Richard E. Beringer, *Historical Analysis: Contemporary Approaches to Clio's Craft* (New York: John Wiley, 1978), 153–57. See also Edward A. Shils, "The Study of the Primary Group," in Daniel Lerner and Harold D. Lasswell, eds., *The Policy Sciences: Recent Developments in Scope and Method* (Stanford: Stanford University Press, 1951), 48. For the relations between Halleck and

The staff effectively performed most of the duties of a modern general staff with Halleck as its de facto chief. It differed, however, in two important respects from the modern United States general staff. After his initial involvement with raising troops, Halleck ceased to be much concerned with the recruitment and formation of troops. Partly a state matter and, after the introduction of the draft in 1863, more strongly a Federal matter, the provision of manpower for the Union armies rested largely in the hands of Stanton and state officials. The Union's informal general staff also differed from its modern American counterpart in the importance of the quarter-master general and the intermingling of operations, intelligence, and logistics, almost in a single unit. In the French staff model used in the United States Army today, these are discrete sections: G-3, G-2, and G-4, respectively.

The contemporary Prussian general staff closely approximated that of the Union. An outgrowth of the importance of the quarter-master in supplying and moving armies, the Prussian model grouped in one section the quartermaster and general staff, the same functions grouped under Halleck.[12]

In the final analysis, the Union's acquisition of a well-structured and functioning general staff, albeit informal, provided an advantage of quintessential importance. The beginnings of a modern general-staff organization had been fostered, partly by design and partly by accident, by Lincoln's war secretary. That the president had chosen so vigorous and capable a man as Stanton to replace the most unwisely selected initial incumbent, Simon Cameron, ranks as a singularly fortunate decision, at least as important as Lincoln's choice of the sagacious and indefatigable Halleck for general in chief. Halleck completed the effective Union command organization when he began exploiting the informal unity of the staff that Stanton had initiated. Lincoln and Halleck made a good team, one

---

Townsend, see E. D. Townsend, *Anecdotes of the Civil War in the United States* (New York: Appleton, 1884), 88.

12. See Hittle, *Military Staff*, 74.

well supported by the excellent headquarters staff. Halleck and the staff effectively implemented Lincoln's plans, especially the war-winning principle of simultaneous advances.

Things changed somewhat in early 1864 after Grant became general in chief. Lincoln, of course, remained commander in chief and continued to keep in close touch with military events, supervising major decisions. He worked with Secretary Stanton and, with Grant absent from Washington, he inevitably continued his contact with Halleck. Halleck changed titles more than jobs; he still functioned as the "military head" in Washington "to keep things from getting into a snarl." He remained the "common head to make the different bureaus act in concert."[13] In a sense, thereafter, the informal organization grew again into a formal one.

Though formally exercising the coordinating role of modern chief of staff, Halleck actually functioned as the chief of staff to Lieutenant General Grant. But the old headquarters staff continued to function. For example, when Grant wished to ascertain whether some of Benjamin F. Butler's troops could be spared for operations north of the James, Halleck sent Meigs and Barnard to investigate and recommend. So, though Halleck's command influence was much curtailed, his staff position changed little from that which he inherited on becoming general in chief in the summer of 1862. Stanton, through his concept of the War Board, had established the essential principle, and Halleck ably carried it out.[14]

The contributions of Halleck and the War Board facilitated Lincoln's use of an administrative style that enabled the president to master in a very short time what others took years to acquire. In spite of, or perhaps because of, Lincoln's lack of prior administrative experience, he did not immerse himself in details of day-to-day decision making. His style gave him the leisure not only to learn but also to think. Largely leaving routine operations to Stanton, Halleck, and the staff, Lincoln concentrated upon fundamental military and political questions. The informal structure of coordination and cooperation made this possible.

---

13. Halleck to Grant, May 2, 1864, *OR*, ser. 1, vol. 36, pt. 2, 328.
14. Sherman to Halleck, July 9, 1864, *OR*, ser. 1, vol. 38, pt. 5, 91–92; Halleck to Sherman, July 16, 1864, ibid., 150–51.

Thus, nearly a century and a half ago, the United States Army created a modern and effective headquarters staff that was strikingly, but coincidentally, similar to von Moltke's contemporary Prussian staff. Because it was entirely informal, however, the model disappeared at the end of the war and, without benefit of this experience, the army had painfully to re-create an effective headquarters staff early in the twentieth century.

◌◈◌ THE CIVIL WAR ARMIES

CREATION, MOBILIZATION, AND DEVELOPMENT

This piece was written at the request of the German Historical Institute and read in April 1992 at a weeklong symposium in Washington, D.C., concerning comparisons and contrasts between the American Civil War and the German Wars of Unification. The star-studded assemblage included just about everyone whose scholarship was pertinent to that topic from America, Germany, and France. The papers were subsequently edited by Stig Forster and Jorg Nagler and published by Cambridge University Press in a book entitled *On the Road to Total War.* I relied exclusively upon secondary sources.

The United States Civil War compelled both North and South to create, mobilize, and develop armies far larger and more complex than ever before had existed in the Western Hemisphere. In the process, armies were molded that in potency and in modernity would become fully equal to those of the great military nations of Europe—but not until after considerable development, which was accomplished only gradually. The Confederacy initially patterned its military system exactly after that of the Union. In both armies, as the war progressed, evolutionary changes occurred—and this is the key to understanding how much more crucial was *development* than was *creation* or *mobilization* in rendering the Civil War armies the potent entities they became.

Since its earliest days, the United States had maintained two separate military forces: an active, regular organization of professionals, and the militia, a volunteer, civilian force to be swelled in size commensurate with any emergency. A major conflict, such as the

Civil War quickly proved to be, had to be fought largely by volunteers, later augmented by draftees. West Point graduates dominated the key command and managerial positions, but their numbers were augmented by volunteer officers. Various reports on file in the War Office indicate that there were 3,163,711 militiamen: 2,471,377 in Union states and 692,334 in Confederate states. But these figures in essence are meaningless, for some of the counts date back as far as 1827.[1]

Each state's militia system, though elaborate, was typically ill-trained, ill-equipped, and poorly organized and managed. Scholarship on these militia is still quite inadequate; we could use some good new works to shed more light upon precise numbers of available personnel and relative soldierly capability. But it was not primarily the regular militia that comprised the bulk of the fighting forces; rather, it was masses of freshly recruited men with absolutely no prior military experience.

On the eve of war, the nation's regular army consisted of 1,105 officers and 15,259 enlisted men, the majority of whom were foreign-born (and some seven hundred were sick or on detached duty). This widely scattered entity was organized into ten regiments of infantry, four of artillery, two of cavalry, two of dragoons, and one of mounted riflemen. Of 197 extant companies, 179 occupied seventy-nine isolated posts in the western territories, and the remaining 18 manned ten garrisons east of the Mississippi River, mostly along the Canadian border and on the Atlantic coast.

The 1860 census indicates that the U.S. population stood at 31,443,321. The eleven states that officially seceded encompassed 9,103,332 of this number: 5,449,462 whites, 3,521,110 black slaves, and 132,760 free Negroes. Some 600,000 whites who resided in Union states cast their sympathies and efforts with the South, bringing the white population in support of the Confederacy to about six

1. See Marvin A. Kreidberg and Merton G. Henry, *History of Military Mobilization in the United States Army, 1775–1945* (Washington: Government Printing Office, 1955), 83–90. See also George T. Ness Jr., *The Regular Army on the Eve of the Civil War* (Baltimore: Toomey Press, 1990); although caustically criticized by some of its reviewers, it is quite useful, long in the making and magnificently researched. Much of the material in the immediately ensuing paragraphs is drawn from Herman Hattaway and Archer Jones, *How the North Won: A Military History of the Civil War* (Urbana: University of Illinois Press, 1983), chap. 1.

million. The North's population therefore stood at 22,339,989 less those estimated 600,000, or an effective 21,739,989.

These figures can be misleading because from the onset there was also much anti-Confederate sentiment within the South, which gradually grew as the war wore on. Some Southerners were starkly opposed to the Confederacy and intent on restoring the Union, and such thought and rhetoric were prevalent in the South throughout the war.[2] In addition, from the Southern totals should be subtracted those people who lived in what during the war became the new state of West Virginia and in areas such as East Tennessee, which contributed substantial support to the Union, and the Southern blacks who were liberated and subsequently saw service in the Union army. Black soldiers became a major factor in the Northern war effort, but not until mid-1863. For the South, the labor provided by masses of blacks (mostly in impressed gangs) was of inestimably great military value from the first.

A crucial demographic statistic, aside from population totals, is relative military population—in other words, white males between the ages of eighteen and forty-five (neither side initially used, nor at the outset intended ever to use, black soldiers). Absolutely accurate data cannot be obtained,[3] but careful estimates suggest that the Confederacy had approximately 1 million potential soldiers, while the North possessed slightly under 3.5 million. To that last number could be added the eventual acquisitions of liberated Southern blacks, as well as the surprisingly high number of more than 100,000 white Southerners who chose to be "loyalists" (the Confederates called them Tories) and fought for the Union. Civil War scholars were relatively ignorant about this group—save for the fraction of them known as "the galvanized Yankees"—until a pathbreaking book by Richard N. Current, *Lincoln's Loyalists,* closed a major gap in our understanding.[4]

2. See Jon L. Wakelyn, ed., *Southern Unionist Pamphlets and the Civil War* (Columbia: University of Missouri Press, 1999), and William W. Freehling, *The South vs. the South: How Anti-Confederate Southerners Shaped the Course of the Civil War* (New York: Oxford University Press, 2001).

3. See E. B. Long, *The Civil War Day by Day: An Almanac, 1861–1865* (Garden City, N.Y.: Doubleday, 1971), 704.

4. Dee Alexander Brown, *The Galvanized Yankees* (Urbana: University of Illinois Press, 1963); Richard N. Current, *Lincoln's Loyalists: Union Soldiers from the Confederacy* (Boston: Northeastern University Press, 1992).

When secession came, regular officers who wished to vacate their commissions were allowed to do so, and some were dismissed under suspicion of disloyalty. A total of 296 officers left the Federal army; 270 of this number eventually joined the Confederate military forces. An effort was made to retain in Federal service all regular enlisted personnel, but at least seventy—and possibly nearly four hundred—enlisted men managed to get out of United States service and go south.[5] During the time span of but a few months in late 1860 and early 1861, eleven states officially seceded from the Union. Both sides later claimed two additional states (Kentucky and Missouri), and the entire border region between the two sections was severely strained with division; in each of the border states, many people chose to support one side and many chose the other side.

Initially, both sides relied upon the state governments as the medium for recruiting and equipping the needed men. Both eventually would shift, though only gradually, toward centralized control over the mobilization process. Ironically perhaps, given its espousal of the state-rights concept, it was the Confederacy that inclined first toward centralization. On March 6, 1861, the Confederate Congress passed two major military laws. The first authorized President Jefferson Davis to call out the militia for six months and to accept 100,000 volunteers for one year in the Provisional Army of the Confederate States. Some 27,200 were inducted prior to the firing on Fort Sumter. The second act authorized the establishment of a regular army of 10,600 men. Five days earlier, the president had named the first general officer, Pierre Gustave Toutant Beauregard, the former United States major of engineers and a West Point graduate whose last assignment had been the superintendency of West Point.

5. This number was asserted by Emory Upton to have been only 26; his assertion long was accepted as correct, and that number appears in a great many works on the Civil War. The higher estimates are underpinned by Richard P. Weinert Jr., *The Confederate Regular Army* (Shippensburg, Pa.: White Mane, 1991).

Much controversy has raged about whether the South garnered a disproportionate share of West Point–trained officers. The regular army was somewhat demoralized by the fact that a seemingly large portion of its officers chose either to resign or to accept dismissal in order to join the Confederate forces. But at the outset, West Point graduates on the active duty list numbered 824; of these, 184 became Confederate officers. Of the approximately 900 graduates then in civilian life, 114 returned to the Union army and 99 others acquired Southern commissions. Thus, the North enjoyed the services of 754 West Pointers, 2½ times as many as the South's 283 West Point–trained personnel.

A closely related controversy has to do with an allegation that, the proportions notwithstanding, the South attracted "the cream" of the old officer corps. A plausible argument in support of this notion can be made, to be sure, and it is strengthened by the obvious high level of quality in command and leadership achieved by the South early on and particularly in the eastern theater of the war. But there are other possible explanations for how and why this occurred;[6] furthermore, the idea has been inflated and badly distorted, not least by the development of the so-called myth of the Lost Cause and the winning of the war—retroactively—by Virginia. I could not possibly settle this issue in so brief an essay as this, if indeed anyone could settle it at all, but suffice it to say that I find the argument to be moot in the present context.

During the crisis between Abraham Lincoln's election as president of the United States and his inauguration, the seceded states formed a joint government, the Confederate States of America. This new government proceeded to seize federal property, forts, and arsenals within the borders of the territory it claimed. Until formation of the Confederate government on February 4, 1861, South Carolina—the first state to secede, and the site early in April of the first significant exchange of hostile gunfire—purported to function as a separate nation. For a brief period following the creation of the Confederacy, South Carolina even maintained its own army, comprising state

---

6. See the relevant works by Thomas Lawrence Connelly, Barbara Bellows, Charles Reagan Wilson, Gaines Foster, William Garrett Piston, John A. Simpson, and myself.

militia, cadets from the Citadel (the Charleston military college), and numerous other volunteers. This polymorphous group was rapidly transformed and much of it absorbed, following the Fort Sumter episode, into the Confederate army. Even at this point in time, the various Southern states probably had larger numbers of men under arms than did the Confederate government, but the speed of national mobilization rapidly increased. On April 16, 1861, President Davis called for another 32,000 volunteers. All of the early calls for manpower were met enthusiastically. A greater problem than getting numbers of men was how to supply them; and still greater was the problem of organization, administration, and training.

The United States potentially possessed an advantage at the outset, for it could have used the regular army as a cadre to train volunteers. This was not done, however, for several reasons: Lincoln did not foresee a long war, the regulars seemed needed on the frontier, and it was politically expedient to appoint new high-ranking officers to command and lead the volunteers. Hence, the United States kept its regular army intact. The Confederacy, of course, initially possessed no regular army at all, and the creation of one never got much beyond the blueprint stage, although six full generals were appointed.

The Union used a departmental system of regional responsibility, initiated in the 1820s by Secretary of War John C. Calhoun and modified in 1850 by Davis when he held the same office. In each department, a senior colonel or general officer by brevet (there were no non-brevet general officers on active duty on the eve of the Civil War) commanded whatever officers and men were stationed therein. The system continued into the Civil War, and this same departmental system, although with some differences in practice, would be used by the Confederacy as well.

Since neither the regular nor the militia organizations provided a suitable base for the huge new armies, the belligerents were obliged to build them from scratch. Both the Union volunteer forces and the Confederacy's provisional army were modeled on the regular army and relied for leadership on a mixture of regular and militia officers, Mexican War veterans, men of political significance, and assorted prominent citizens. When a nation so construed as was the United States finds itself in a large war, it must rely heavily upon volunteer officers. The mass of these will, to be sure, remain at company-grade levels, but the better of them may rise to field grades, and some even might attain general-grade ranks, as was the case in the Civil War. The general topic of the Civil War volunteer officer still awaits a good scholarly treatment.[7]

Many of the volunteer officers, the future president Rutherford B. Hayes among them, had no prior military knowledge whatever. But many other nonsoldiers at least had attended one of the numerous private and state military schools that had proliferated since the Mexican War. The great majority of these were located in the South, though Norwich University, a private military institution in Vermont, furnished 523 Northern officers and 34 Confederate subalterns.[8] Also, many more Southern young men had attended, though not necessarily graduated from, such institutions than did Northern men. Thus, in addition to the oft-cited fact that more Southern boys than Northern ones experienced hunting and other outdoor adventures, a large number also attended a military school. The important thing to remember is: when a volunteer attained high rank, there was a good reason for it.

Only a small fraction of the volunteer officers who attained very high rank, such as the North's Alexander Schimmelfennig, made real asses of themselves—and most of the incompetents were weeded out or reassigned to a job where they were not terribly dangerous. I will venture one speculation concerning the relative merits of the North's and South's pools of potential volunteer officers: Since the South had a greater number of men with some military schooling, its pool probably provided for better leadership at company-grade and staff positions. But at general-grade ranks, if it is fair to posit that two quintessentially representative samples from each

7. Thomas J. Goss's *The War within the Union High Command: Politics and Generalship during the Civil War* (Lawrence: University Press of Kansas, 2003), may well prove to be the book that fills the bill. My late professor T. Harry Williams was much interested in this subject, and intended his *Hayes of the Twenty-third: The Civil War Volunteer Officer* (New York: Knopf, 1965) to be a case study. Rutherford B. Hayes, incidentally, did not hanker for a star on his collar (although he eventually got one), preferring, as he put it, "to be one of the good colonels to being one of the poor generals" (ibid., 18).

8. Recent research indicates that Norwich was the *only* military school in the North.

side were, say, Joshua Lawrence Chamberlain and Rutherford B. Hayes for the North and Nathan Bedford Forrest and James Johnston Pettigrew for the South, we see a significant contrast. The South's better volunteer general officers tended to be eccentric geniuses or brooding intellectuals, often with an aristocratic bent, while the North's were more likely to be professional men with more universally applicable managerial skills.[9]

Initially, state and individual initiative played a large role in the formation of regiments, the basic units of the armies. The voluntary infantry regiment comprised ten companies with no battalion organization intervening between the colonel and the ten captains and their companies, each numbering between fifty and one hundred men. Usually four to six regiments, grouped together, formed a brigade under a brigadier general. The next higher unit, the division, commanded by a major general, was quite unstandardized, as was the next larger unit, the corps. Once the fighting commenced in earnest, battle losses often made a mockery of organizational ideals. Sometimes a division was reduced to a size that rendered it hardly as large as a proper regiment.

The esprit of a regiment was of crucial significance during the Civil War. Men had an intense affinity with their regiment, and regiments typically were formed from men who came from the same geographic area and who had known each other in civilian life. Whatever other loyalties one might espouse, one's pride depended most upon his regimental identity. The Union created 3,559 separate units, while the Confederacy spawned probably 1,526.[10]

Armies usually were named for the military department in which they operated or were expected to operate when initially formed.

9. See Williams, *Hayes of the Twenty-third*; Alice Rains Trulock, *In the Hands of Providence: Joshua L. Chamberlain and the American Civil War* (Raleigh: University of North Carolina Press, 1992); Clyde N. Wilson, *Carolina Cavalier: The Life of James Johnston Pettigrew* (Athens: University of Georgia Press, 1990); and Brian Steel Wills, *A Battle from the Start: The Life of Nathan Bedford Forrest* (New York: HarperCollins, 1992).

10. Long, *Civil War Day by Day*, 716–17.

Military departments tended to be named by the Union for rivers, while the Confederacy typically named them for states or regions. There eventually were sixteen Union and at least twenty-five Confederate field armies—the latter number is unclear because the complexity of the Confederate Military Department System renders it impossible to say with certainty, in some cases, what was and what was not a field army. Official records indicate that the total enlistment in the Federal forces was 2,778,304, but scholars dispute this figure. Of course, many thousands of individuals enlisted more than once, and some troops served only for very short periods. Estimates of how many individuals served run from 1,550,000 to 2,200,000. The greatest student of Civil War minutiae who ever lived, E. B. Long, suggested that "probably something over 2,000,000 would be as accurate a figure as possible on total individuals in the Federal armed forces." Confederate totals are even more in dispute. Numerous scholars believe that the Southern forces comprised no more than 600,000 individuals; other estimates range upward to 1,400,000. Long judiciously asserted that "perhaps 750,000 individuals would be reasonably close." James M. McPherson, however, puts the number at 900,000 and thinks that even this may be too low because of uncertainty as to precisely how many Southern militia might, if only for brief episodes, actually have gotten into combat.[11]

The armies, alike in their personnel—at least until after the midwar Northern augmentation of black troops—and alike in their organization, also resembled each other in doctrine. Again, this was because of the domination of the highest commands on both sides by West Point graduates. Modeled on the École Polytechnique in France, the West Point curriculum emphasized engineering. It provided an excellent technical education, and the best graduates were selected for service as engineers. Its military education instilled a good understanding of weapons and of army routine, making the graduates adept at map reading, drill, and small-unit tactics. Thereafter, service in the regular army provided West Pointers

11. Ibid., 705; James M. McPherson, *Ordeal by Fire: The Civil War and Reconstruction* (New York: Knopf, 1982), 181; James M. McPherson, *Battle Cry of Freedom: The Civil War Era* (New York: Oxford University Press, 1988), 30 n. See also Maris A. Vinovskis, *Toward a Social History of the American Civil War: Exploratory Essays* (New York: Cambridge University Press, 1990), 11.

with a knowledge of troop leading, logistics, and small-unit staff duties.

In the months that followed the fall of Fort Sumter, both sides steadily groped toward full mobilization. Two days after the fort's capitulation, President Lincoln issued a proclamation declaring the existence of an insurrection in the then only seven Confederate states, called out 75,000 militia for three months' service, and scheduled a special session of Congress to convene on July 4, 1861, a little more than six weeks away. On April 29, Jefferson Davis sent a lengthy message to his Congress, meticulously detailing the history of the establishment of the Southern government and terming Lincoln's proclamation a presidential declaration of war, which indeed it was.[12]

The strongly pro-Union Northern states immediately wired their acceptance of the call for troops, but the border states balked. Virginia seceded on April 17 and promptly raised forces to protect her borders. North Carolina state troops mustered, and seized Fort Caswell and Fort Johnson. Meetings of patriotic groups stirred attention in both the North and the South, and efforts everywhere were concentrated upon mustering and organizing militia. Lincoln was intensely worried about the possibility of a rebel incursion in Washington, but on April 18, to his great relief, five companies of Pennsylvanians numbering about 460 men (known thereafter as the First Defenders) reached the capital, the vanguard of troops to defend the District.

On the same day, General in Chief Winfield Scott—himself too old and infirm to take the field—held a conference with his former engineer staff officer from the Mexican War, brevet Col. Robert E. Lee, and offered him command of the Union army. But Lee declined, resigned his commission two days later, and within a week became major general in command of all of Virginia's military forces. Lee, of course, ultimately emerged as the preeminent Southern general—

---

12. Much in the immediately ensuing paragraphs is drawn from Hattaway and Jones, *How the North Won,* chap. 2.

but not until after a lackluster early performance in western Virginia, coastal defense duty in South Carolina, and staff work in Richmond. The North placed first reliance for major field command upon a former major elevated to major general, Irvin McDowell—and, after McDowell's debacle at the Battle of Bull Run, upon thirty-six-year-old George B. McClellan. First in the West Point class of 1846, McClellan had resigned from the army a captain in 1857 to become chief engineer of the Illinois Central Railroad.

The swelling size of the opposing armies forced Lincoln and Davis to elevate numerous individuals to general-grade ranks. Lincoln could select almost two-thirds of his general officers from numbers of regulars because, contrary to traditional supposition, he had three times as many regulars as Davis from whom to choose. Yet Lincoln, lacking Davis's regular military background, sometimes gave less recognition to military professionalism. His nation suffered from far more division than Davis's, and he used the appointment of general officers as patronage in enlisting support for the war among the various political, ethnic, and other interest groups.

Actually, for a variety of reasons, the South had a keener appreciation for military professionalism than did the North. It has been asserted that early in the Civil War the South did a better job than the North in identifying its more able officers and getting them sooner into high levels of command. More to the point is that the South, from the outset, welcomed its military professionals and capitalized upon their talents. Sixty-four percent of the regular army officers who went South became generals, while fewer than 30 percent of those who stayed with the Union did so.[13] But all of this was something that came after the war had commenced.

In appointing generals Lincoln sought a broad base of support for the war, drawing appointees from the hard-core abolitionists, the high-tariff advocates, the War Democrats, and the foreign-language immigrant groups. In 1861 alone he made generals of two Dutchmen, two Germans, a Hungarian, an Irishman, and a Pole. Yet Lincoln also recognized the professional expertise of the regulars and

13. Samuel P. Huntington, *The Soldier and the State: The Theory and Politics of Civil-Military Relations* (New York: Vintage, 1957), 213.

appointed, proportionally, half again more career soldiers than did Davis, handicapped as Davis was by a far smaller number from whom to choose.

We do not know nearly as much about Civil War basic training as might be useful for us; here is another great topic awaiting its student.[14] While it is true that masses of soldiers got no basic training at all and learned on the job, even sometimes being committed to combat literally from the first moment of their service, basic training did take place for some troops. The Confederacy, at least early in the war, maintained a number of basic-training camps, the most notable one being located on the fairgrounds just outside of Richmond, Virginia. Another, and ill-fated, Confederate basic-training facility was Camp Moore, near Kentwood, Louisiana, where the entire garrison was wiped out by an epidemic of measles. Following the first Battle of Bull Run in July 1861 and the commencement of the Peninsular Campaign in May 1862, the principal Union army remained so long in garrison near Washington, D.C., that the experience constituted an extensive and convoluted episode of basic training. The commander of that force, the Union Army of the Potomac, was George B. McClellan—called by T. Harry Williams and other detractors "the problem child of the Civil War." His many egregious flaws notwithstanding, though, students usually agree that he was the most keenly able organizer and administrator that the war produced. Aside from McClellan, William Tecumseh Sherman, and George G. Meade, no high-level Union officers accomplished much in the way of setting up practical training programs.[15]

14. For a good start, see William J. Miller's *The Training of an Army: Camp Curtin and the North's Civil War* (Shippensburg, Pa.: White Mane, 1990).

15. Kreidberg and Henry, *History of Military Mobilization,* 121–22. Many useful insights on McClellan can be gleaned from Stephen W. Sears, *George B. McClellan: The Young Napoleon* (New York: Ticknor & Fields, 1988), but Sears is blatantly anti-McClellan. Much older but still useful is Fred A. Shannon, *The Organization and Administration of the Union Army, 1861–1865,* 2 vols. (Cleveland: Arthur H. Clark, 1928). My doctoral student Ethan S. Rafuse wrote a brilliant dissertation on McClellan at the University of Missouri–Kansas City (2000) which he is revising for publication.

Training camps followed no normative standard. There was no prescribed length of training. For some men, their time in training camp was measured in hours, but others spent months in one training camp or another. The vast majority of training camps existed only early in the war. North or South, they might spring up anywhere: on fairgrounds, vacant lots, train yards, parks, or village greens. Some of them remained in existence only a few weeks or months. Nearly all of them that were developed with much in the way of physical facilities, especially those in the North, ultimately were converted into places of incarceration for prisoners of war. Camp Curtin, located about a mile north of Harrisburg, Pennsylvania, was a notable exception. It remained in operation as a training center throughout the war, and more than 300,000 troops from Pennsylvania, Maryland, Michigan, Minnesota, New Jersey, New York, Ohio, and Wisconsin spent some time there during the conflict.

Some lower-level officers took the initiative, during lulls between battles, to institute training programs on their own. We know in some detail about the activities of a few such noteworthy individuals; for example, I have written much about the training activities of the Confederate Stephen D. Lee during the nearly yearlong period that he was a field-grade officer. While he often was compelled by circumstances to go into battle at the head of green troops, he never left himself in so unfortunate a position as to have to commit *raw* troops to a fight, because he insisted upon some training from the instant they came under his purview.[16] Doubtless there were a number of other similarly judicious-minded officers. (Here again is an underworked topic awaiting a good synthesizer.) But whatever the amount of training in the field that was prescribed, the most effective training in most cases came from the experience of combat itself.

When it comes to studying particular armies, there are a number of possible approaches: investigations of personnel from the bottom

16. See my book *General Stephen D. Lee* (Jackson: University Press of Mississippi, 1976) and the essay on Lee in this volume.

rank up, investigations from the top-ranking people down, institutional delineations (especially regimental histories), or some combination of these. Probably the best-known and best-loved study of a single army is Bruce Catton's vivid and emotionally moving memorial to the Federal Army of the Potomac: *Mr. Lincoln's Army* (1951), *Glory Road* (1952), and the Pulitzer Prize–winning *A Stillness at Appomattox* (1953). Catton used all four of the variant approaches to some extent, but more than any other his is primarily an institutional approach. While justly popular, Catton was somewhat opinionated, always slightly pro-Northern in viewpoint, and much of his work is only lightly documented, being based largely on regimental histories.

The Northern armies have not yet been compared and contrasted with each other at the macrocosmic level nearly to the same degree as have at least two of the Southern armies. Douglas Southall Freeman in the mid-1930s made a magnificent pioneering study of the Confederate Army of Northern Virginia, albeit through a complex delineation of its commanders.[17] (I note Freeman's approach because, in all fairness, it is probably true that any army can be studied effectively through the biographies of its leaders.) Thomas Lawrence Connelly, in the late 1960s and early 1970s, set a new standard for histories of Civil War armies with his two volumes on the Confederate Army of Tennessee.[18] But Richard M. McMurry, probing these same two armies from an entirely fresh perspective, performed a transcendent achievement in comparative analysis in his 1989 book *Two Great Rebel Armies*.[19]

McMurry intended his short book to be "a philosophical and historiographical introduction" to his projected magnum opus: a history

17. Douglas Southall Freeman, *R. E. Lee: A Biography*, 4 vols. (New York: Charles Scribner's Sons, 1934–1935), and *Lee's Lieutenants: A Study in Command*, 3 vols. (New York: Charles Scribner's Sons, 1946).

18. Thomas Lawrence Connelly, *Army of the Heartland: The Army of Tennessee, 1861–1862* (Baton Rouge: Louisiana State University Press, 1967), and *Autumn of Glory: The Army of Tennessee, 1862–1865* (Baton Rouge: Louisiana State University Press, 1971). These two volumes eclipsed Stanley F. Horn's well-documented *The Army of Tennessee: A Military History* (Indianapolis: Bobbs-Merrill, 1941), which remains popular because of its readability.

19. Richard M. McMurry, *Two Great Rebel Armies: An Essay in Confederate Military History* (Chapel Hill: University of North Carolina Press, 1989).

of the Civil War in the West.[20] This is a worthy goal, one on which I wish him well. Until rather recently, far too much emphasis has been put upon study of the war in, and the armies of, the eastern theater. Connelly was something of a modern harbinger of a more proper and balanced perspective, aided by a handful of like-minded zealots like Archer Jones, Albert Castel, the Reverend Larry J. Daniel, William Garrett Piston, and, I humbly submit, myself.[21]

McMurry sheds edifying new light on the perplexing contrast between the accomplishments of the two principal Confederate armies, the Army of Northern Virginia and the Army of Tennessee. The former, under Robert E. Lee for nearly all of the war, enjoyed much success; the latter, under six different (and relatively incompetent) commanders, enjoyed almost no successes at all. This was not, as has been typically surmised, because of the huge difference in operational area. McMurry posits that "the Army of Tennessee was not unsuccessful because it campaigned over a vast area; it campaigned over a vast area because it was unsuccessful."[22] But why?

Many factors apply: the amorphousness of boundaries, the effect of waterways and railroads, and differences in quality and availability of command and leadership, as well as organization and execution. Most significant was that far more personnel who found their way into the Army of Northern Virginia had some previous military experience or training than did those who served in the Army of Tennessee. Ultimately, the Army of Northern Virginia was far superior to the Army of Tennessee because of the latter's less-qualified lower-level officers. This affected leadership at all levels, but the contrast was greatest with respect to commanding generals. Robert E. Lee and Virginia Governor John Letcher made a good team, as did Lee and President Davis. Lee was self-effacing, cooperative, and communicative. He constantly tinkered at improving administration, organization, and articulation. For much of the war,

20. Ibid., xiii.
21. Since writing this, the Society of Historians of the Western Theater has been formed; it is small but growing, and holds an annual convention. At the very least I should add to my list Steven D. Woodworth, Michael Ballard, and John F. Marszalek.
22. McMurry, *Two Great Rebel Armies*, 150.

he faced inferior opposing commanders in the Federal army. In every way, the reverse was true in the West.

It is also possible to begin the study of an army not from the top down, via looks at the lives of its commanders, but rather from the bottom up—to investigate the common soldier.[23] The great pioneer of this technique was Bell I. Wiley, whose classic works on the common soldier include *The Life of Johnny Reb* and *The Life of Billy Yank.* Wiley's student James I. Robertson Jr. offered a good supplement to the master's work in 1988 with *Soldiers Blue and Gray,* but a new and higher level of achievement in this regard was reached that same year by Reid Mitchell with his much superior book, *Civil War Soldiers.*[24]

Mitchell began by depicting the North and the South as much more alike than different. But shared national identity does not necessarily prevent violent conflict, and, assuredly, it did not in this case. Hatred for the enemy became a reality; it either existed at the outset or it developed. Soldiers projected stark differences upon the individuals and culture of the other side, and that helped them not only to nurture hatred, but also to be fomenters of depravity and destruction. And, too, the war itself engendered and fed an ensuing mythology. If, for example, at the outset the South did not possess an internal force powerful enough to tie its whites together, it did have that by 1865.

Brave deeds, and above all a shared military experience, bred a potent brotherly affinity. The war profoundly changed its participants.

23. In "Have Social Historians Lost the Civil War?" (the lead essay in his *Toward a Social History of the American Civil War*) Maris A. Vinovskis cites the pioneering work in this regard by Earl J. Hess and W. J. Rorabaugh. Elsewhere in the book Vinovskis makes a few references that reinforce the concept, but they are too arcane and tentative to warrant being taken into account within the scope of this essay.

24. Bell I. Wiley, *The Life of Johnny Reb: The Common Soldier of the Confederacy* (Indianapolis: Bobbs-Merrill, 1943); and *The Life of Billy Yank: The Common Soldier of the Union* (Indianapolis: Bobbs-Merrill, 1952); James I. Robertson Jr., *Soldiers Blue and Gray* (Columbia: University of South Carolina Press, 1988); Reid Mitchell, *Civil War Soldiers* (New York: Viking, 1988).

More than anything else, it welded the loyalties of combatants to each other and alienated them from society at large. The war was hell, but those who endured it tended to internalize a certain indifference to brutality and savagery. Further, a soldier's own virtue and courage and that of his fellows, in contrast to the evil cruelty (real or imagined) of those on the other side, provided a sustaining element. Mitchell concludes that "fraternizing between the armies was not as prevalent as postwar myth would have it."[25] On the other hand, Civil War soldiers usually were willing to give quarter, to take prisoners and not to abuse them. But brutality, especially in the prisons, apparently increased toward the war's end.

The most significant of all puzzles concerning the Civil War are the questions of loyalty, tenacity, and will. Mitchell is fascinated with these matters and deals much with them. His interesting conclusion is that "the North had a superior will to fight the war it had to fight than the South had to fight its war."[26]

We know a good deal about the black soldiers thanks to two outstanding books: Dudley T. Cornish's 1956 classic, *The Sable Arm,* and Joseph T. Glatthaar's prize-winning 1990 work, *Forged in Battle.* The black troop units mostly were outstanding outfits. This resulted in part because blacks were highly motivated and strove mightily to be good soldiers and also because generally their officers—almost all of them white—were particularly well qualified. White men were drawn as candidates for commissions in the United States Colored Troops by a variety of motivations: "I would drill a company of alligators for a hundred and twenty a month," confessed one, and some were men whose previous units wanted to dump them.[27] But the majority were keenly able. One famous institution that helped many of them to qualify was the Free Military School for Applicants

25. Mitchell, *Civil War Soldiers,* 37.
26. Ibid., 183.
27. Dudley T. Cornish, *The Sable Arm: Black Troops in the Union Army, 1861–1865* (New York: Longmans, Green, 1956); Joseph T. Glatthaar, *Forged in Battle: The Civil War Alliance of Black Soldiers and White Officers* (New York: Free Press, 1990), 41.

for Commands of Colored Troops, in Pennsylvania, a precursor of Officer Candidate School.

More than 34,000 Northern blacks served in the Union army, over 15 percent of the 1860 free black population. The precise total of all black troops cannot be ascertained. An officially recorded number is 178,892; hence some 80 percent of the black troops were former slaves. Donning the Federal uniform was rather an esoteric experience for blacks. "This is the biggest thing that ever happened in my life," commented one.[28] They encountered all manner of trial: racism, prejudice, negative stereotypes, doubts about their worth, and outright hostility. But they persevered, and they turned in a collective war record marked by honor and valor. They also provided the ultimate psychological blow: in the end—because of appalling rates of Confederate battle casualties combined with egregious numbers of desertions—there were about as many blacks serving in the Union army as there were whites remaining on active duty in the Confederate forces.

Until recently, little has been done to delineate the specific differences, as groups, between common soldiers who comprised the various armies spawned by the two sides. A step in this direction has been taken by the Reverend Larry J. Daniel, whose *Soldiering in the Army of Tennessee* has done much, as Gary Gallagher put it, to bring "these western Confederates out from the shadow of their more famous counterparts in Lee's army."[29]

It is striking that the western army retained cohesiveness despite its lack of strong leadership and its frustrations on the battlefield. This resulted, Daniel concludes, from fear of punishment, a fortuitous religious revival that stressed commitment and sacrifice, and a

28. Glatthaar, *Forged in Battle*, 79.
29. Larry J. Daniel, *Soldiering in the Army of Tennessee: A Portrait of Life in the Confederate Army* (Chapel Hill: University of North Carolina Press, 1991); the quotation from Gallagher is from a blurb used in advertising Daniel's book. It is amusing to wonder whether Gallagher, since moving to the University of Virginia and nearly exclusively touting the war in the East, would still stand by these words.

strong element of comradeship that was engendered in large part by the common experience of serving for so long under losing generals. Nevertheless, the ultimate reality is that the Civil War was decided in the western theater, where the principal Union army came to far outclass any of the Confederate forces.

A crucial reality with respect to the ongoing development of the opposing principal forces in the western theater is that, with the passage of time, the Confederate forces did not improve as much as the Federal forces, which continued to evolve and become quintessentially effective. This, really, is the key, as I see it, to the topic of this essay. Late in the war, even Confederate Gen. Joseph E. Johnston asserted of his adversarial force that "there had been no such army since the days of Julius Caesar," and one member of that army said "it is not likely that one equal to it will be seen again in this country in our day and generation."[30]

Two recent books tell much about this process. The first is Charles Royster's *The Destructive War*, in which, in a complex and stimulating long essay of the same name that comprises Chapter 8, he attempts to explain how the war came to be so violent and how the people who waged it, both soldier and civilian, became able to accept that level of violence. In the process, Royster winds up describing within a sociocultural context quite a bit about Americans of the Civil War era in general, and in particular Thomas J. "Stonewall" Jackson and William T. Sherman.[31]

Rather more pertinent to the subject of this essay is Glatthaar's superb *The March to the Sea and Beyond*, which delineates much about the internal and institutional development of Sherman's army—really an "army group" comprising three field forces. I perhaps have yielded too much in the remainder of this essay to the temptation to

30. Johnston and Union soldier quoted in Joseph T. Glatthaar, *The March to the Sea and Beyond: Sherman's Troops in the Savannah and Carolinas Campaigns* (New York: New York University Press, 1985), 15.

31. Charles Royster, *The Destructive War: William Tecumseh Sherman, Stonewall Jackson, and the Americans* (New York: Knopf, 1991); see my review of this book in *The Washington Times*, March 22, 1992.

quote from this intriguing work.[32] I am attracted, I think, by the art-fulness of Glatthaar's approach. It is through such an approach, I am convinced, that one can best grasp the significance and impact of Sherman's achievement. To that end, I also highly recommend Keith F. Davis's *George N. Barnard: Photographer of Sherman's Campaign*.[33]

Sherman's March to the Sea late in 1864 and his subsequent campaign in early 1865 into the Carolinas was an integral part of the grand strategy formulated by the Union's general in chief, Ulysses S. Grant. The strategy aimed at overcoming a significant twofold advantage enjoyed by the Confederacy: of being on the defensive, and being able to use interior lines. Grant envisioned army-sized raids rather than penetrations (for example, invasions and occupations) of enemy territory. Concomitantly, in order to preclude the South's ability to redeploy to counter any significant threat of the moment—as it had managed to do, rather spectacularly, on several occasions—Grant prescribed something that Abraham Lincoln long had advocated: simultaneous advance along several fronts. Such advances could in effect be holding actions in favor of the one advance that would become the Union's principal hammerblow against the South's will to continue making war. This one advance, this will-breaking venture, became Sherman's March.

It was a march conducted by an army of veterans. This "army had more actual campaign experience than any other Federal command," for it was a group of men who had learned the art of soldiering through several years of actual, often hard, campaigning.[34] Nearly all the troops had received their training in the western theater,

32. Much material in the ensuing paragraphs is also based on John G. Barrett, *Sherman's March through the Carolinas* (Chapel Hill: University of North Carolina Press, 1956), and Richard E. Beringer, Herman Hattaway, Archer Jones, and William N. Still Jr., *Why the South Lost the Civil War* (Athens: University of Georgia Press, 1986).

33. Davis's book was published in 1990 by his employer, the Hallmark Card Company Archives. It was personally and professionally gratifying to me to have had the opportunity to assist in the preparation of this work as an editorial advisor. Davis also prepared a touring exhibit of photographs from the book, and I spoke at the exhibit's opening at the Amon-Carter Museum in Fort Worth, Texas.

34. Glatthaar, *March to the Sea*, 17.

where prolonged campaigns, lengthy marches, supply shortages, and success in battle were the rule rather than the exception.

It was a march destined to have amazing psychological impact upon the Southern people. As Glatthaar observes, "the Civil War historian Frank E. Vandiver once said with tongue-in-cheek that communities from Texas to Virginia swear that Sherman's army marched through them. Beneath the lighthearted side to that statement, however, is a very powerful message. It clearly indicates the enormous effects of total war as implemented by Sherman's army, both in actual devastation and in the generation of fears" in the hearts and minds of the civilian populace. Resolved to "make the march and make Georgia howl," Sherman's object was not only to destroy resources but also, as Sherman himself put it, to "illustrate the vulnerability of the South. They don't know what war means; but when the rich planters of the Oconee and Savannah see their fences, and corn, and hogs, and sheep vanish before their eyes, they will have something more than a mean opinion of the 'yanks.' "[35]

It is worthwhile to remember that Sherman's men were not only experienced veterans, but also citizen soldiers and for the most part intensely patriotic. Southerners anxiously had awaited the November 1864 Union presidential election, hoping for Lincoln's defeat as a sign of the failure of the North's determination to triumph over the Confederacy. But they did not receive much help from Sherman's men, who overwhelmingly favored reelection and cast a staggering 86 percent of their ballots for Lincoln. As Glatthaar says, "In a sense, the Lincoln victory at the polls, coupled with the fall of Atlanta, renewed the commitment of Sherman's troops to the cause."[36]

Wisely, "Sherman realized from the start that in [the] campaigns [ahead] the burdens were going to shift from headquarters to lower-grade officers and enlisted men":

One key element in the success of Sherman's army was the astonishing amount of experience in the officer corps. Nearly all the officers had served for several years, many of them having worked

35. Ibid., xiii; Beringer et al., *Why the South Lost,* 329.
36. Glatthaar, *March to the Sea,* 49.

their way up from the enlisted ranks. . . . Ninety-six percent of the regimental commanders had served previously in companies, with one in six coming from the enlisted ranks. More revealing are the statistics on company-grade officers [captains and lieutenants], the men who dealt directly with the rank and file. Almost 50 percent of the captains and over 90 percent of the lieutenants served at one time as enlisted men. The result, then, was the formation of a body of ingenious young officers with a wealth of experience who, Sherman insisted, "accomplished many things far better than I could have ordered."[37]

Sherman also carefully limited the *kind* of men who would make up his expedition: he believed that he had to have soldiers who knew what to do and how to care for themselves, and he was willing to "take 'only the best fighting material,' soldiers accustomed to hardship and disease. All others had to remain behind." Before the March to the Sea commenced, "Sherman ordered his senior officers and medical staff to undertake what one soldier called 'a rigorous weeding-out process.'" As Glatthaar observes:

> From a medical standpoint the results were astounding. During the Savannah campaign, Sherman's entire army averaged less than 2 percent of its men unfit for duty due to sickness on any given day, and on the much more demanding march through the Carolinas the average was a fraction over 2 percent. In comparison with all other Union troops, Sherman's army suffered 46 percent fewer illnesses per 1,000 men during the campaign months. . . .
> . . . The army began to believe itself invincible, and with each day's march confidence in its own abilities grew. A veteran recorded in his journal: "We have weeded out all the sick, feeble ones and all the faint hearted ones and all the boys are ready for a meal or a fight and dont seem to care which it is."

These were men who *wanted* to go on the campaign: "'I wouldn't miss going on this expedition for 6 months pay,' jotted an ecstatic officer in his diary."[38]

Sherman himself was quite a remarkable man. His "nickname,

37. Ibid., 15, 21.
38. Ibid., 19–20, 44.

'Uncle Billy,' signified both familiarity and respect." Like some quintessential Boy Scout leader, Sherman had become

> the premier veteran, a man who awed his troops with his vast knowledge of the terrain of Georgia and the Carolinas and all aspects of campaigning. Whether it was showing a soldier how to mend a harness, teaching several drummer boys how to light a fire in the pouring rain, or guiding his army through the swamps . . . without suffering heavy losses, Sherman always seemed to know exactly what to do and how to do it. The end result was an unfailing confidence in his generalship.[39]

The operation was unprecedented: no longer did Sherman have any communications to protect, nor any for his principal adversary, Confederate Gen. John Bell Hood, to threaten. Sherman led his "army group" of more than sixty thousand men unmolested to the coast and reached Savannah, Georgia, in time to present it to President Lincoln as a "Christmas gift." On the way, he had created such ambiguity about his route that he had no difficulty avoiding the meager forces available to oppose him. His army moved rapidly, easily living off the country and destroying in its path anything of value to the Confederate war effort. Sherman's raid was aimed as much at Confederate morale and will as it was at the South's railroads and granaries.[40]

(Contrary to the beliefs of many Southerners, then and ever since—and even the beliefs of many ill-informed students—Sherman did not unleash his force in wanton, uncontrolled destruction. The violence was measured. Doubtless it could have, and probably would have, been intensified if circumstances had suggested that to be appropriate. The historian Mark Grimsley well elaborates on this in *The Hard Hand of War*.)[41]

---

39. Ibid., 16.
40. Beringer et al., *Why the South Lost*, 328–29.
41. Mark Grimsley, *The Hard Hand of War: Union Military Policy toward Southern Civilians, 1861–1865* (New York: Cambridge University Press, 1995).

Sherman's March presented the Confederates with a serious di-lemma: what could possibly be done in effective response? General Hood chose to disengage from Sherman and to march into Middle Tennessee. While Sherman marched virtually unopposed through Georgia toward the coast, Hood planned not a raid but a reconquest of Middle Tennessee. The two regions—the one into which General Hood moved and the one into which Major General Sherman moved—were not of equal value. Middle Tennessee could not pos-sibly contribute as much to sustain Confederate armies as the rail-ways in Georgia, severed by Sherman, had provided throughout the war. As a raider, Sherman had the goal and the opportunity to avoid the enemy's army. But Hood, aiming to conquer territory, had to engage Union forces in his path. The advantage of the defense thus accrued—and thereafter continued to belong—to the Union.[42]

Hood seemed determined to help the Union make the most of its advantage. On November 30, 1864, he made a costly frontal at-tack against his entrenched opponent at Franklin, Tennessee. In this engagement he had an army roughly the same size as that of his opponents, but the power of the defense, here enjoyed by the Union, proved decisive as Hood lost 15 percent of his force, in-cluding six generals killed or mortally wounded. His capable adversary, the seasoned Union Maj. Gen. John M. Schofield, with-drew even though he had resisted Hood's attacks successfully and his casualties numbered barely a third of his opponent's. Schofield fell back to Nashville, where he joined his superior, Maj. Gen. George H. Thomas, with a still-larger force in well-entrenched po-sitions protected from turning movements by the Cumberland River, patrolled by Union gunboats. Very soon thereafter, in freez-ing weather on December 15 and 16, Thomas, in an essentially frontal battle, easily defeated Hood's already demoralized army and drove what was left of it into northern Mississippi. Superior in numbers, morale, and cavalry, Thomas conducted a damaging pursuit. Discredited and disgraced, Hood resigned as army com-mander; his army had lost so heavily in numbers and morale that it effectively had ceased to exist.[43]

42. Beringer et al., *Why the South Lost,* 329–30.
43. Ibid., 330–31.

It was not just Confederate armies that had to be vanquished, however, for as Sherman wrote Union chief of staff Maj. Gen. Henry W. Halleck: "We are not only fighting hostile armies, but a hostile people, and must make old and young, rich and poor, feel the hard hand of war, as well as their organized armies. I know that this recent movement of mine through Georgia has had a wonderful effect in this respect. Thousands who had been deceived by their lying papers into the belief that we were being whipped all the time, realized the truth." President Davis succinctly summed up the non-material impact of this significant march: "Sherman's campaign has produced [a] bad effect on our people. Success against his future operations is needed to reanimate public confidence." By this point in time, Grant and Sherman both had come to envision a second thrust to be made by Sherman's army: northward, through South Carolina.[44]

Sherman's men had by now come to reflect in their appearance the kind of life they had been leading and that Sherman intended for them to continue to lead. Again, I quote Glatthaar:

At first glance, the men looked more like a mob than an army. They were an unkempt, boisterous, seemingly unruly lot, in no way resembling the stereotypical professional army of the mid-nineteenth century or even their counterpart at Petersburg.[45] Yet they were an army, superbly skilled in both marching and fighting. While other Union commands took pride in their spit-and-polish dress and expertise in marching drills, Sherman's men cared little for that; instead, they took extra pride in their ability to endure all hardships and still achieve in battle and on the march. The sinewy frames, bronzed skin, scraggly beards, and dilapidated clothing were merely trophies from the last successful

44. Ibid.
45. The Army of the Potomac, then besieging Petersburg, Virginia, was under the leadership of Gens. George G. Meade and Ulysses S. Grant. As my friend Russell Weigley, the eminent military scholar, and I observed together in conversation at the conference where this essay was first presented, Grant had an "army group" too, and his situation was made still more complex by his also being in command over *all* the Union armies.

campaign. Upon their arrival in Beaufort, South Carolina, one member of Sherman's army overheard a black soldier in a shiny, new uniform comment, " 'they alls are about as black as we alls,' which," he felt, "though not very complimentary told something how we did look."[46]

Despite how the hearer of the remark assessed it, perhaps the black soldier had meant to utter the greatest compliment he could. One of the things that Sherman and his army did was to bring about the de facto emancipation of many thousands of blacks from slavery. On one occasion, Sherman measured in *miles* the blacks who trailed behind the raiding infantry of his army.

Somewhat counter to popular myth, Sherman's "troops had surprisingly infrequent contact with Southern whites on the march. . . . it was not unusual, particularly in South Carolina where thousands throughout the state evacuated to 'safer' areas, for some troops to go several days without seeing any white inhabitants. Only in the larger towns and cities of Georgia and the Carolinas did Sherman's men find Southern whites in sizable numbers."[47]

Glatthaar writes: "Rumors of mistreatment by Sherman's troops, whether or not they had any basis, had spread throughout Georgia and the Carolinas and left the people frantic. . . . South Carolinians were particularly susceptible to such tales, for they had good reason to fear Sherman's army, especially after they learned of the fate of Columbia and other towns." Sherman's men had entered Columbia, the state capital of South Carolina, on February 17, 1865. Not far outside town, Sherman spent one cold night sleeping on the floor of an abandoned country mansion. The fire burned low, and he awakened uncomfortably cold. He arose and renewed the flames with an old, wooden mantel clock and a bedstead: "the only act of vandalism," he later asserted, "that I recall done by myself personally during the war." Yet about one-third of the city of Columbia was destroyed by fire before Sherman pushed on. In 1976, in a brilliant piece of historical detective work, Marion B. Lucas demonstrated that the fire was not the fault of Sherman or his troops. But Southerners

46. Glatthaar, *March to the Sea*, 37.
47. Ibid., 66–67.

then and since have typically equated the fire with Sherman's willful policies of war making.[48]

As Glatthaar observes, the fear of terror and destruction was always a key element:

> A handful of Union soldiers actually went out of their way to propagate the myths [of Yankee ferocity] by telling South Carolina women stories intended to terrorize them. At Barnswell two soldiers told some women that there were no gentlemen in Sherman's army, as convicts released solely to subjugate the South constituted the entire enlisted population. . . .
>
> Of course, not all Southern women cowered . . . Some defiantly displayed their anti-Union sentiments at every opportunity and, at times, without regard to the consequences. . . .
>
> . . . A South Carolina woman tried to drive away some foragers by throwing scalding water in their faces but instead got a dunking in a barrel of molasses to sweeten her temper.
>
> Many of these women possessed a bitter hatred of Union soldiers . . . [W]artime propaganda at home intensified their burning hatred for the Union Army. . . . [A] North Carolina woman told a soldier that she would not give a cup of water to a dying Yankee. Later, after becoming better acquainted with the man, she admitted, "I would give you a cup of water to soothe your dying agonies, and, as you are a yankee *I wish I had the opportunity to do so.*"[49]

In general, however, "Sherman's army treated Southern civilians well." In fact, "three prominent Confederates—Lt. Gen. William J. Hardee, Maj. Gen. Gustavus W. Smith, and Col. Edward C. Anderson—left their wives to the care of Sherman's occupation forces in Savannah" and "Time after time, members of Sherman's army performed acts of kindness for southerners, especially the poor." In addition, "Many of Sherman's troops were eligible bachelors, and since there were very few Southern men outside the Confederate Army, they found in Georgia and the Carolinas a

---

48. Ibid., 70–71; Sherman quoted in Hattaway and Jones, *How the North Won,* 666; Marion B. Lucas, *Sherman and the Burning of Columbia* (College Station: Texas A&M University Press, 1976).

49. Glatthaar, *March to the Sea,* 71–72.

considerable number of unattended and unspoken-for women. Soldiers of every rank commented on the attractiveness of Southern women . . . Once both parties got over their initial hesitancy, all sorts of relationships blossomed, from lifelong friendships to marriages."[50]

Because Confederates now were concentrating fragments of forces—mostly remnants of the bedraggled and battered Confederate Army of Tennessee—and the next raid would bring Sherman toward Lee's army in Virginia, the situation was significantly different than it was during Sherman's March to the Sea. Grant prepared for the probable use by Confederates of interior lines to achieve dangerous concentration against Sherman. Wanting Sherman to have a supply line this time so he could remain stationary and hold his ground if attacked, Grant sent Major General Schofield with part of Major General Thomas's army by rail and water to the North Carolina coast to take Wilmington and establish a line of communications with which Sherman could connect if necessary. Fort Fisher—the principal Confederate defensive emplacement at Wilmington—fell to a combined assault in the middle of January 1865. Schofield's Twenty-third Corps reached the North Carolina coast on February 9 and, along with the troops of Maj. Gen. Alfred Terry, occupied Wilmington eleven days later. The Union force, some 30,000 effectives, then moved up the Cape Fear River to secure Fayetteville, North Carolina, for Sherman's approaching army.[51]

By the winter of 1865, Federal efforts to improve the cavalry, which had been markedly inferior to the Confederate cavalry earlier in the war, at last had created a well-led force, numerically superior and better armed than its Confederate counterpart. Grant used this force to make several minor and two major cavalry raids. Both major raids began in March 1865. One, under Philip Sheridan, went from Winchester, Virginia, through that state to the Federal army at Petersburg. This raid successfully disrupted Richmond's rail and canal communications with the western part of Virginia.[52]

50. Ibid., 74–75.
51. Beringer et al., *Why the South Lost*, 330–31.
52. Ibid., 331–32.

The other raid, under James H. Wilson, an 1860 West Point graduate and now a brevet major general, moved from Tennessee into Alabama and captured Selma, an important war industrial center on a rail route connecting Georgia and Mississippi. In the desperate defensive operations, the famed genius Nathan Bedford Forrest at last met his match. Thanks to Wilson's insistence and perseverance in the matter, almost all of the Federal cavalrymen were armed with Spencer seven-shot repeating carbines. In addition, the men carried a six-shot revolver as well as a light cavalry saber. Each division was equipped with a battery of horse artillery. And most significantly, Wilson had a pontoon train outfitted with enough equipment to enable his pontonier battalion to build a four-hundred-foot bridge. Forrest was outnumbered as well as outfought, for Wilson's compact force of 13,480 men moved with a swiftness not achieved by any of Forrest's previous foes. The Federal troopers were not dependent upon the land for food or forage, for each carried on his mount five days' light rations, twenty-four pounds of grain, one hundred rounds of ammunition, and a pair of extra horseshoes. It is not without reason that a standard book on this campaign is entitled *Yankee Blitzkrieg*.[53] After defeating Forrest and smashing the industrial installations at Selma, Wilson's men continued on to take Montgomery, Alabama, Columbus and Macon, Georgia, and eventually to capture the fleeing Jefferson Davis near Irwinville, Georgia, on May 10, 1865.

All the while, prior to the final capitulation of the western Confederate army late in April, Sherman's men had continued their march. "By the time Sherman's army reached Goldsboro, North Carolina, it was in all its glory. Hatless heads, frazzled pants, threadbare shirts, torn shoes or barefoot, faces blackened by Carolina pine smoke, they looked, as a member of Schofield's army noted, 'very hard.'"[54]

By the end of March 1865, Sheridan had completed his destructive raid and joined Grant at Petersburg, the army from the trans-Mississippi was besieging Mobile, the Selma cavalry raid was in full swing, and Sherman and Schofield had united in North Carolina. Sherman had beaten off a feeble attack at Bentonville March 19–21 by

---

53. James Pickett Jones, *Yankee Blitzkrieg: Wilson's Raid through Alabama and Georgia* (Athens: University of Georgia Press, 1976.)
54. Glatthaar, *March to the Sea*, 38.

a small, patchwork Confederate army under General Johnston. Grant was clearly attaining the object of his raids—to "leave the rebellion nothing to stand upon."[55]

> Sherman's Savannah and Carolina campaigns were very different from any other campaign in the war. . . . [S]uccess did not depend upon victory in combat; . . . the enemy was not just the Confederate Army. Sherman's objective was to demonstrate to the Southern people that the Confederate armies were no longer capable of protecting its citizens and that life outside the Union was much worse than life within the Union. The march itself, then, determined the success of the campaign, and its primary enemies were the mud and hunger rather than the Confederate troops. . . .
>
> For the most part . . . campaigns were arduous at best and frequently very dangerous. As Sherman's army marched to Savannah and through the Carolinas it had to deal with an increasingly larger and highly mobile Confederate force. . . .
>
> The Confederates had little success delaying Sherman's army with gunfire, but they did slow the march somewhat through the use of other tactics. One practice was to fell trees across the road . . . Another tool that the Confederates employed . . . was land mines . . . These subterranean explosives . . . had a crippling, sometimes fatal effect on their unsuspecting victims, prompting Sherman, strangely enough, to declare them a violation of civilized warfare. . . . Confederates also lit barrels of turpentine or pine trees . . . These fires blocked off the roads and scared the horses and mules as the "air filled with pitch pine smoke made it almost unbearable to breathe."[56]

The capitulation of the Confederacy was but a symptom of the defeatism that had by this time triumphed throughout the South. Grant's strategy of simultaneous army-sized raids had provided a useful solution to the military stalemate. But a broken stalemate dictates only that military activity, if it continues, will become more fluid, unpredictable, and irregular. It does *not* dictate the defeat of one side or the other. Even when the Union armies accepted the surrender of the Confederate armies, the latter had still other alternatives open to them. But very few Southerners wished to continue the fight.[57]

55. Beringer et al., *Why the South Lost,* 332.
56. Glatthaar, *March to the Sea,* 101, 108.
57. Beringer et al, *Why the South Lost,* 334. Subsequent scholarship has shed

For now, even if the Confederacy did continue to exist, slavery was gone. The preservation of slavery was not precisely and openly what the Confederacy had come into being primarily to protect, but it certainly had not come into being with any expectation that the institution soon would be demolished. Neither did the Union have the extinction of slavery as its original war aim; *that* had been the preservation of the Union. "As the war progressed, however, most [Union] troops began to see emancipation as a powerful tool in crushing secession. . . . [A]s Sherman's troops passed through Georgia and the Carolinas, opposition to slavery grew stronger and stronger."[58]

Somewhere along the way, just as the Union had added the extinction of slavery to its original war aim, so too had the Confederate leadership altered its concept of the political goal of the war. Beyond the loss of slavery, much else previously dear to Confederates seemed now to have been demolished. State rights appeared to be gone. Soul-searing casualty lists indicated the loss of a staggeringly large portion of the region's young men. Even God seemed to be turned against the South. In the late summer of 1864, one Confederate citizen prayed: "Oh God, wilt thou hear the prayers of Thy people who daily say, Lord, give us peace."[59] This supplicant meant peace with a tinge of satisfaction; peace at least in part on the South's terms. But the depression of the Southern people, and their desire for peace on *any* terms, deepened. This was especially so after the fall of Atlanta (which helped assure the re-election of President Lincoln) and the start of the siege of Petersburg, for any siege is liable to be long, bitter, and very costly, and inevitably the besieger will win, unless the siege is lifted from the outside—and there was no chance of that. By 1865, Southern morale was beyond recovery. The armies had not yet surrendered, but the people were beaten. At last, the days of sacrifice ended.

---

much light upon the improbability of guerrilla success and the utter impossibility that white Southerners would submit to the bitter privations and inevitable changes that such an attempt would wreak in their society.

58. Glatthaar, *March to the Sea*, 41.
59. Beringer et al., *Why the South Lost*, 335.

THE EVOLUTION OF
TACTICS IN THE CIVIL WAR

This essay was solicited by Keith Poulter, the editor of *North & South* magazine, for a special issue on the general topic of tactical evolution.

It is important that the reader understand what the definition of *tactics* is, as opposed to *strategy* and *operations*. Strategy is "the big picture," or "the art of the general." It is distinguished from tactics primarily in scope, but in truth, the ultimate differences between them sometimes blur. Strategy has to do with applying the principles of war, of selecting how one's military forces may be arrayed so as to counter or defeat the enemy regardless of whatever he might do. Operations falls in between the other two: it has to do with moving men and material in such a manner as to place them where they can apply and fulfill the aims of the strategy. Tactics can be defined as what the men are instructed to do and how they do it once they come into close proximity with the enemy's forces.

Sir Archibald Wavell opined that "tactics is the art of handling troops on the battlefield; strategy is the art of bringing forces to the battlefield in a favorable position." Carl von Clausewitz suggested that "tactics is the art of using troops in battle; strategy is the art of using battles to win the war." There is a difference between offensive tactics and defensive tactics. The first aims at gaining the desired goal by aggressively attacking; the second is used when one hopes or expects (or knows) that the enemy is going to attack, and aims at inflicting such damage upon the enemy while he is attacking as to bring victory to the defender.

This essay first appeared, in shorter form and under the title "The Changing Face of Battle," in *North & South* 4:6 (2001).

The primary combat arm in the Civil War was infantry, but infantry usually was augmented by artillery and cavalry. Inherited from the days of Napoleon Bonaparte was the concept of advancing in long lines of battle, typically two ranks deep. One could elect to employ an alternative that relied more on mass: the column. This varied from one to ten or more companies wide and eight to twenty ranks deep. Less typical was another possibility, a version of what was referred to as deploying skirmishers. This was an "open order," strung-out, irregular single line of deployment, suitable only for advance elements intended to guard against the main force being surprised and to identify enemy emplacements by drawing early fire.

There are only a small number of maneuvers that are possible in bringing a body of troops into close proximity with an enemy force for the purpose of attacking it. One can advance directly in frontal attack. One can try to envelop left or to envelop right. Still more daring is the double envelopment—trying to hit an enemy emplacement on both of its flanks. While offering the possibility for inflicting the greatest damage upon the defender, such a maneuver is difficult to execute and dangerous to try, owing to the challenge of jointly timing two large troop movements and to the necessity of dividing the attacking force, rendering both elements susceptible to being "defeated in detail." Lastly, one might move far to the rear of an enemy emplacement with the aim of cutting its lines of communications and supply. This can reasonably be expected to induce the enemy to disengage and retreat from its position—on preselected ground prepared to resist an onslaught—to a less-desirable site, where the advantage may shift to the attacker.

A basic idea behind these tactics before the Civil War was that the firepower available to infantry was such that advancing troops could close with those on defense and fight hand-to-hand. But the introduction of the longer-range rifled musket allowed such a potent degree of firepower that Civil War troops rarely came into close contact: an advance either would be stopped before closure occurred, or defenders would be routed in retreat or surrender as captives.

Firepower thus also rendered frontal attack the least likely tactic to produce the desired result, and yet that was the attack most often attempted by Civil War officers. Why? It's simple and uncomplicated: they are there and we are here, why not just charge 'em with overwhelming fortitude and ferocity? More often than not it did not work, but many an officer continued to try just that.

Once it is established that firepower will limit the possibility of closing with the enemy for hand-to-hand combat, a basic law of physics dictates that flanking attacks promise greater chance of success than frontal ones. It is simply a fact that, given any soldier's ability to aim, more rounds will fall long or short than will fall wide right or left. A volume of fire directed to the front (whether by an individual or a mass of soldiers) will result in an elliptical "beaten zone." But when a flanking attack is successfully executed, the result is enfilade fire. This is defined as "when the long axis of the beaten zone coincides with the long axis of the target zone"—that is, the defending troops. If the flanking movement is executed with celerity, spectacular results can be achieved, unless the enemy has made preparations to defend his flanks as well as his front.

It is a pure and simple truth that in modern war (however one defines that term) cover and concealment are useful in combat. Cover provides some physical protection from incoming fire; concealment does not do that, but rather hides all or part of the defender's body. Both have their desirable aspects.

Dennis Hart Mahan, who taught at the U.S. Military Academy at West Point from 1824 to 1871—a remarkable forty-seven-year career—preached that "celerity is the secret of success." He tried to instill in his students the importance of mobility, surprise, and boldness. Nonetheless, he also keenly stressed the importance of digging in when on static defense. His admonitions induced mixed responses from his former charges when they fought in the Civil War. Many of them much eschewed using any form of entrenchment, because they thought it would lower the élan of the defending troops. Some officers actually opined after the war was over that troops which had served behind entrenchments never again fought with the zest and unalloyed enthusiasm they had before the experience. But experience after experience in the Civil War showed these officers to be wrong in their denigration of entrenchments.

Logic dictates that an attack column offers the greatest chance for success, but only if the attacking movement is accomplished with celerity and at least some measure of surprise. However, geographic conditions in America at the time of the Civil War tended to render the use of an attack column relatively impracticable, if not quite impossible. There was much wooded countryside, and this dictated that open order was best.

There were some meaningful limits, too, on the width of an attacking front that might be practicable or even possible. A coherent corps was, of course, desirable (and in accord with Napoleonic maxims). Then the corps commander could give overall tactical direction. But this almost never was possible under the conditions extant during the Civil War. Logically, the next best step was to rely upon divisions as principal tactical units, but more often than not, even that was not possible. Brigades, and sometimes even regiments, became the principal maneuver elements. It was brigades for the most part that did the tactical fighting in the Civil War; sometimes it was a regiment or even a company.

The difficult terrain also dictated that the artillery and cavalry play lesser tactical roles than under Napoleonic conditions. Firepower, as much as terrain difficulty, necessitated that artillery or cavalry not usually be principal attacking elements. Save for independent, relatively smaller operations, cavalry especially had a new and more limited role: scouting and screening, flank protection, and augmenting pursuit when and if attack had been successful. As for artillery, it was now best used in bolstering the defense—not, as it was distributed at first, in a piecemeal array, with single batteries widely scattered among the infantry units they were supporting. Increasingly as the war progressed, artillery was best employed when massed in concentrated elements.

But Civil War commanders were slow to learn the new realities. Some *never* did. The better ones, who would eventually chalk up the more significant achievements, did learn—but only after a surprisingly large number of experiences offered practicable examples of the new realities.

The major episode in the Battle of Shiloh, April 6–7, 1862, was just such an illustration. The Confederates were so fortunate as to engage an unentrenched, considerably unready enemy force and to do so with a substantial element of surprise. The Confederate advance went well for most of the morning of April 6. But then the advance stalled. Many men were simply exhausted. Many could not resist feasting on what they found in the abandoned Federal campsites. Many were short on, or out of, ammunition. The Federals received the gift of a window of opportunity to stabilize their lines and to bring up fresh troops. A 1,200-man force commanded by Brig. Gen. Benjamin M. Prentiss took position in a protruding—and, as it would turn out, crucial—salient. Ulysses S. Grant visited the spot and gave Prentiss the order to "hold at all hazards."

The troops had aligned along an eroded wagon trace, the old Purdy-Hamburg Stage Road, about two-thirds of a mile long. Later this road would be redubbed the Sunken Road. It offered the cover of a ready-made entrenchment. Prentiss was subsequently augmented with much more force: in the end the salient was held by some 10,200 infantry and eight artillery batteries with thirty-three guns. Theirs was the position that the Confederates would call the Hornet's Nest. Again and again, rebels hurled themselves haplessly against this strong line, and the casualties began to pile up.

Confederate brigades long since had become intermingled, and there was much confusion. In one bizarre episode, the Thirteenth Arkansas and the Fourth Louisiana, each mistaking the other for the enemy, exchanged "friendly fire"—which assuredly is the most unfriendly kind there is. The self-destruction might have gone on longer than it did, but a woman in a sunbonnet appeared, seemingly out of nowhere, and wandered between the lines.

Hours slipped by while the Confederates formed, reformed, and assaulted, ultimately a total of eight times. The final attack was launched at 3:30 P.M., when some ten thousand Confederates were thrown into the Hornet's Nest. One student of the episode places their casualties at about 2,400, or 24 percent. Flanking movements probably could have produced the same outcome with less loss, but the Confederates tended in this battle to try brute strength over finesse. By more modern standards, the general advance should not have been halted in other sectors simply to await reduction of the

Hornet's Nest, but the prevailing norm then was to not leave any major pocket of resistance in one's rear.

The Hornet's Nest was finally taken after a barrage from fifty-three artillery pieces, firing at a range of five hundred yards. The Federals managed to offer some potent return fire, but the massed Confederate pieces were the final scale-tipper. In truth, the Yankee salient was already beginning to crumble even before the barrage began. The defenders had held out just about as long as they could have in any event. They had bought six hours of time, and this clearly saved the day for the Federal army, allowing the tide to turn in Grant's favor.

This was a spectacular lesson in the western theater on what could come from defending with the benefit of some cover and concealment—provided in this case by a fortuitous thicket and sunken road. The next two lessons of this type came in the eastern theater, the first in the Second Battle of Bull Run (Manassas) August 29–30, 1862.

Here, Federal Maj. Gen. John Pope was duped into thinking that he had succeeded in moving with sufficient celerity to launch an attack upon Stonewall Jackson's corps while James Longstreet was still trying to come up. As it turned out, Longstreet arrived in time, and the artillery battalion under Col. Stephen D. Lee seized the opportunity to pour a searing and punishing (partially enfilade) fire into the assault that Pope fomented.

By this time, however, the attack upon Jackson's corps had brought some of the combatants into close enough proximity to engage in hand-to-hand combat. Many of Jackson's men enjoyed the cover and concealment provided by a cut that had been prepared for a railroad that was being built. These Confederates were much more secure than those who were not provided with such entrenchment. The Federals directed musketry fire at the defenders in long, cascading rolls. From the woods, Jackson's veterans stepped forward. Twice, Federal Maj. Gen. Fitz-John Porter's assaulting troops faltered and scurried back from the searing return fire, but still they came onward for a third time. Hand-to-hand combat broke out in sectors of the line. Some of the Confederates, out of ammunition, threw rocks at their attackers. More Federals were sent into the fray, but Jackson's men held firm.

Then came the punishing enfilade fire from S. D. Lee's guns, and that halted the Federal advance. Soon thereafter, anticipating that Robert E. Lee would so direct, Longstreet took the initiative and unleashed a furious counterassault, most of his men having been well concealed until they stormed forward. Some Federal units simply dissolved. It was one of the war's greatest counterassaults, and most of the Yankee army fled in disarray. Only a spirited and dogged defense on Henry House Hill prevented a thorough disaster for the Federals. When night fell, the Union force was in full retreat to Centerville.

The second big eastern lesson came just a few weeks later, at the Battle of Antietam on September 17, 1862, in and around Sharpsburg, Maryland. In this daylong engagement, the Confederates defended entirely unentrenched. Union Maj. Gen. George B. McClellan had planned a masterful (in his mind—then and forever after) double envelopment with a diversionary assault upon the rebel center. But events unfolded unpredictably from north to south.

At the lower point of the battle lines, the Rohrbach Bridge proved difficult for the troops under Ambrose E. Burnside to secure and pass over. Later redubbed the Burnside Bridge, this obstacle held up the Union advance for a number of hours. The Confederates found it practicable to diminish their forces facing Burnside and to redeploy them at more seriously threatened points.

By midmorning the focus had shifted to the rebel center. There, a farm lane, worn down below the surrounding land by weather and long use, formed a natural trench. This the Confederates bolstered with a breastwork of fence rails. Later called the Sunken Road and by some the Bloody Lane, this sector became the scene of the most awful slaughter: one Federal division lost 40 percent, another 10 percent. A Confederate officer wrote that his unit's first volley "brought down the enemy as grain falls before a reaper."

It could have been an even more spectacular example of the value of cover and concealment, but there was considerable "dead space" beyond the Confederate front. Dead space is an area behind the defender's front where, because of some oddity or variation in the terrain, an advancing attacker can find respite, safe from direct fire from the defensive lines. Sometimes dead space can be reduced simply by advancing some defensive emplacements, but the safest and most effective way to do it is with high-angle indirect fire—either from howitzers or, more typically, from mortars.

Suddenly, however, some mishap in Confederate command caused the fortuitous position to be abandoned. Luckily for the hard-pressed rebels, this was their only serious tactical error of the day. McClellan could have exploited his good fortune—the position was clearly visible from his headquarters—but he did nothing, relying instead on the success he erroneously assumed Burnside was achieving.

Aside from this error, which caused the Confederates to receive a major assault on the defensive while completely unentrenched, General Lee handled each tactical challenge as it arose with an impressive response. But Bloody Lane should have been a more widely received lesson in tactical reality than it proved to be.

Photographers reached the scene of the battle before the dead and wounded were tended to or disposed of. This was a first in American history, and the widely published and much circulated scenes of grisly slaughter and destruction shocked a horrified public. Even today, viewing pictures of the dead near Bloody Lane can give one a jolt.

The next example came in the Battle of Fredericksburg, on December 13, 1862. Lee had time to prepare his defenses before Burnside's rash assault along a wide front. Barely contesting the Federal crossing of the Rappahannock River, Lee fortified the heights west of the city, which were from one to two miles away from the river. Lee stretched his approximately 75,000 men along a seven-mile front stretching from the Rappahannock on the west to Massaponax Creek on the east. Three hundred pieces of artillery were arrayed in support. The dead space to the front of these positions was covered to such an extent that one Confederate officer gave assurance that not even a chicken could get across the battleground.

The key to the defense was a sunken road and a stone wall at the base of the heights. The stone wall provided a great place for the Confederate defenders to conceal themselves: the ground behind the wall was much lower than that in the front, allowing the Confederates to not just crouch behind the wall but actually to stand.

All day the Federals charged what proved to be an almost impregnable position, and they were beaten back each time with heavy losses. Only darkness put an end to the essentially useless slaughter. It was during this battle that Lee and Longstreet sat atop their horses looking down from a high eminence at what was happening and Lee said to his principal subordinate: "It is well that war is so terrible, lest we grow too fond of it." Later, when Gen. Joseph E. Johnston read about this battle, he proclaimed his sorrow that "no one will attack *me* in such a position." The Federals had suffered 12,653 killed, wounded, or missing; the Confederates, 5,309.

The supreme lesson came on the third day of the Battle of Gettysburg, July 3, 1863. On the two previous days, Lee had hit the Federal right and then the Federal left. Both attacks seemed to produce promising results, but not the conclusive results the rebels desired. This led Lee to suppose that the Federals must be weakest in the center. What could have made Lee feel that it was propitious for an assault wave to cross a little more than a mile of artillery-swept open ground, slightly uphill? How could this eighteen- to twenty-minute rapid walk directly into fierce enemy fire be made, and the attackers arrive with enough cohesion and vigor to break a line of determined defenders? The plan was not totally without recent precedent. It was, after all, less than four years since Napoleon III, at Solferino, had smashed the Austrian center by commencing with a heavy artillery bombardment and then following up with a vigorous frontal assault.

The charge was co-led by one of Longstreet's division commanders, Maj. Gen. George E. Pickett, whose division comprised about one-third of the assault force, and Maj. Gen. James J. Pettigrew, who commanded the wounded Henry J. Heth's division, which comprised the main assault force. The name Pickett's Charge, first given to the attack by the *Richmond Press,* is a misnomer. In the bitter aftermath, Pickett came to wish that the attack had been more accurately named Longstreet's Assault.

An artillery bombardment preceded the charge, but the shots mostly went long, and few Federal infantrymen were hit. Blue-clad gunners responded to the fire, and for a time there was a terrific noise—so loud, it was alleged, that it could be heard 150 miles away. Then the Federal artillery chief, Brig. Gen. Henry J. Hunt, pulled his gunners back to safety, and the Confederates wrongly concluded that they had disabled the enemy's guns. When the Southerners charged, they met an unexpected and murderous Federal artillery barrage. Hunt later claimed, perhaps with but scant exaggeration, that had his superiors allowed him, he could have stopped Pickett's Charge with artillery alone.

"General, shall I advance?" Pickett asked Longstreet. So overcome by his feelings that he could not speak, Longstreet simply bowed his head. The lines were dressed, the flags unfurled. At ten minutes past three in the afternoon, 10,500 men moved forward, in two main ranks followed by a thinner rank of file closers. They walked deliberately, at route step—110 paces per minute. In perfect order and steady advance, they covered a hundred yards with each passing minute.

In the first part of the charge, the Confederates were hit by long-range artillery, then by salvos of rifle fire, and ultimately by brass Napoleon field cannon firing canister. Major General Pettigrew was riding on horseback, close behind his line, when his horse was hit. Dismounting, he sent it back with a wounded man, and stayed with his line. Grapeshot smashed the fingers of his right hand. On and on, he and his men pressed forward. He could see clearly the stone wall on Cemetery Ridge.

After they had crossed nearly half the distance, the Confederates reached a swale that sheltered them from much of the incoming fire. There they halted, and redressed their lines. Up to this point, the losses, while far from insignificant, were by no means crippling or demoralizing. The men would go on.

But the fire got hotter, the losses mounted, and the formations mostly were broken. Still, some five thousand of the attackers got to Cemetery Ridge. There was hand-to-hand fighting with the advance Federal skirmishers. A small breach opened in the Federal line. Confederate Brig. Gen. Lewis Armistead, his hat stuck on the end of his sword, led the advancing rebels. A handful of them swarmed over the stone wall, but Federal reinforcements rushed into the melee. There was more hand-to-hand fighting, lasting somewhat less than two minutes—later declared to be the most dramatic "hundred seconds of the Confederacy." Armistead was mortally wounded. The "high tide of the Confederacy" began to recede as the crushed and vanquished remnants made their way back. Relatively little musketry fire hampered them as they went, for many Federals stopped shooting—partly out of chivalry, partly from the feeling that there had been quite enough killing, and largely because many were busy rounding up prisoners. Some of the captives still had spunk. "Every rooster fights best on his own dunghill!" shouted one. "Fredericksburg . . . Fredericksburg . . . Fredericksburg," shouted the elated Federals, taunting the rebels for having made, in an even starker manner, the same kind of costly mistake that the North had made.

"Too bad . . . too bad . . . oh, *too bad*," Lee cried out in anguish. "The task was too great," he told the survivors of the assault, and admitted that it was all his fault. And indeed it was Lee's fault: he had fought his worst battle, his egregiously flawed tactics dictating that he lose miserably.

The problem, of course, was not the presence or lack of cover and concealment; *that* was part of the *solution*. The problem was the unprecedented increase in the rapidity and range of the defense's firepower, which greatly enhanced their strength.

John K. Mahon elaborated on this, emphasizing the impact of rifling and conoidal projectiles, in a 1961 article titled "Civil War Infantry Assault Tactics."[1] These innovations made it necessary for

---

1. John K. Mahon, "Civil War Infantry Assault Tactics," *Military Affairs* 25 (summer 1961): 57–68.

armies to assemble farther apart than formerly and for the density of men in combat zones to be reduced, as well as rendering shock action, particularly assault in columns, much less viable. Battles became not only longer but also typically less decisive: a vanquished commander who elected to start a retreat would know he had sufficient firepower to provide protection for a forced disengagement. A defeated Civil War military force almost always could end the battle, get away, and salvage some fighting capability, which then could be nurtured to be used on a future date.

Could any tactical innovation or variation lessen the impact of the new weaponry? Edward Hagerman discussed this question at length in his 1960s doctoral dissertation, belatedly published in 1988 as *The American Civil War and the Origins of Modern War.*[2] Hagerman pointed to the admonitions given by West Point professor Dennis Hart Mahan, who had begun to extol the value of field fortifications even before the introduction of the minié ball (which solved the problem of difficulty and slowness in preparing to fire a round from a muzzle-loading rifle). Mahan also was insightful enough to predict that any big war would necessarily involve many inexperienced citizen soldiers who would be called up to augment the rather small regular forces. He was correct in opining that Napoleonic assaults would not be effectively executed by citizen soldiers, thus wasting the lives of many people valuable to society. Some of Mahan's students began using field works early in the Civil War, while others, as we have seen, were leery of them and their potential negative effects on morale and efficiency. But even these students were thoroughly convinced of the necessity of cover and concealment by the latter part of the war.

Grady McWhiney and Perry D. Jamieson agree with both Mahon and Hagerman in their book *Attack and Die.*[3] Technological innovations bestowed tremendous advantages upon the side on the defensive, and McWhiney and Jamieson suggest that Northerners perceived this rather quickly, while Confederates took a much longer

---

2. Edward Hagerman, *The American Civil War and the Origins of Modern War: Ideas, Organization, and Field Command* (Bloomington: Indiana University Press, 1988).

3. Grady McWhiney and Perry D. Jamieson, *Attack and Die: Civil War Military Tactics and the Southern Heritage* (Tuscaloosa: University of Alabama Press, 1982).

period of time and, in some cases, never did so. Why? Northerners, by and large, were of Anglo-Saxon stock, while Southerners' heritage was Celtic. Celts throughout history, observe McWhiney and Jamieson, display a rash and uninhibited preference for offensive operations and tactics. Hence, Southerners, as did their ancestors, had a fatal propensity to "attack and die." (The authors draw an interesting parallel between the practice of some warring Celts of stripping and painting their bodies blue—to achieve some measure of shock, revulsion, surprise?—and Stonewall Jackson's proposal to stage a night attack in the nude!)

Whether Southerners' predominantly Celtic heritage rendered them inclined to bleed themselves to death is, as one might expect, a controversial question. But the scholarly bickering has tended to obscure the truly great contribution made by McWhiney and Jamieson, who produced the best survey of tactics in warfare from the time of Napoleon I to the Civil War. (Jamieson, in a subsequent volume, traced the unfolding search for tactical solutions to the problems produced by technological innovation up to the Spanish-American War.[4] He concludes that while intelligent thought was applied, an adequate solution was not reached.)

In 1986, my collaborators and I included in our book *Why the South Lost the Civil War* an appendix directly refuting the *Attack and Die* thesis. The following year, Albert Castel published his impressive and thoughtful article "Mars and the Reverend Longstreet," which looks at available options to assaults and attempts to explain why various specific assaults took place.[5] Once forces engage in combat, Castel argues, commanders have only four options: they may fight on the defensive; they may attack on a broad front; they may attack directly with a narrow front; or they may attempt to strike their opponent's flank or flanks (or, alternatively, get far to the enemy's rear in a turning movement). Once one opts for the defensive, he has surrendered the initiative. Attacking with a broad front offers the

4. Perry D. Jamieson, *Crossing the Deadly Ground: United States Army Tactics, 1865–1899* (Tuscaloosa: University of Alabama Press, 1994).

5. Richard E. Beringer, Herman Hattaway, Archer Jones, and William N. Still Jr., *Why the South Lost the Civil War* (Athens: University of Georgia Press, 1986); Albert Castel, "Mars and the Reverend Longstreet; or, Attacking and Dying in the Civil War," *Civil War History* 33 (1987): 103–14.

promise of success only when one possesses some overwhelming numerical and/or topographical advantage. Flanking movements and turning movements are difficult to execute because of the deficiencies of timing and precision which volunteer troops can manifest. (Indeed, terrain often renders any of these last options impossible anyway.) Hence, more often than a casual observer or student might suspect, a frontal assault is the only viable option.

Paddy Griffith, in his 1989 book *Battle Tactics of the Civil War,* takes totally tangential and challenging directions in interpretation. He does not believe that the rifle produced much new effectiveness in firepower; indeed, he denigrates the concept that the Civil War was the first modern war and calls it instead the last Napoleonic war. He emphasizes the frequent presence of wooded and/or brush-encumbered battle areas, which cut down on the long-range effectiveness of firepower. He stresses the limitations imposed by the fact that most soldiers were poorly disciplined and inexperienced and most officers nothing more than rank amateurs trying to make war—and that these twin realities, more than defensive firepower, were what necessitated the failure of most assaults. Earl J. Hess, in his 1997 book *The Union Soldier in Battle,* tends to second Griffith's theses. But Reid Mitchell, a fellow contributor to this special issue, strongly disagrees with many of Griffith's conclusions.[6]

Many other arguments have tended to look for one prevailing tendency or another and to weigh its relative significance and impact. It is all, after all, an impossible argument to win. To what degree was the Civil War "old," to what degree was it "modern"? One can easily argue for both extremes. To what degree, further, was it "total"? It assuredly was not *totally* total—for there never has been such a conflict fought, save possibly in prehistoric times or perhaps in the ancient world.

But the Civil War was indeed a very hard-fought war. The men on both sides believed deeply in their cause. James M. McPherson has done much to discover and shed light on the motivation of the various soldiers. Still, he notes in *For Cause and Comrades,* the

6. Paddy Griffith, *Battle Tactics of the Civil War* (New Haven: Yale University Press, 1989); Earl J. Hess, *The Union Soldier in Battle: Enduring the Ordeal of Combat* (Lawrence: University Press of Kansas, 1997); Reid Mitchell, "The Infantryman in Combat," *North & South* 4:6 (2001).

citizen-soldiers were a complex lot. This meant that while military discipline and the rigors of army life during combat could strip them of some of their individualism, they never could be turned into disciplined military cogs. It added also to the improbability of frontal assaults producing successful results. Nonetheless, they did work sometimes. This was due not so much to luck, nor to the propitiousness of the maneuver, but to the comparative degree of élan, dash, and determinism that commanders sometimes managed to elicit— usually by showing it in themselves as a motivating example.[7]

Another thing that augmented defending infantry was effective artillery. Again, however, the situation is beclouded: all too often, artillery ammunition was defective, and precious few Civil War artillerymen were sufficiently skilled in using their pieces for indirect and longer-range fire. This dictated that short-range canister was the most frequently used kind of artillery augmentation for defending infantry. It was very difficult (but not totally impossible) to use artillery in the attack. When it was used, it helped a lot.

Cavalry, on the other hand, had lost nearly all of its traditional function, which was to aid in the attack. Now it was almost totally relegated to scouting, screening, protecting flanks, and aiding in the mop-up or pursuit of the enemy in the event of a successful assault. It could, of course, be used as mounted infantry, adding a measure of mobility and firepower to any command's combat capability. Stephen Z. Starr, however, offers some thoughtful counterarguments in his three-volume *Union Cavalry in the Civil War*.[8] Emphasizing that there was a considerable break with traditional European uses of cavalry, Starr outlines some much more complicated employments of cavalry in the Civil War. Again, limitations were imposed by the fact that neither the horses nor the men had sufficient training to be maximally effective as cavalry forces. The South possessed some early advantage in this category—owing to the reality that Southern youths had considerably more horseback-riding experience than Northerners—but in time the Northerners learned as much as the Southerners, and thereafter the Federal cavalry was every bit an equal, and sometimes a superior, arm.

7. James M. McPherson, *For Cause and Comrades: Why Men Fought in the Civil War* (New York: Oxford University Press, 1997).
8. Stephen Z. Starr, *Union Cavalry in the Civil War*, 3 vols. (Baton Rouge: Louisiana State University Press, 1979–1985).

It was mainly a question of what the commander of a sufficiently small cavalry unit (not, to be sure, diminutive, but definitely smaller than army-sized or even corps-sized units) could do by taking advantage of speed and surprise. The Confederate Nathan Bedford Forrest was clearly the Civil War's most able example of such a commander. Unlike far too many of his infantry counterparts, Forrest reached and did not surpass his maximal level of competency. He could not have effectively commanded greatly larger units than he did. Jubal Early was of no small significance too, but in the end he failed. Improved armaments, particularly repeating weapons, rendered his Federal counterparts, especially Philip Sheridan and James H. Wilson, better masters of horse-riding commands late in the conflict.

With the passage of time the combat effectiveness of forces on both sides increased greatly. Each year of the Civil War was marked by more aggressive and violent war-making. So it is no surprise that the 1864 campaigns were particularly destructive. In Virginia, the war's two best generals, Ulysses S. Grant and Robert E. Lee, heading the two best armies, were pitted against each other. Both sides were giving prominence in their thinking and deployments to the politically critical eastern theater. But Richard M. McMurry, in his *Two Great Rebel Armies*, gives a thorough explanation of why the Army of Northern Virginia outshone the Army of Tennessee.[9]

By this latter part of the war, soldiers on both sides thoroughly had learned the importance of cover and concealment. Hence, at the end of every day's marching or maneuvering, much use was made of entrenching tools. It was simply no longer possible to punch through a prepared defensive position. In the Battle of the Wilderness, May 5–6, 1864—the opening engagement of the forces now overseen by Lee and Grant—the results were inconclusive; the Confederate lines were much threatened, but they held. The casualties were staggering: of over 100,000 Federals engaged, 2,246 were killed, 12,037 wounded, and 3,383 missing; Confederates numbered over

9. Richard M. McMurry, *Two Great Rebel Armies: An Essay in Confederate Military History* (Chapel Hill: University of North Carolina Press, 1989).

60,000, and their losses, while uncertain, probably totaled over 7,500. Instead of retreating, Grant (unlike his predecessors) sidled off and thrust farther southward, thus forcing Lee to counter by riposte.

Few officers on either side had any inkling of what might be done to overcome the tactical standoff, but one who did was young Federal Col. Emory Upton. Having graduated from West Point eighth in his class shortly before the war began, Upton encountered numerous opportunities for getting ahead during the conflict. He took various staff and line appointments early, and then went into the volunteer service and became colonel of the 121st New York. He was a good leader of men, and a thoughtful and scientifically oriented soldier. He harbored a deep suspicion that there was a better way to deal with the solid trenches that the rebels prepared every time they drew up on defense.

He spoke about his ideas to his superiors on May 10, 1864, and they decided to give him twelve specially chosen infantry regiments to try whatever he might. The Battle of Spotsylvania was set to commence that day; it began late in the afternoon and continued into the early evening. Upton was expected to foment some kind of column maneuver. The spot picked for him to assault was foreboding: there was a 200-yard upward slope to the front of the rebel position, and a heavy abatis, felled trees with their sharpened branches pointing outward toward the Federals. The Confederates had fashioned a solidly constructed trench, using logs and banked-up earth. There was a head log atop, so the rebels could stand and fire, through slits about three or four inches tall. Heavy traverses— mounds of earth running to the rear at right angles from the main embankment—appeared at frequent intervals, protecting the rebels from envelopment and the possibility of enfilade fire.

In Upton's mind, speed was essential to his planned column assault: a mass of men had to get atop the parapet quickly. For this to be possible, the assaulters should not stop in their advance to exchange volley fire. Every man was to have his musket loaded and bayonet fixed, but only the men in the three leading regiments were to cap their pieces. If those soldiers with uncapped pieces could run fast enough and get into proximity with the rebel defenders, it would be easy for them then to cap their rifles and engage in close-range shooting.

Upton's advancing force met sharp fire, but with painful sacrifice they got through the abatis and swept forward without halting. There followed some desperate hand-to-hand fighting. The rebels easily shot or bayoneted the first Yankees who reached the parapet, but the weight of numbers finally began to yield costly results: many defenders were killed, and at last, those remaining began to break and run rearward. The next wave of Upton's assaulting force swept forward and secured a second trench to the rear of the initial rebel front. The scheme had worked: twelve blue-clad regiments had burst the Confederate line wide open and at a place where it had been strongest. A considerable number of prisoners were taken.

But Upton's men now were three-quarters of a mile ahead of the rest of the Union army, and the rebels began to bring up strong reinforcements. The Confederates doggedly reclosed the gap in their line, and Upton, with no help coming from his rear and unable to go any farther to the front, began to try leading his men back to their own main lines. They brought about a thousand prisoners with them.

Grant was impressed and rather encouraged. What twelve regiments had done might be repeated on the morrow with a much larger force. "A brigade today—we'll try a corps tomorrow," one of Grant's orderlies heard him say. But tomorrow proved to be a bit too soon: it took time to mount an attack of the size envisioned. So May 11 passed with the troops holding their lines; a train of wounded men started toward Fredericksburg, and the Federals did their planning.

Grant and Maj. Gen. George G. Meade in joint conference chose a new spot for their attempted breakthrough. The Confederate lines covering Spotsylvania Court House were formed in two tangents— a long one, opposite the Federal right, and a shorter one somewhat to the east of the first. The two lines did not intersect, but rather were joined by a great loop of entrenchments, which jutted toward the north to cover some high ground: it was a huge salient nearly a mile deep and a half-mile wide that the Confederates named the Mule Shoe, which seemed apt from its outline on the map.

If this salient could be broken, the Confederate army would be cut in half. Technical teaching suggested that the point of a salient was difficult to defend, owing to the fact that the defenders' fire, limited in delivery, tended to diverge. For that reason twenty-two heavy guns were brought up and emplaced to aid in defense of the Mule Shoe.

The Federals knew the guns were there, but their thinking led them to suspect that a solid corps of infantry making a quick rush in column, with no firing and no stopping, could overrun the salient before the guns chewed them up too badly. The guns became moot anyway, for when rebel scouts saw the Federal trains moving off toward the northeast on the afternoon of May 11, Lee deduced that Grant was starting another shift around the Confederate right, which he would have to move sufficient force to meet and counter. The artillery pieces were limbered up and taken to the rear before midnight.

As the daylight assault commenced and the struggle continued to unfold, probably the only thing that kept the Federals from experiencing utter disaster was that the rebel guns were gone. As the Federals ran madly forward, the rebels countered by trying to get the twenty-two guns back in their Mule Shoe emplacements. If the guns had been in position, the blue-clad targets would have constituted an artillerist's dream. But only two or three of the pieces got into the gun pits, each firing one or two rounds, before the massed Federals came flooding over the trenches. Between three and four thousand Confederate infantrymen were quickly taken captive.

But the Federals did not continue the advance as they should have. They now constituted what amounted essentially to an excited mob. All organization and control seemed to disappear. Then, suddenly, an ably led Confederate counterforce slashed into the Mule Shoe (Lee among them) and commenced driving the Yankees back. There was bitter and confused fighting, while rebel troops shouted, "Lee to the rear!" Twenty-four Federal brigades had slammed into only a few hundred yards of entrenchments. The weight of their numbers had produced some desirable results at first, but now their numbers were a handicap. Reforming and organizing proved to be just too difficult. Things were happening too fast, and no one knew quite what they ought to do next. Close-in clashes continued, perhaps the wildest and bitterest in-fighting of the entire war.

Here, at what would become known as the Bloody Angle, about the only thing that kept the opposing forces from mutual annihilation was that men were firing so fast that they failed to aim. Upton, though, was pleased with the way his men were desperately continuing to fight, and he had the idea that they could do even better if they had some artillery to help them. He sent back for a section of guns, and two brass fieldpieces came wheeling up. Here was something startlingly new: attacking infantry augmented by advancing artillery, firing double charges of canister and plowing into entrenched rebel infantry. When the guns finally ceased their fire, they could not be removed because all the horses were dead, and only two of the twenty-four artillerymen were unwounded.

There was more hand-to-hand fighting, but it produced no victory and no defeat; it was just fighting. It went on all day and continued after dark. The scene was awful: the trenches had corpses in them piled four and five deep. The Confederates were forced to yield perhaps a square mile, and then re-mended their lines. The Federals lost perhaps 6,800 men, and the Confederates about 5,000. One Southerner wrote of Grant, "We have met a man this time, who either does not know when he is whipped, or who cares not if he loses his whole army." But Grant was not going to lose his *whole* army, and in any event, if things did continue like this, the attrition factor alone would yield a Federal victory and eventually end the war.

And so the war ground on, with neither side able to demolish the other. Lee's men always managed to survive, but then were forced southward by Grant's sidling. The Confederates actually could inflict great damage upon the assaulting Union forces, as happened in the Battle of Cold Harbor on June 1–3 (which Grant later wrote he had always regretted). But the two armies gradually moved southward as far as Petersburg, where, on June 18, after assaults failed to break the rebel lines, Grant commenced a siege. The nine-month siege was costly and bitter, but the Union army never was able to break meaningfully through the lines. Instead, the much more numerous Union force ever so gradually extended the length of the siege lines, forcing Lee's army to stretch farther and farther, until at last they had stretched too far.

Was the Civil War's outcome decided by Northern tactical

superiority? No. It was decided by Grant's superior strategy: the use of simultaneous advances in several widely separated scenes of action. Did the military powers of the world learn much about the realities of tactical stalemate now prevalent? No, because the three Wars of German Unification, in which the Prussians proved able to demolish the armies of France so rapidly, fooled military thinkers into believing that mass and élan *could* break lines of well-armed defenders. World War I produced some sad illustrations to the contrary. There was a crying need for new tactical innovation, but as yet, it had not come.

Epilogue
On Remembering and Reliving History

This was a speech I prepared for a weeklong seminar on the Civil War at Hillsdale College, Hillsdale, Michigan, in February 1994. My friend Albert Castel, who with his wife lives in retirement in Hillsdale, was behind my being invited. I was pleased with how the piece turned out, and was extremely gratified by its reception. The speech was videotaped, but has never before been published. I have updated the section about my career.

Between Friday, April 12, 1861, when Fort Sumter was fired upon and replied, and Monday, April 2, 1866, when President Andrew Johnson proclaimed that the "insurrection is at an end . . . peace, order, tranquillity, and civil authority now exist in and throughout the whole of the United States of America," 1,816 days elapsed. During that time the American Civil War was fought: 10,455 battle actions of one kind and degree or another, variously described then and later as campaigns, battles, engagements, combats, actions, assaults, skirmishes, operations, sieges, raids, expeditions, reconnaissances, scouts, affairs, occupations, and captures.[1]

"The Civil War is at the center of our national psyche. Each year more than 100 new Civil War books are published. Tens of thousands of people devote their spare time to its study—collecting memorabilia, reenacting battles, touring historical sites, discussing causes," considering alternative outcomes, dissecting each campaign and battle.[2]

---

1. Herman Hattaway, "The Embattled Continent," in *Touched by Fire: A Photographic Portrait of the Civil War,* 2 vols., ed. William C. Davis (Boston: Little, Brown, 1985).

2. From the description of *Long Shadows: The Legacy of the American Civil War* (1987) in the *James Agee Film Project* catalog.

And people love to visit the actual battle sites: millions go every year to Gettysburg—two million per annum at this most-visited battlefield alone—and, in descending order by number of visitors, to Fredericksburg-Spotsylvania, Chickamauga, Chattanooga, Vicksburg, Kennesaw Mountain, Harpers Ferry, Petersburg, Fort Donelson, Antietam, Richmond, Tupelo, Fort Pulaski, Appomattox, Shiloh, Fort Sumter, Stones River, and Brice's Crossroads.

The Civil War affected in some way almost all of the embattled continent, the large pro-Virginia crowd notwithstanding. "We can't help it that the war after all was fought in Virginia," a defensive lady once said in reaction to criticism of the frequent overemphasis by some students of the war in that state. Assuredly, many of the war's epochal events did occur in Virginia: 2,154 military actions, or 20.6 percent of the total. But Tennessee, Missouri, Mississippi, and Arkansas, the next four leading theaters of the war by state, together were the scenes of 4,167 military actions. Every Confederate state had hundreds of engagements on its soil—except Florida, which had 168, and Texas, which had 90. There were even 88 in California (largely against Indians), 75 in the New Mexico Territory, and one in Vermont, when a small band of Confederates thrust from Canada to rob banks at St. Albans and a firefight ensued with the local militia. (Most of the money was recovered, but the rebel leader, Lt. Bennett H. Young, escaped with some of it. He made his way from Canada to England, where he spent the rest of the war attending university!)

The hills around Vicksburg and Chattanooga were as fateful as those in Pennsylvania, and huge numbers of Americans "remember and relive history" by visiting these sites, as well as the nearly numberless other sites where some engagement of the war took place. People enjoy ruminating upon what occurred at such obscure places as Pigeon's Ranch, New Mexico; Honey Hill, South Carolina; and Amelia Springs, Virginia; they are edified at the skirmish sites of Turkeytown, Alabama; Pea Vine Ridge, Georgia; Crab Orchard and Barren Mound, Kentucky; Pest House, Louisiana; Klapsford, Missouri; Moccasin Swamp, North Carolina; Whippy Swamp, South Carolina; and Shanghai, West Virginia.[3]

3. The preceding two paragraphs are taken from Hattaway, "Embattled Continent"; the data is from E. B. Long, *The Civil War Day by Day: An Almanac, 1861–1865* (Garden City, N.Y.: Doubleday, 1971).

This was a war—in some instances, literally—of brother against brother, or more typically, family member against family member. It had a tremendous cast of intriguing characters, and these people, and what they did, mattered as much or more than did the impact of modern technology. Technology *was* of great significance, though: steam power and iron, railroads and epoch-changing new war vessels—even submarines; air power, in the form of balloons, and all that goes with it, from plans for dropping poison gases to deceptive techniques like the construction of "Quaker guns" (black-painted tree trunks to make airborne spies think one was better armed than one actually was); the telegraph, and even the use of telegraph wire for entanglement purposes (barbed wire did not yet exist); and myriad powerful new weapons such as rifles—most of them muzzle-loaders, but some early versions of repeaters and breech-loaders—mortars, explosive mines, and hand grenades. The increase in available firepower caused troops to seek, or to devise, some kind of cover: foxholes, trenches, and field fortifications.

The war was tragic—it was the result of our ancestors' failure to settle their deeply felt differences in the typically American way: by debate and ballot and compromise. It has aptly been called, by various historians, our "American Iliad," the "Ordeal of the Union," and the "great crimson gash in American history." And, while it left some crucial matters unsettled (some of which remain unsettled even to this day), it did settle two troublesome matters decisively: it made a permanent Union (the phrase "the United States *are* . . ." forever after became "the United States *is* . . ."), and it ended therein the anachronistic and unacceptable institution of human slavery. How poignant is history lived, and how compellingly interesting, inspiring, and instructive it is to relive the unfolding moments of the Civil War.

I did not pick this topic. It came printed next to my name in the initial correspondence inviting me to participate in this symposium. I was subsequently told that I could change it if I wanted to. Well, after the initial jolt—the thought of preparing a speech on a topic of someone else's choosing is always a bit daunting—the idea more and more appealed to me. The topic is so nebulous! Why, with a title like this, I can talk about any of a huge number of possible alternatives—anything I want! So what I am going to try to do is to explore several different avenues.

The Spanish-born poet and philosopher George Santayana—who, incidentally was born in 1863, the middle year of our Civil War—is famous for his observation that "those who cannot remember the past are condemned to repeat it." Contemplating that remark and extrapolating its possible extended meaning tells much about what historians assert to be the value of studying the past: we may, through historical awareness and understanding, be able to avoid our previous pitfalls and those of our predecessors; on the other hand, if we remain ignorant of them, it is almost certain that we shall suffer quite avoidable agonies that already have been suffered. One thing that may be safe to say about the Civil War is that some persons who have "remembered" it have not always remembered it correctly—or, perhaps fairer and more on the mark, they have not remembered it in as complete, honest, and unbiased a manner as possible. In any event, the Civil War—as much as or more so than any other episode—falls into a category of history that both has been *lived* and, for person after person and time after time, *relived*, in the sense that when we study the past, we make it a part of our present; the past becomes momentarily "alive" again for us, because being aware of it is how we are alive at that moment.

I suppose the first thing many people think of when they hear the term *living history* is some form of reenactment: a costumed presentation of persons and events from the past, either in a tableau or animated performance. "Living history" of this sort has been quite the rage in recent years; there is even a popular magazine of that title devoted to the topic. Reenactors, especially Civil War reenactors, are often seen camping, parading, demonstrating, or restaging Civil War battles.

Civil War reenactors have been with us since the war itself, or very shortly thereafter. The late Thomas L. Connelly, my much-admired professional friend, spoofed them—delightfully, I have always thought—especially those reenactments that from time to time have been major social events in the South. "The typical reenactment," Connelly wrote, "might include the following line-up of characters. The commanding general, General Leonidas Ham Hock, . . . portrayed by some prominent county lawyer and candidate for county judge. The Confederate soldiers would be portrayed by volunteer state highway patrolmen, members of plumbers union local 101, students from Little Lord Fauntleroy Riding School. The Union soldiers are obtained from the state prison farm."[4] This is a caricature of reenactments in the *deep* South! Now, there are reenactment buffs all over the country and of every stripe.

(*Buff* is a term I dislike and certainly do not apply nor tolerate being applied to myself. It is short for "buffoon" and is similar to *fan*—which, after all, is short for "fanatic." The reenactors have a term they apply, in condemnatory deprecation, to anyone in their midst who dares to stray from strict standards of historical accuracy in such matters as using period-acceptable fabrics in one's costume, or, say, avoiding twentieth-century equipment in their camp display: *FARB,* or foolish and ridiculous buffoon.)

I might be a fairly well-qualified person to make a few observations about Civil War reenactors, because (1) I am not one of them, (2) I have been attending, observing, and enjoying their activities for more than thirty years, and (3) I know a lot about what it is they think they are trying to do.

Their primary stated goal is to help make history "come alive" (Ken Burns places much value upon this). They do not seek so much to entertain (although they do) as to impart knowledge, and to do so in a deeply personal, profoundly moving manner. They do not want to simply inform people about the past; they want to inspire them, and, as closely as possible, to show them what it was like to have been there. One reenactor interviewed in the film *Long Shadows* says that "for a moment, you're translated into the past . . . it *is* 1862." (I find this bizarre, but part of the goal for the more extreme reenactors is to be damned uncomfortable; they want to suffer like the Civil War participants did!)

The reenactors' *unstated* goal—which, I am convinced, is always present and powerfully operative—is to find *themselves,* to nurture their own personality, to "be" who they truly perceive themselves to be. This can be elusive, and I may not have enough time or material here to be adequately convincing, but what I am suggesting is that the reenactors are practicing a variant form of civil religion. They are sacerdotalizing aspects of the past: they, and only they, by

4. Thomas Lawrence Connelly, "That Was the War That Was," *Journal of Mississippi History* 30 (1968), 123–33.

how they do it, can bridge the gap between the essence of which they are aware and the minds and hearts—and, indeed, the souls— of their audience. Further, and this is crucial, it is the way in which they find meaning in their own lives.

The most extreme example of this that I have observed was in someone I'll call Private Smith, a Civil War Roundtabler and reen- actor whom I encountered while out at Riverside, California, in 1987 at one of Jerry Russell's West Coast Civil War Conference pro- grams. Smith was atwitter about the 125th anniversary of the Battle of Gettysburg the following summer. It was, he asserted, absolutely necessary to his peace of mind that he be at Little Round Top for the anniversary observation. Why? Because his great grandfather had fought there, and if he, the direct descendant in the late 1980s, was not there, his whole life would be without meaning. Perhaps, in fairness, he was merely being hyperbolic, but in honesty, I do not think that he was!

It might be amusing, as well as instructive, if you do not already know, to hear that the first Civil War battle reenactors were veterans themselves. Now, why did they do that? What drew them to such an activity? At times the reenactments were staged as fund-raisers, to generate monies for veterans' eleemosynary endeavors for wounded or indigent veterans, widows, and orphans. At times they just seemed like a fun thing to do. And eventually they became very symbolic: memorial rituals, love feasts—or at the very least, peace- ful manifestations of reverential observance shared by former com- batants. Two of the most famous of the veteran-staged reenactments were the fiftieth and seventy-fifth anniversaries of the Battle of Gettysburg, in 1913 and 1938, respectively. Some 53,000 veterans participated in the fiftieth, and the official count for the seventy- fifth was 1,845—most of them in their nineties and some of them over one hundred years old. There is an interesting picture book about these events called *Hands across the Wall;*[5] the title refers to the reenactment of Pickett's Charge with the Southern and Northern veterans shaking hands across the wall near the top of Cemetery Ridge. (At the 1913 reunion, the recently formed Boy Scouts of

5. Stan Cohen, *Hands across the Wall: The 50th and 75th Reunions of the Gettys- burg Battle* (Charleston, W.Va.: Pictorial Histories Publishing Co., 1982).

America got a heady dose of national publicity when one Scout was assigned as an aide to each veteran.) The Gettysburg reunions were but the most well-covered in the news; countless other veterans participated in reenactments.

In the intervening years, nonveterans have continued the practice. Many reenactments have been staged on or very near to the ground where the original episode took place. But that has become the exception in recent times, as the National Park Service, though it does occasionally allow "living history demonstrations" on Park property, now forbids any reenactment—not for the good reason that such activity could damage historical property, but because reenactors are not always careful and sometimes are badly injured. More to the point, they actually have been known to *try* to hurt, maim, or even kill the persons portraying enemy soldiers!

In our time, reenactors unquestionably have provided useful services, not least being to supply myriad properly costumed and equipped "extras" for such motion pictures as *Glory* and *Gettysburg*. When *Glory* began filming, it was found that there were not a whole lot of black Civil War reenactors. There were some Revolutionary War and War of 1812 black units, however, that were induced to retool—at least they already knew how to handle muzzle-loading firearms—and enough new black recruits eventually were found. I am happy to report that a number of them continued in the activity. (A significant portion were recruited from among college students in Arkansas, and it was my pleasure to meet one of their principal organizers when I was down there for a symposium at the University of Arkansas.) This added a new group of participants to Civil War reenactments.

Reenactors—some, to be sure, more than others—seem to get into their roles with commitment and gusto. While *Gettysburg* was being made, the reenactor extras tended to remain "in character" even while off camera, saluting and calling the officer-actors "sir," and cheering wildly whenever Martin Sheen, who portrayed Robert E. Lee, appeared.

While there are lots of Northern reenactors, and some of them can get pretty emotional, I think that for many Southern reenactors there is an added dimension—what C. Vann Woodward referred to as "the burden of Southern history." The added poignancy that comes from commemorating the defeated, the whole set of baggage that goes with "the cult of the Lost Cause" . . . Here is the perfect point to make reference to that famous passage in William Faulkner's *Intruder in the Dust*. "Every Southern boy fourteen years old" is capable of reliving the moment just before Pickett's Charge at Gettysburg as if the issue had not been decided and its success were still a possibility: "the guns are laid and ready in the woods and the furled flags are already loosened to break out and Pickett himself . . . [is] waiting for Longstreet to give the word and it's all in the balance."

Or, to take another tack, if there still is a cult of Lincoln and Lee, as historians tell us there was late in the nineteenth century (an outgrowth of the nationalism and unity that underpinned the New Manifest Destiny and U.S. participation in the Spanish-American War), which aspect of it stirs the most emotional reaction, Lincoln or Lee? In a recent newsletter of the Civil War Roundtable Associates, the popular Ed Bearss is quoted as observing that "Lincoln doesn't sell as well as battlefields." In any event, I'll bet he doesn't sell as well as Lee. In fact, I bet nothing in Civil War lore "sells" as well as Lee! Unless it might be Miss Scarlett, and Ashley, and Rhett, and Mammy, and all those marvelous characters from *Gone with the Wind*.

If you want to read what I regard as the most remarkable annotated bibliography of all time (how much competition could there be?), take a look at Douglas Southall Freeman's *The South to Posterity* (1939). Freeman wrote this fascinating book after having been asked innumerable times, "What shall I read next?" by people who had just finished either Margaret Mitchell's marvelous tome or Clifford Dowdey's *Bugles Blow No More*—which *might* have been the great Civil War book if not for its being overshadowed by *GWTW*.

The work of Douglas Freeman—to which I shall return—stands as one of several catalysts that induced more intense and sometimes extended periods of interest in the Civil War (in addition to the ambient one that always has been present ever since the conflict occurred). I think the first of these commenced in November 1883. It was then that the first of a three-year-long series of articles appeared in the *Century Magazine* (so named because it had begun publication in 1876, the one-hundredth anniversary of the founding of the Republic) that later would be republished in the massive four-volume set *Battles and Leaders of the Civil War.*

Many aging warriors who had participated in the conflict had been for some time recounting their versions of what had happened in the war, "to themselves, their cronies, and their children." Some were trying to clarify their own uncertainty as to what their roles had been, and some were trying to justify what they had done. Some, of course, were rekindling old animosities and refighting old struggles with personal rivals, while others were inclined either to boast or to praise. The reason there were so many of these "historically active" veterans was not just that the Civil War was a big war, with many participants, but also that it was the first big war in human history in which the mass of participants were literate. Two of the *Century*'s associate editors, Clarence Clough Buel and Robert Underwood Johnson, and their chief, Richard Watson Gilder, were the driving forces behind the creation of a "series of articles on the principal battles" of the Civil War "by the leaders of both sides."[6] It was an enormously successful venture.

"Buel and Johnson and Gilder had chosen the [correct] psychological moment; the generals were ready to write and the public to read. Five years earlier the passions would still have been too hot; five years later the generals lost in aged garrulousness." Not only did a large number of the war's participants "re-live what they had lived,"[7] and in the process create a crucially valuable source for historical study, but they spawned an aftermath of intense interest by the reading public in the Civil War that continued for the better part of two decades.

Another extended period of interest came in the 1930s. Who can say why, precisely, the time was ripe? The Great Depression induced many people to find solace in escapist literature, and, perhaps, in contemplation of the past. This was when Margaret Mitchell brought forth her magnum opus, *Gone with the Wind.* Three years later, David O. Selznick turned a part of that opus into a grand and

---

6. Roy F. Nichols, introduction to new edition of *Battles and Leaders of the Civil War* (New York: Yoseloff, 1956).
    7. Ibid.

successful motion picture. In addition, 1934–1935 saw the publication of Douglas Southall Freeman's incomparable biography, the four-volume *R. E. Lee.*

"Freeman's biography is great because in spirit and in blood he also has marched with Lee," commented William Allen White, editor of the *Emporia (Kan.) Gazette.* "It is a great book, made in the grand manner," declared the *London Observer.* Civil War historian Lloyd Lewis admitted, "I found my eyes pretty wet after his pictures of Gettysburg." And Stephen Vincent Benét summed it all up by saying that "there is a monument—and a fine one—to Robert E. Lee at Lexington. But this one, I think, will last as long."[8]

Clearly Douglas Freeman—son of Walker Freeman, a veteran of the Army of Northern Virginia and a former commander in chief of the United Confederate Veterans—knew something about remembering and reliving history. Freeman, in tandem with Mrs. Mitchell, produced a renewed spirit of voracious reading about the Civil War that slackened only slightly when World War II commenced. Freeman's second magnum opus, the three-volume *Lee's Lieutenants,* appeared during the years 1942–1944. Among other things, it induced a consideration of leadership—of what the Civil War leaders had shown that might be of help to the leaders of World War II.

World War II itself was a catalyst that brought about a major change in the prevailing scholarly and historiographical interpretation of the Civil War era, ushering in the New Nationalist school of thought, which, with some additional sophistication, is essentially still in vogue. But my purpose here is not to run through the various and changing schools of historiographical thought. I mention historiography only in passing. I do want to suggest that while all historical manifestation is subject to historiographical analysis and categorization, it is important to beware the temptation to assert that anyone, or anyone's presentation—especially of something so rich and complex as is the Civil War—is the final word.

That is what most surprised me about the Ken Burns television series *The Civil War*—and, to a lesser extent, the companion book that sold so many millions of copies: the implication, if not the

8. Quotations are from the dust jacket of Richard Barksdale Harwell, *Lee: An Abridgment in One Volume of the Four-Volume R. E. Lee by Douglas Southall Freeman* (New York: Charles Scribner's Sons, 1961).

assertion, that nothing more ever needed to be said, that this was the final and essential word on the Civil War. This is not even to mention the artistic license that Burns and company occasionally took, or that they had an ax to grind: to promote an underlying theme of antiwar philosophy and a certain civil-rights agenda. I *liked* the Burns series, but I was amazed at how many people seemed to think (1) that there was nothing wrong with it, and (2) that there was nothing more that needed to be said.

Since the Mitchell/Freeman era, there have been two extended renewals of intense interest in Civil War history. The first was during the war's centennial, 1961–1965. Much good stuff came out just before and during the centennial, including perhaps the greatest of the centennial-era Civil War writings and a corpus of work that must be mentioned here, the books by Bruce Catton. His three-volume *Centennial History of the Civil War* is noteworthy; the narrative he wrote for the *American Heritage Picture History of the Civil War* is timelessly brilliant; and his trilogy on the Union Army of the Potomac will always be worthy of notice: *Mr. Lincoln's Army, Glory Road,* and the Pulitzer Prize–winning *A Stillness at Appomattox.* But much drivel came as well, and by the time the centennial drew to a close, many Americans were growing jaded, if not bored, with Lincoln and Lee, Longstreet and Jackson, Sherman and Sheridan, and so on. Even Charles Schulz expressed this in the cartoon *Peanuts,* showing Linus singing "Just Before the Battle, Mother," Charlie Brown singing, "Yes, We'll Rally 'Round the Flag, Boys," and Snoopy thinking, "I'll be glad when the centennial is over."

Civil War book sales slackened and production of new ones decreased markedly; numerous fair-weather Civil War roundtables became defunct. But then, suddenly, splendidly, along came Burns. His series hit like a lightning bolt. Even before the Christmas season following the initial television showing in 1990, booksellers noticed a renewed interest in the Civil War. Publishers began rushing new titles into print and reprinting a rich matrix of formerly revered studies. (I myself profited from this phenomena, most notably in that the University of Illinois Press was induced to issue a paperbound edition of my collaboration with Archer Jones, *How the North Won: A Military History of the Civil War.*) Happily for those of us who care about the war, the trend is continuing.

In any field of history, the questions that scholars are most interested in tend to change over time. This phenomenon is perhaps more pronounced in Civil War studies, since that war is the most written-about event in American history. Hence the endlessly variant kaleidoscopic picture we get of the era. I find that now, for example (and the Burns series certainly echoed, if not reinforced, this), many people equate Civil War studies with studies in the history of civil rights.

This theme dominated the discussions at a symposium in November 1993 at Mississippi State University where the general panelists were Carl Degler, Hans Trefousse, and myself. I was very honored, but I must admit to having done a little squirming on the stage while young black members of the audience sparred with ultraconservative Professor William Kauffman Scarborough over whether the Reverend Dr. Martin Luther King Jr. is or is not a hero to white Americans as well as to blacks, and over the relative merits and demerits of recent attempts to prohibit display of the Confederate flag (more typically, the Confederate battle flag and not the national ensign) in such places as the Georgia state flag, atop the Georgia Dome while the Super Bowl was being played, atop the Alabama state capitol, and on the logo of the United Daughters of the Confederacy.

Still another package of controversies in recent years swirls around the image and memory of the Confederate general Nathan Bedford Forrest, one of the war's most colorful and intriguing figures. An untutored military genius who went into the army as a private and came out a lieutenant general, he was called "that Devil Forrest" by William Tecumseh Sherman and "the war's greatest general" by none other than Robert E. Lee. Forrest is vilified in some quarters today because he had been a slave trader, asserted bluntly that the South was fighting the war to preserve slavery, was in command during the April 1864 Confederate storming of Fort Pillow and the alleged "massacre" of its largely black garrison, and because he was active—perhaps even the Imperial Wizard—in the Ku Klux Klan.

A statue of Forrest in a park in Memphis, Tennessee, long has been the center of bitter argument and struggle—one group wants to have it preserved, and another wants it removed from public prominence. A huge painting of Forrest, one of three portraits of Civil War generals that graced the main administration building of

Mississippi State University (the others being of Stephen D. Lee and Joseph E. Johnston) has been forced off campus to safer display in a museum at Columbus, Mississippi, twenty-five miles to the south. Interestingly, for many years the three portraits hung unmolested—perhaps because there were no identifying plaques to indicate who the subjects were. But after such plaques were installed, the Forrest portrait repeatedly became the subject of attempts by vandals to deface it. Administrators tried removing the portrait to the archives, but even there it was slashed. So the General Stephen D. Lee Home and Museum underwrote a restoration, and now has it on permanent loan.

My own feeling is that most people's interest in the Civil War does not originate in a concern for the story of civil rights in America, and that even if somehow, someway, someday, we manage to transcend the difficulties that sprang from our collective failure to resolve all the problems that have to do with civil rights, interest in remembering and reliving the history of the Civil War era will still be extant and strong. I might say too, that I consider myself more of a J. H. Hexter type than a Carl Lotus Becker type insofar as my own composition affects the way I feel about the war, or, vice versa, the way I feel about the war tends to affect and mold me in the present. Becker asserted that one's view of the past inevitably is shaped and even blurred by one's present, by who and what one is; Hexter strongly suggested that it is the other way around, that one's present is shaped and shaded by what one knows about the past. In other words, just as Hexter asserted that he knew more about the Elizabethan Poor Laws than he knew about welfare legislation in his own time, so do I know and care more about the Democratic and Republican parties of the 1860s than I do about those of recent decades.

Perhaps you would be interested to hear how my interest in this field originated. Despite the fact that my great-granduncle John Nick Coiner rode with John Singleton Mosby and I have his gun and one of his Civil War letters,[9] and that Cornelius Coiner, my first

9. I have since given the gun to my first doctoral student, Mark Snell, and he has it on display at the George Tyler Moore Center for the Study of the Civil War, which he heads, in Shepherdstown, West Virginia. The letter was published in *We Remember,* a compendium of letters by ancestors of members of the Kansas City Civil War Roundtable.

cousin three times removed, was also in the war, I did not grow up in a family, nor in a community (Houma, Louisiana), in which the Civil War was an often-mentioned topic.

But in the fall of 1960, nearing the end of my time as a college undergraduate, I encountered T. Harry Williams. He changed my life. His brilliant lectures on the Civil War and his dynamic and magnetic personality drew me to him and to his field, making me want to spend my career as an historian specializing in this fascinating subject. He became my graduate major professor and directed my dissertation on the life of Confederate Gen. Stephen D. Lee. Williams was a colorful, loquacious, and lovably egomaniacal character who was universally known as T. Harry. I have since gotten a few laughs with my assertion that I, like the other thirty-five people who completed their doctorates under his direction, am a "Wee Harry."

My wife, Margaret, and I were married in August of 1961, and among the activities I planned for our wedding trip (many of them unwisely and poorly chosen, I eventually learned) was to spend several hours of our first full day of married life touring Vicksburg National Military Park. We hired a most energetic little old lady in tennis shoes to guide us, and spent a hot afternoon thoroughly engrossed in scenes of struggle, siege, and commemoration. I doubt that I noticed the statue there of Stephen D. Lee, for he as yet did not mean as much as he soon would in my life.

I have returned to Vicksburg several times during the years that have elapsed since that first visit. The BBC hosted me in the vicinity for several days while shooting my appearance in its excellent series *The Divided Union*. (As it turned out, it was a very brief appearance; much of my footage wound up on the cutting-room floor.) I was recognized by the park officials when I paid a quick visit to headquarters, and one of them asked what I was doing there. I quipped that I had some time on my hands and thought that I would "make a meditation" at the base of the S. D. Lee statue. To my amusement, no one batted an eyelid—how logical that Herman Hattaway would come to meditate at the statue of the man whose biography he wrote!

I remember, on another visit to the park on a dreamy, almost majestic sunny afternoon, taking a long and, yes, meditative drive past all the monuments and along the siege lines, contemplating what a total commitment I had made in my career, and, indeed, in my life, to studying—to remembering and reliving—the history of the Civil War.

Sometime in the mid-seventies I encountered Archer Jones. Professor Williams introduced me to him at a meeting of the Southern Historical Association. Jones changed my life almost as much as had Williams. He became my inspiring mentor, helping me to shape the Lee biography into the prize-winning book that it finally became. Then we together produced *How the North Won*, which was well received. I am particularly proud that the U.S. Army has this book on its recommended reading list for career officers. I suspect that *HTNW*, as I refer to it (à la *GWTW* for *Gone with the Wind*), will remain the magnum opus of my career.

Subsequently Jones and I worked with Richard E. Beringer and William N. Still Jr. to write *Why the South Lost the Civil War*. Both *HTNW* and *WTSL* were quite successful, won several prizes, and attracted much favorable attention. The Atlanta Historical Society hosted Beringer and me at a well-attended session to discuss *WTSL*, and the Southern Historical Association held a session dedicated to a critique of the book.

In 2002, Beringer and I—after being under contract for seventeen years—finally published our *Jefferson Davis, Confederate President*. My third doctoral student, Michael J. C. Taylor, now at Dickinson State University in North Dakota, firmly predicts that this latest book will become my new magnum opus, or at least regarded as coequal with *How the North Won*.

It will have to be very successful for that to become so. *How the North Won*, first published in 1983, is still in print, both in hardbound and paperbound editions, and in 1995 the Easton Press issued it in a special edition. It is something of an ego trip to have your book bound in beautifully embossed leather. I have framed a copy of the Easton Press's advertisement for its Library of Military History, which it describes as the forty best books ever published on that subject. Also framed is a letter Jones and I received from the director of a university press. As it happened, we first submitted the typescript for *HTNW* to Alfred A. Knopf, and after being turned down, we sent it to this press, which also turned it down. But when life hands me lemons—as often has been the case—I try to secure some ice, sugar, and good spring water to make lemonade. The director's letter concludes with this paragraph: "Congratulations, one more time, on having written such a successful book. I'm sure that if [the previous director] was aware of how well this book has been received and how well it has sold he would want to kick in the butt the guy who wrote such a nasty critique for the press! Of course we have made mistakes too, but I can't think of any that were as big as this one. Best wishes to you both."

So: Williams, Jones, Stephen D. Lee, *How the North Won,* and most recently, Jefferson Davis. What a marvelously interesting, fulfilling, and fun way to have spent the past four decades!

INDEX

Hunt, Henry J., 209
Hunter, Lloyd, 99

Illinois, 78, 154–55
Illinois Central Railroad, 179
Immigrant groups, 179
Imperial Wizard, 232
Indiana: 53, 58–59; militia, 59
Indiana Legion, 56
Indianapolis, Indiana, 58
Indians: Comanche, 70; Seminole, 68
Industry: Confederate, 197, 218
Infantry: 201, 218–19; mounted, 214
Innovations, tactical, 210–11
Institute of Aerospace Sciences, 149
Intelligence, military, 165
Interest groups, 179
Interior lines, 79
Intruder in the Dust (Faulkner), 228
Irish general, 179
Ironclads, 139
Irwin, William J., 56
Irwinville, Georgia, 197

Jackson, Ohio, 61
Jackson, Thomas J. "Stonewall":
    equated with Sherman, 187; loses
    battle at Martinsburg, 72; in Mexi-
    can War, 33; and reorganization of
    Army of Northern Virginia, 21–22;
    in Second Manassas campaign,
    26–30; as symbol of "Lost Cause,"
    107–8; as symbol of the war, 231;
    Valley campaign of 1862, 81
Jamaica, 135
James River, 87, 152, 167
Jamieson, Perry D., 211–12
Japan, 143
Jefferson Barracks, Missouri, 70
Jefferson Davis (Hattaway and
    Beringer), 235
Jefferson Davis Award, 19
Jefferson Mills, New Hampshire, 148
Jensen, Lesley D., 115
Johnson, Adam R. "Stovepipe," 54, 62
Johnson, Andrew: appoints Holden
    provisional governor of North
    Carolina, 120; and G. H. Thomas,
    66, 77; and pardons, 46; proclaims
    end of war, 221

Johnson, Robert Underwood, 229
Johnston, Albert Sidney: in command
    of western theater, 42; death, 51; as
    friend of Davis, 15; at Shiloh,
    42–43; son's biography of, 48;
    statue of, 50
Johnston, Joseph E.: capitulates at
    Bentonville, 197–98; commands
    Georgia state forces, 129;
    commands Western Confederate
    Army, 75; disputes with Davis,
    15–16, 49; does not seek pardon, 46;
    envies R. E. Lee, 208; in First
    Manassas campaign, 40; memoirs,
    48; in Mexican War, 36–37; opposes
    Sherman, 12; portrait of, 233;
    praises Sherman's army, 189; re-
    places Hood in army command,
    45; wounded at Fair Oaks (Seven
    Pines), 21
John T. McCombs (steamboat), 56
Jomini, Antoine Henri, 90
Jones, Archer: 13, 78, 121, 158, 183,
    235; *Elements of Confederate Defeat*
    (with Beringer et al.), 40; *How the
    North Won* (with Hattaway), 235;
    The Politics of Command (with
    Connelly), 11, 44
Jordan, Tyler Calhoun, 23
Jordan's Battery, 23
Judah, Henry M., 54–55, 60
Judah's Cavalry, 55

Kellogg, Frances Lucretia, 70
Kelton, John C., 165
Kemper, Delaware "Del," 23
Kemper, William H., 25
Kennesaw Mountain: battle site, 222
Kentucky, 15, 52–53, 55–56, 58, 73–74,
    76, 172, 222
Kentwood, Louisiana, 180
Keyes, Erasmus D., 69
King, Martin Luther, Jr., 110, 144, 232
King Cotton Diplomacy (Owsley), 113
Kingston, Ontario, 134, 142
Kintner Hotel, 58
Kirby Smith, Edmund, 50
Klapsford, Missouri: battle at, 222
Knoxville, Tennessee, 54
Krick, Robert K., 24